Tony Harrison

Classical Receptions in Twentieth-Century Writing

Series Editor: Laura Jansen

Each book in this groundbreaking new series considers the influence of antiquity on a single writer from the twentieth century. From Woolf to Walcott and Fellini to Foucault, the modalities and texture of this modern encounter with antiquity are explored in the works of authors recognized for their global impact on modern fiction, poetry, art, philosophy, and socio-politics.

A distinctive feature of twentieth-century writing is the tendency to break with tradition and embrace the new sensibilities of the time. Yet the period continues to maintain a fluid dialogue with the Graeco-Roman past, drawing on its rich cultural legacy and thought, even within the most radical movements that ostentatiously questioned and rejected that past. Classical Receptions in Twentieth-Century Writing approaches this dialogue from two interrelated perspectives: it asks how modern authors' appeal to the classical past opens up new readings of their oeuvres and contexts, and it considers how this process in turn renders new insights into the classical world. This two-way perspective offers dynamic and interdisciplinary discussions for readers of Classics and modern literary tradition.

Fellini's Eternal Rome, Alessandro Carrera
Virginia Woolf's Greek Tragedy, Nancy Worman
James Joyce and Classical Modernism, Leah Culligan Flack

Editorial Board

Prof. Richard Armstrong (University of Houston)
Prof. Francisco Barrenechea (University of Maryland)
Prof. Shane Butler (Johns Hopkins University)
Prof. Paul A. Cartledge (University of Cambridge)
Prof. Moira Fradinger (Yale University)
Prof. Francisco García Jurado (Universidad Complutense de Madrid)
Prof. Barbara Goff (University of Reading)
Prof. Simon Goldhill (University of Cambridge)
Dr. Constanze Güthenke (University of Oxford)
Prof. Edith Hall (King's College London)
Prof. Judith Hallett (University of Maryland)
Dr. George Kazantzidis (University of Patras)
Prof. Andrew Laird (Brown University)
Prof. Vassilis Lambropoulos (University of Michigan)
Prof. Charles Martindale (University of Bristol/University of York)
Dr. Pantelis Michelakis (University of Bristol)
Prof. Neville Morley (University of Exeter)
Prof. James Porter (University of California, Berkeley)
Prof. Phiroze Vasunia (University College London)

Tony Harrison

Poet of Radical Classicism

Edith Hall

BLOOMSBURY ACADEMIC
LONDON • NEW YORK • OXFORD • NEW DELHI • SYDNEY

BLOOMSBURY ACADEMIC
Bloomsbury Publishing Plc
50 Bedford Square, London, WC1B 3DP, UK
1385 Broadway, New York, NY 10018, USA
29 Earlsfort Terrace, Dublin 2, Ireland

BLOOMSBURY, BLOOMSBURY ACADEMIC and the Diana logo are
trademarks of Bloomsbury Publishing Plc

First published in Great Britain 2021
This paperback edition published 2022

Copyright © Edith Hall 2021

Edith Hall has asserted her right under the Copyright, Designs and Patents Act,
1988, to be identified as Author of this work.

For legal purposes the Acknowledgements on p. vi–vii constitute an extension of this copyright page.

Cover design: Terry Woodley
Cover image © English poet and stage writer Tony Harrison on the South Bank,
London, 1990. (Photo by Gemma Levine/Hulton Archive/Getty Images)

All rights reserved. No part of this publication may be reproduced or transmitted in any form or by any means, electronic or mechanical, including photocopying, recording, or any information storage or retrieval system, without prior permission in writing from the publishers.

Bloomsbury Publishing Plc does not have any control over, or responsibility for, any third-party websites referred to or in this book. All internet addresses given in this book were correct at the time of going to press. The author and publisher regret any inconvenience caused if addresses have changed or sites have ceased to exist, but can accept no responsibility for any such changes.

A catalogue record for this book is available from the British Library.

Library of Congress Cataloging-in-Publication Data
Names: Hall, Edith, 1959– author.
Title: Tony Harrison : poet of radical classicism / Edith Hall.
Description: London ; New York : Bloomsbury Academic, 2021. | Series: Classical receptions in twentieth-century writing | Includes bibliographical references. | Summary: "This is the first book-length study of the classicism of Tony Harrison, one of the most important contemporary poets in England and the world. It argues that his unique and politically radical classicism is inextricable from his core notion that poetry should be a public property in which communal problems are shared and crystallised, and that the poet has a responsibility to speak in a public voice about collective and political concerns. Enriched by Edith Hall's longstanding friendship with Harrison and involvement with his most recent drama, inspired by Euripides' Iphigenia in Tauris, it also asserts that his greatest innovations in both form and style have been direct results of his intense engagements with individual works of ancient literature and his belief that the ancient Greek poetic imagination was inherently radical. Tony Harrison's large body of work, for which he has won several major and international prizes, and which features on the UK National Curriculum, ranges widely across long and short poems, plays, translations and film poems. Having studied Classics at Grammar School and University and having translated ancient poets from Aeschylus to Martial and Palladas, Harrison has been immersed in the myths, history, literary forms and authorial voices of Mediterranean antiquity for his entire working life and his classical interests are reflected in every poetic genre he has essayed, from epigrams and sonnets to original stage plays, translations of Greek drama and Racine, to his experimental and harrowing film poems, where he has pioneered the welding of tightly cut video materials to tightly phrased verse forms. This volume explores the full breadth of his oeuvre, offering an insightful new perspective on a writer who has played an important part in shaping our contemporary literary landscape"– Provided by publisher.
Identifiers: LCCN 2020034885 (print) | LCCN 2020034886 (ebook) | ISBN 9781474299336 (hardcover) | ISBN 9781474299343 (eBook) | ISBN 9781474299350 (ePDF)
Subjects: LCSH: Harrison, Tony, 1937–Criticism and interpretation. | Classicism in literature.
Classification: LCC PR6058.A6943 Z64 2021 (print) | LCC PR6058.A6943 (ebook) | DDC 821/.914—dc23
LC record available at https://lccn.loc.gov/2020034885
LC ebook record available at https://lccn.loc.gov/2020034886

ISBN:	HB:	978-1-4742-9933-6
	PB:	978-1-3501-9458-8
	ePDF:	978-1-4742-9935-0
	eBook:	978-1-4742-9934-3

Series: Classical Receptions in Twentieth-Century Writing

Typeset by RefineCatch Limited, Bungay, Suffolk

To find out more about our authors and books visit www.bloomsbury.com
and sign up for our newsletters.

Contents

Acknowledgements	vi
Timeline of Tony Harrison's Classics-Informed Works	viii
Series' Editor Preface	xi

1	'Models of eloquence': Radical Classicism	1
2	'Stone bodies': Statuary and Classicism in *The Loiners* (1970) and *Palladas* (1975)	19
3	'Frontiers of appetite': *Phaedra Britannica* (1975)	35
4	'Shaggermemnon': Aeschylus' *Oresteia* and *Continuous* (1981)	59
5	'All the versuses of life': '*v.*' and *Medea: A Sex-War Opera* (1985)	79
6	'Bookworm excreta': *The Trackers of Oxyrhynchus* (1988) and Other Plays and Poems	97
7	'End to end in technicolour': *Prometheus* (1998) and Other Films	123
8	'Witnessed horror': *Fram* (2008) and Harrison's Euripides	147
9	'Surviving the slopes of Parnassus': 'Polygons' (2015) and Other Poems	167

Notes	179
Bibliography	199
Index	213

Acknowledgements

Conversations with many people have gone into the making of this book. I am particularly grateful to Barrie Rutter, Yana Sistovari, Emma Harding, Oliver Taplin, Fiona Macintosh, Henry Stead, Paul Cartledge, David Braund, Jane Harrison, Dinah Wood, the attendees at a seminar organised by graduates at King's College London in early March 2020 and my former PhD students Matt Shipton, Helen Eastman, Caroline Latham and Lottie Parkyn. I learned much from correspondence and sharing ideas and work with Cécile Marshall, Blake Morrison, Giovanni Greco, Christine Regan, Sandie Byrne, Rachel Bower, Hallie and Toph Marshall, Lorna Hardwick, Richard Eyre, Antony Rowland, Claire Armitstead, Jo Balmer, Lee Hall, Simon Armitage, Melvyn Bragg, Andy Burnham, Jasper Britton, Jacob Blakesley, Oswyn and Penny Murray, Lawrence Evans, Jimmy Walters, John Kittmer, Margaret Silver, Joan Winterkorn, Robert Crawford, Emily Pillinger-Avlamis, William Fitzgerald and Peter Parsons. Sarah Prescott, a Harrison specialist at the Brotherton Library, and the exceptionally friendly staff at the Premier Inn in Leeds in different ways made my week in the archives in September 2019 a delight; Dan Orrells and the Arts and Humanities Faculty at King's College London made it possible for me to fund that trip. Faber & Faber kindly gave permission to quote from Harrison's published works, and the Brotherton Library at Leeds University gave me permission to quote from his Notebooks, which he produced while working on each of his texts. Peter Symes enabled me to study all of Tony Harrison's film-poems. Lily Mac Mahon at Bloomsbury and Laura Jansen, the series editor, have been wonderfully supportive, and Juliet Gardner a kind and meticulous copy-editor. Merv Honeywood at RefineCatch has been his usual friendly, prompt and professional self. I have revelled for many years now in the friendship of Sian Thomas as well as Tony Harrison himself; Tony's many typewritten postcards and gifts of amusing classics-related ephemera have made their way, in a subterranean fashion, into the argument everywhere. This was a Covid-19 lockdown book only made possible by the endless good humour and companionship of Richard, Sarah and Georgie Poynder. I heartily thank each and every one of the people named here. I am grateful to Taylor and Francis Ltd. For permission to reproduce as Chapter 2 a version of my article 'Statuary and classicism in Tony Harrison's *The Loiners* and beyond' from *English Studies* 99:1 (2018) 77–91 (reprinted by permission of Informa UK Limited, trading as Taylor & Francis Group, www.tandfonline.com), and to Nicholas Poburko, editor of *Arion*, for permission to reproduce parts of 'Tony Harrison's *Prometheus*: a view from the Left', *Arion* 10.1 (2002) 129–40 and 'Classics, class and Cloacina: Tony Harrison's humane coprology', *Arion* 15.2 (2007) 83–108 in Chapters 7 and 6 respectively.

Timeline of Tony Harrison's Classics-Informed Works

Date	Title	Genre/Medium	Classical Source(s)
1964	*Aikin Mata*	Stage adaptation	Aristophanes' *Lysistrata*
1969	'Newcastle is Peru'	Published poem	Numerous classical allusions
1970	*The Loiners*	Published poetry	Numerous classical allusions
1975	*Phaedra Britannica*	Stage adaptation	Phaedra-Hippolytus plays by Euripides, Seneca and Racine
1975	*Palladas: Poems*	Published translation	Palladas' epigrams
1978	*From the School of Eloquence and Other Poems*	Published poetry (the first of several editions)	Numerous classical allusions
1981	*Continuous: 50 Sonnets from The School of Eloquence*	Published poetry (the second of several editions)	Numerous classical allusions
1981	*The Oresteia*	Translation for stage	Aeschylus' *Oresteia*
1981	*U. S. Martial*	Published translation	Martial's *Epigrams*
1984–5	*The Common Chorus*	Stage work adapting ...	... *Lysistrata* and Euripides' *Trojan Women*
1985	'v.'	Published poem	Numerous classical allusions
1985	*Medea: A Sex-War Opera*	Opera libretto	Many *Medea* plays
1990	*The Trackers of Oxyrhynchus*	Stage play with embedded translation	Sophocles' *Trackers* fragments
1991	'A Cold Coming'	Published poem	Numerous classical allusions
1992	*The Gaze of the Gorgon*	Film poem	Numerous classical allusions especially to the *Iliad*
1994	*A Maybe Day in Kazakhstan*	Film poem	Athenian setting and numerous classical allusions

Timeline of Tony Harrison's Classics-Informed Works

1995	*The Kaisers of Carnuntum*	Stage play with embedded classical texts	Marcus Aurelius and many other classical authors
1995	*The Labourers of Herakles*	Stage play with embedded translations	Phrynichos' tragic fragments
1998	*Prometheus*	Film poem	Aeschylus' *Prometheus Bound*
2000	*Laureate's Block*	Published poetry	Numerous classical allusions
2000	*Metamorpheus*	Film poem	Numerous classical texts about Orpheus
2005	*Under the Clock*	Published poetry	Numerous classical allusions
2005	*Hecuba*	Translation for stage	Euripides' *Hecuba*
2008	*Fram*	Stage play with numerous classical allusions starring Gilbert Murray	Euripides' plays
2013	'Black Sea Aphrodite'	Published poem	Classical content throughout
2015	'Polygons'	Long published poem	Classical allusions everywhere. About Delphi
2017	*Iphigenia in Crimea*	Radio play with embedded translation	*Iphigenia in Tauris* by Euripides
2017	*Inky Digit of Defiance*	Edited prose essays	Many discussions of Classics

Series' Editor Preface

The present volume marks the fourth innovative contribution to the series *Classical Receptions in Twentieth-Century Writing* (*CRTW*), a project that seeks to explore the modalities and textures of modern classicisms in the works of writers recognized for their global impact on modern poetics, philosophy, politics and the arts. *CRTW* approaches this aim from two distinct yet interrelated perspectives: it asks how modern authors' appeals to the classical past open up new understandings of their oeuvres and contexts, and it considers how this process in turn renders new insights into the classical world. In plotting twentieth-century receptions of Graeco-Roman antiquity from this two-way perspective, the series aims to promote dynamic, highly interdisciplinary discussions for readers of Classics and Literary and Classical Studies. Indeed, a key feature of the series is its extensive range and scope. It looks at both Anglophone and non-Anglophone writers from modernities around the globe, as well as writers still or until recently active in their field, as is the case of Tony Harrison in the present volume, or our forthcoming studies in Wole Soyinka, and Simon Armitage. Each of these authors is considered primarily as a writer whose interest in antiquity has contributed to a significant revision of aesthetics, philosophical and political thought, identity studies, gender studies, translation studies, visual culture, performance studies, urban studies and cultural criticism, amongst other areas of knowledge. In this sense, *CRTW* aspires to promote a new intellectual space and critical direction for those producing research on Twentieth-Century Studies with a focus on Classics and vice versa.

The series furthermore aims to re-energize aspects of reception premises and practice. Over the last two decades, Classical Reception has developed broadly into four main fruitful areas of investigation: periods and/or movements (e.g. Humanism; the Enlightenment; the Victorians), media (e.g. film; sculpture; painting; the stage; musicology; comics), theory and criticism (e.g. psychoanalysis; gender studies; deconstruction; postcolonialism); and geopolitical regions (e.g. Africa; the Caribbean; Latin America; Eastern Europe; Australasia). These lines of enquiry have been instrumental in shaping methodological agenda and directions, as well as offering tremendous insights into discourses of Graeco-Roman antiquity in space and time. Yet, within the histories of classical receptions focusing on periods and regions, the twentieth century has been underexamined as a thematic unit. On the one hand, there has been a preponderance of focus in studies in English on Anglophone, Francophone and Germanophone receptions. This has been in part corrected by postcolonial reception studies with a focus on geopolitical regions outside of Western Europe. What has been missing is a perspective that combines not only an appreciation of Western and non-Western receptions, but also an understanding of these reception phenomena within a global, and not merely regional, framework. *CRTW* seeks to address this tangible gap, moving beyond isolated treatments and into full-scale investigations of authors recognized both for radical re-readings of the classical past and for challenging received ideas about the identity and cultural mobility of antiquity in the Western tradition. Interdisciplinarity is at the heart of such a reconsideration of reception in the series. Instead of treating reception as a sub-discipline of Classics, or as an expansion of the disciplinary boundaries of Classics, *CRTW* conceives it as a hub for interdisciplinary exchange amongst multiple subjects, disciplinary practices and scholarly expertise. It addresses some of the most profound shifts in practices of reading, writing and thinking in recent years within the arts and humanities, as well as in the poetics of reading the classics that one finds in twentieth-century writing itself.

Beyond reception, each individual study in the series draws attention to the specific quality of a modern author's classicism, as well as the ways in which that author negotiates classical ideals and values. Such is the case with the outstanding oeuvre of award-winning poet Tony Harrison (Leeds, 1937–). In *Tony Harrison: Poet of Radical Classicism*, Edith Hall offers a distinct reading of how classical antiquity informs key aspects of this author's poetics and identity politics, from his classical education at Leeds Grammar School and the University of Leeds, to the extraordinary breadth and scope of his artistic production, most notably, 'Newcastle in Peru (1969)', *The Loiners* (1970), *Phaedra Britannica* (1975), '*The Oresteia* (1981), *v.*' (1985), *Medea: A Sex-War Opera* (1985), *The Trackers of Oxyrhynchus* (1990), *Prometheus* (1998),

Metamorpheus (2000) and *Iphigenia in Crimea* (2017). Instead of simply concentrating on the presence of the classics in his writing, Hall draws strategic attention to how Harrison carefully selects Graeco-Roman materials as 'models of eloquence', which he experimentally adopts to develop his public voice about social and political concerns of his time. At the heart of this enterprise is what Hall identifies as Harrison's 'radical classicism'. This is by no means a mere slogan. In fact, it emerges as a shorthand for an approach that requires careful consideration. As Hall puts it, Harrison's brand of classicism is 'radical' in the 'special sub-sense of containing a commitment to 'root-and-branch' socio-political change of a left-wing rather than right-wing nature'. It is from the perspective of the radical left that Harrison's 'classicism' thus acquires certain semantic inflections which dramatically depart from other connotations of the term. Most notably, readers of Hall's chapters will not find an author whose love for the classics serves to idealise Graeco-Roman antiquity or to portray its literary and material productions as qualitatively superior to those of other cultural traditions or subsequent periods in Western history. On the contrary, in each of her nine chapters one discovers a refreshing profile of a poet who treats 'ancient writers and figures as equals speaking to the contemporary public in vibrant living voices from the transhistorical community of authors with whom he interacts in diverse but never deferential ways'. From this angle, Hall explores the multiple ways in which Harrison combines the formalistic controls found in Graeco-Roman textual, visual and epigraphic culture with a distinctive form of colloquialism that revolves around aural echoes and soundscapes, syntactic economy and experimentation, and rhythms close to what has been characterised as a 'jazz-like spontaneity'. Examples of this combination abound Hall's chronological structure, which moves from her explorations of the interplay of statuary and classicism in Harrison's early poetry, through his experiments in verse drama and Aeschylus' *Oresteia*, to his 'prosodic motions' of the figure of Prometheus and his classically-informed poetic autobiography. In her close analyses of Harrison's poetry, translations, poetic films, and other materials, Hall presents us with a writer who constantly recalls classical myths, history, artifacts, and the authorial voices of the ancient Mediterranean, from Aeschylus to Martial and beyond, to articulate local and global social and political agenda, in particular. Here, readers can effectively trace Harrison's uses of antiquity as a rhetorical conduit for his ongoing concerns about class and gender inequality and exclusion, the impact of oppressive regimes, the plight and deprivations of war, and the injustices suffered by minority groups, to name just a few. If one returns to the intellectual ambitions of the present series discussed above, Hall's volume makes for a timely contribution. It introduces a contemporary author whose radical aesthetics prompt us to a substantial rethinking of the classics and the practice of reception. But it also crucially suggests new ways of questioning the uses of the classical past, as well as the place and roles this past can (or should?) have in the shifting ethical and political codes of our new century.

Laura Jansen, University of Bristol

1

'Models of eloquence': Radical Classicism

Idiosyncratic classicism

These are the extempore words with which Tony Harrison introduced some of his poems at an event organized by the campaign to save the Classics Department at Royal Holloway, University of London, in 2011:

> I owe a huge debt to the Classics. Classics has been in my bloodstream since I was eleven. I absolutely absorbed it greedily. It gave me all kinds of models of eloquence I've been mining ever since, in my poetry, my theatre work, and in my films.[1]

He used four successive metaphors to describe his personal relationship with Classics: a financial one (debt), two physiological ones (bloodstream, greedily) and an industrial one (mining). These offer insights into his subjective feelings about classical literature, but also into the scope of his poetry, where economics, work, material production and corporeality are constant concerns. Classics gave him 'models of eloquence' – a carefully chosen phrase.

'Eloquence' has been one of Harrison's signature nouns ever since his second book-length volume of poetry was published in 1978 under the title *From 'The School of Eloquence' and Other Poems.* 'The School of Eloquence' was one of the revolutionary London Corresponding Society's euphemisms for their meetings, necessitated by the censorship laws of the 1790s. As members of the School of Eloquence they pretended to be assembling innocently to study rhetoric via classical authors, especially Cicero. But the real purpose was to plan republican constitutional reform.[2] The word 'eloquence', in Harrison's speech, is always suggestive of his identification with the history of democratic republicanism.

This book addresses the relationship between Harrison's poetry and the ancient Graeco-Roman world, between the Bronze-Age backdrop to the myths enacted in Homer and ancient tragedy, and the triumph of Christianity around the end of the fourth century CE. The shorthand for that relationship in this book's title is 'radical classicism'. The uses to which Harrison puts the classical worlds are undoubtedly 'radical' in the special sub-sense of containing a commitment to 'root-and-branch' socio-political change of a left-wing rather than right-wing nature. By 1822 the term 'radical' was intuitively paired with 'Jacobinical';[3] the 1841 autobiography of the Lancashire Chartist Samuel Bamford was entitled *Passages in the Life of a Radical*. But 'classicism' is ambiguous. It is not an ancient concept. Rival terms have been coined, such as Thomas Mann's 'classicity' (Klassizität) in 1911.[4] As Theodore Ziolkowski writes in his study of Modernism, every 'classicism' is embedded in its own era, and is 'always a synthesis of past and present and never simply a restoration of antiquity'.[5]

Harrison's idiosyncratic classicism eludes analysis according to many resonances of the term, such as the principles of proportion, moderation, simplicity, order and quiet dignity.[6] The earliest instances, in the nineteenth century, emerged in response to the term 'Romanticism'. In an 1826 review of an edition of Alberto Nota's comedies, the author says that the Italians' 'national character and literature' contains 'classic elements' (by which he means elements inherited from classical Latin literature), so that, for Italians, in what he calls 'regular composition', 'Romanticism ... will always be tempered by classicism'. He alludes to the Italians' insistence that plays must have aesthetic unity, an inheritance of the Aristotelian tradition.[7] Harrison certainly adheres to one of the formal tenets of 'regular composition' in his relishing of the constraints imposed on the poet by formal metre, as we shall see. He could loosely be accommodated by Sherard Vines' definition of English classicism, which, despite its great 'elasticity', he says displays 'correctness, good sense, grandeur and dignity'.[8] Harrison's 'correctness' does not extend beyond formal restrains, although his consistent outlook might well qualify as expressing 'good sense', and despite its earthiness, his poetry is often both grand and dignified. But he breaks all other rules ever invented by self-appointed policemen of literary form and content; he has no interest in nationalism or national literatures. His poetry is as informed by Romantic poets (Byron, Keats and Shelley; Hugo and Rimbaud; Goethe and Heine) as 'Augustan' or 'classical' ones.

His is not the impersonal, intellectual, morally didactic classicism associated with French authors of the later seventeenth century, however much he learned from translating Molière's *The Misanthrope* and Racine's *Phèdre* in the 1970s. Nor is it not the learned, crafted but critical and often satirical English classicism of Jonson, Dryden, Addison and Pope, however much he has absorbed from reading them immersively. Even less does Harrison's classicism imply that he regards certain Greek or Roman artefacts 'as the best of their category, often with the implication that their heyday is past'.[9] He never glorifies classical antiquity, being aware, like the English radical Tom Paine, that idealizing it prevents living generations from conceiving a better future.[10] Nor does he regard ancient texts as either qualitatively superior or 'over and done with'; he treats ancient writers and figures as equals speaking to the contemporary public in vibrant living voices from the transhistorical community of authors with whom he interacts in diverse but never deferential ways. Harrison's ancients speak to him in the present tense.

Nor is composer Wolfgang Rihm's diagnosis of 'classicism' as the monopoly of the past relevant to Harrison. Rihm proposes that 'something of the present can never be classic. Classicism always *is* when it *has been*.... Classicism *becomes*.'[11] But Harrison's poetry has often been of such terrifying immediacy that it is classical, in his sense, at the moment of first publication or performance, especially his 'news poems' for *The Guardian* in the 1990s.[12] By being commissioned to write precisely about headline issues, such poetry has led to him being described as 'a public poet in the classical tradition'.[13] In 'A Cold Coming' (taking its title, ironically, from the first line of T. S. Eliot's 'The Journey of the Magi'), which the newspaper published in 1991, Harrison makes the 'charred Iraqi' in his burnt-out vehicle assume that the Western press had avoided images of Gulf War Iraqi dead for the same reason that he doubts 'victorious Greeks let Hector join their feast as spoiling spectre'.[14] This use of the *Iliad* in a newspaper shares something with the 'mass classicism' which Jonathan Awtrey sees 'was an essential component for social cohesion' in New England in the 1770s, when Joseph Warren was using Ciceronian oratory to forge a 'familiar language' through which Bostonians were enabled to 'understand their revolution and to imagine a republic of equal citizens' during a turbulent historical moment.[15]

For a similar reason, Harrison's classicism is not illuminated by Salvatore Settis' claim that the 'uniqueness' of Western classicism, in comparison with Chinese, Indian and other great but 'static' civilizations, lies in its notion of the cyclical return of classical periods.[16] Harrison is not particularly absorbed by the Renaissance or other periodic revivals of interest in the ancient world; his work contains nothing equivalent to Ezra Pound's *Canto* I, which reworks Odysseus' visit to the Underworld through Andreas Divus' Renaissance Latin translation of the *Odyssey* (1538).[17] Although Harrison engages, sardonically, with the great Modernists, Eliot as well as Pound,[18] he would contest Alexander Kluge's claim that for contemporary artists, early twentieth-century Modernists are our equivalent to classical authors and that engaging with them is our classicism.[19]

The transhistorical republic of writers

Harrison departs from earlier post-Renaissance classicisms in his lack of interest in religion and commitment to candour; he embraces the frank voices of the ancient Greek and Roman lyric, comic and satirical traditions, before they were silenced by Christianity, about both sex and excretion. He could never relate to Eliot's Catholicism or even Pound's anti-Christian Confucianism. He is fascinated by every feature of Milton's poetry except its ardent Protestantism. His poems rarely engage with biblical literature except when regretting the 'droning vicar' at his mother's funeral who 'misquotes *Ecclesiastes* Chapter 3'.[20] He resents the historical connection between the classical curriculum and the Anglican hierarchy, 'the vicar teaching Classics' representing sexual and colonial repression in his 'Doodlebugs' and the prurient 'Classics/RI master' of 'Wordlists'.[21]

The poem 'The Pomegranates of Patmos' (1989) is a satire on the Christian tradition that God ordered St John ('a batty old bugger') to write the 'Apocalypse' on the island, and that he dictated it to his disciple Prochorus. This tradition is weighed against Harrison's heady and verbally explicit sex with his lover there, entailing a ribald invitation to think of Sappho's erotic poems by inverting the loneliness of her haunting fragment about sleeping alone after the moon and the Pleiades have set.[22] It contains one of his most outrageous stanzas (the Greek word is the divine imperative, 'write!' pronounced 'GRAPSON'):

> And the God with gargantuan ΓΡΑΨΟΝ
> commanding that crackpot to write

is a Big Daddy bastard who craps on
the Garden of Earthly Delight.

Made the same year, the film-poem *The Blasphemers' Banquet*, broadcast on BBC 1 on 31 July 1989, criticized Islam during the furore surrounding Salman Rushdie's 1988 publication of *The Satanic Verses*. The novel, which deals with the life of Muhammad, was condemned by many Muslims as blasphemous. The Iranian Ayatollah Khomeini issued a fatwa encouraging Rushdie's murder.

The film-poem is set at the Omar Khayyám restaurant in Bradford where Harrison holds a banquet for invited guests who have been 'damned by some priest': Omar Khayyám, Salman Rushdie, Voltaire, Molière and Byron. The film's refrain is 'this fleeting life', a reference to the Koran, Al-Insan 76.27, which condemns unbelievers who 'love this fleeting life' rather than concentrating on the afterlife. In bypassing the entire history of Christianity and Islam and embracing the pagan ancient Greeks and Romans, Harrison divests his poetry of metaphysical apparatus except insofar as his commitment to savouring every joy and sensation 'this fleeting life' offers often feels like a spiritual position.[23] As we shall see in Chapter 7, the nearest to a classifiable philosophy of life in Harrison's poetry is the Epicureanism of Lucretius.

In 'The Grilling', first published in *London Review of Books* on 6 June 2002, we are invited into Harrison's transhistorical 'republic of artists', who are vibrantly alive to him, at a Dionysiac symposium. Harrison imagines himself sitting beneath Mount Vesuvius, listening to Goethe and the artist Tischbein converse; Tischbein sketches Harrison, and recites, in Latin, Martial's epigram on the devastation caused to Vesuvius by the eruption which destroyed Pompeii and Herculaneum in 79 CE. The Germans 'improvise translations', we are told, but Harrison provides us with three translations into English, 'Thomas May's then Addison's then mine'. His own reads,

Vesuvius, green yesterday with shady vine,
    where the crushed grape gushed vast vats of wine,
ridges, Bacchus loved and put before
    his birthplace Nysa, Venus favoured more
than Lacedaemon, and where Satyrs stomped,
    till now, and Herculaneum, all swamped,

> engulfed by cinders in a flood of fire:
> > power like this not even gods desire.
>
> (Tony Harrison, 1937–)²⁴

By appending his vital date(s) (his date of death still to be determined), Harrison is equating himself with both May and Addison, whose dates follow their translations.

Harrison's version reveals several of his trademarks, notably rhyming couplets and the intrusion of a 'low', colloquial word ('stomped') into elevated classical subject matter. A word in May's translation gives the poem its title and unifies its twin themes of catastrophe and applied heat. The Latin of the last line, 'nec superi vollent hoc licuisse sibi', literally 'nor do the gods want to be allowed this [power]', is translated by May, 'the gods are grill'd that such great power they had'. Harrison's follows May's translation with this explanation:

> (*grill* as in to hurt, give pain,
> *Grill* as in 'The grones of Sir Gawayne
> does my heart grille'. But *grill* as well has heat
> and whatever gods there were have blistered feet.)

To illustrate May's verb 'grill'd, meaning 'pained', Harrison cites a line from *The Awyntyrs off Arthure*, a medieval romance in alliterative northern English rhyming verse,²⁵ thus exemplifying another trademark – a joy in flamboyant displays of erudition and lexicography.²⁶ The poem also contains his customary wine theme and personal touch, expressed in his increasing inebriation, reminiscent of Tibullus' elegy I.2, and self-description as a 'life-affirming drinker'. But it develops into a lament for two further fire-related catastrophes in wine-producing communities. They span history from Bronze Age Greece to the Second World War: the eruption on Thera (Santorini) that destroyed the Knossos-based civilization, and the dropping of incendiary bombs which flattened Würzburg, killing more than 5,000 Germans, on 16 March 1945. Harrison has said that the carnage of the Second World War, the backdrop to his childhood, provided him with his lifelong commitment to poetry. When watching newsreel footage from Belsen in 1945, he wondered how he 'could measure even simple pleasures against such images – when the violent events of history seem to cancel out joy and meaning'.²⁷

The Grilling exemplifies and clarifies the distinctive nature of Harrison's classicism. It positions him in dialogue with a genealogy going back via canonical German and English poets, including an early Arthurian author, to the Latin of Martial and the Minoan-Mycenaean civilization reflected in Homeric epic. It shows him revelling in his own control of classical languages, craftsmanship and erudition, but explaining arcane references for a general public. It also reveals him offering glimpses of his personal lifestyle and personality while addressing human suffering and issues of public moment today.

The trapeze of poetic form

Harrison's answer to human suffering is to frame horror, memory and emotions within strict verse forms. He has written a few fascinating prose essays, mostly as introductions to his poetry,[28] but is uncomfortable except when writing in metre. He has said that he was originally drawn to verse because he 'wanted to "occupy" literature', and 'learned it as skilfully as I could in order that people would have to pay attention', but added that verse has a more primal source connected with the human life force: 'it's associated with the heart beat, with the sexual instinct, with all those physical rhythms which go on despite the moments when you feel suicidal';[29] his poem 'On the metre' expresses this in sonnet form.[30]

He wrote in 1964 that that translating poetry into English poetry would improve his own poems;[31] 'I learnt all the metres by imitation; it gives you a structure from which to venture out, like being on a trapeze but having a wire to catch you if you fall.'[32] In this he shares what Dominique Secretan has identified as the time-honoured emphasis of classicism, especially French classicism, on learning a craft – becoming a skilled word-artisan by immersion in the masters of the medium.[33] His sonnets reveal his absorption of exponents of the fourteen-line form from Dante to Yeats and Auden, but his chosen model in many poems, including '*v.*', is the sixteen-line sonnet of George Meredith's *Modern Love* (1862). Harrison realized that double octets, alternatively divisible as four quatrains, allowed a stronger dialectic, and therefore enriched potential for polemic. He sometimes breaks the lines up differently to underscore the sense of an argument developing. 'On Not Being Milton', for example (see p. 12), is divided unevenly as 4-7-1-3-1 and printed as such.[34] The sonic syncopation reflects the contrast between Miltonic formality and Harrison's theme of inarticulacy. Rhyme further controls Harrison's poetry in sonnet and other verse structures. Alan Young was surprised, when he read Harrison's first major collection, *The Loiners* (1970), by its 'almost exclusive use of rhymed forms to convey experiences of raw and often appalling character as well as wild and rollicking ones. It is as if these forms were used by Harrison as non-literary (or even anti-literary) devices, enabling him to avoid "literature" as he created poems of jazz-like spontaneity.'[35]

'Strong, powerful emotions,' says Harrison, 'are very difficult to articulate and measure without some kind of form.'[36] He takes the creation of verses, whether in translations or new poems, with such single-minded seriousness that he dismissed his mammoth achievement in creating powerful drama out of the English Mystery Plays as merely the work of the man who 'came in to read the meter/metre'.[37] When translating the *Oresteia* into Old English verse forms, he wrote to director Peter Hall, quoting Stravinsky's working manifesto:

> *My* freedom thus consists in my moving about within the narrow frame that *I* have assigned myself for each one of my undertakings. I shall go even further: my freedom *will* be so much the greater and more meaningful the more narrowly I narrow my field *of* action and the more I *surround myself with obstacles. Whatever diminishes constraint, diminishes strength.*[38]

Despite his colloquialism, and emotional immediacy, Harrison never uses free verse. Even where he employs flexible and varied rhythms, for example in his translation of selected epigrams by Palladas (1975), he introduces rhyme to control the form. When translating the Latin epigrams of Martial into New York dialect, Harrison expanded elegiac couplets into strictly rhyming tercets.[39]

One sub-category of classicism entails an author identifying with a classical literary figure, as Victoria Moul has argued that Jonson 'liked to think of himself as Horace', and that his relationship to Horace involved modelling 'his own self-conscious poetic "authority"'.[40] Harrison identifies with the low-status satyr Marsyas who dared to challenge the patrician Apollo to a musical competition;[41] he has absorbed aspects of many poets, and sometimes temporarily experimented with a partial identification with them, especially

Keats and Rimbaud. As a youth, he had an intense relationship with Virgil. In the 1960s, he published, as 'T. W. Harrison', two academic articles on the eighteenth-century reception of Virgil;[42] in 1999–2000, he served as president of the Virgil Society. But he has moved from admiration of Virgil's dazzling craftsmanship towards unease with his political stance as celebrator of the Augustan imperial project.[43] Harrison is constitutionally incapable of using poetry to celebrate any political regime, let alone an empire on a massive scale. He often indicates that his endeavour is shared with all other republican, rebellious and revolutionary wordsmiths who have used their art as a vehicle for public dissent, and thereby suffered marginalization, ridicule or even persecution: Milton and May, Shelley and Hugo, Heine and Brecht, Holub, Ritsos and Zargana.

He absorbed the snarling tonality of both Palladas and Martial after translating them; 'Harrison's pain, like Palladas's, is not usually borne either with stoical resignation or gentlemanly decorum. There is a good deal of deliberate bad taste.'[44] Yet he has not invited identification with earlier poets by extensively translating any other since, although his one-off version of a fragment of the comic poet Amphis, the second stanza of 'Wine and Poetry', has been identified by Harrison's admirers as his personal manifesto:

> One glass and no refill
> Is life for men.
> So keep on pouring till
> Death says *when*.[45]

When searching for a 'barbarian', northern diction into which to translate Aeschylus' *Oresteia* for the National Theatre, he discovered the visceral 'kennings', neologisms compounded out of two existing elements, in Old Norse and Icelandic; he identified a linguistic ancestor for his own raw, consonantal version of Aeschylus in the tenth-century Icelandic poet Egil Skalla-Grimsson, who once lived in England. He riffed on a symbiosis between himself and the early tragedian Phrynichos in *The Labourers of Herakles* (1995). But he has never consistently emulated any author; his authorial presence, voice, consciousness and style are emphatically his own, indeed exceptionally clear-cut and consistent across his entire *oeuvre*. Nobody coming across one of his couplets could ever mistake it for one by Ted Hughes or Seamus Heaney.

Like the ancient Greeks lyric poets, and the vase-painters who proudly inscribed their names on pots, he is at ease with his own persona and subjectivity. The self-conscious theorizing of the personal 'I' voice was developed in the discourses of Plato, and through Greek philosophy, which encouraged individuals to develop their interior selves as moral agents. This in due course produced the first surviving examples of individuals constructed and preserved through their writings in St Paul's Epistles and the Stoic emperor Marcus Aurelius' *Meditations*, which Harrison was to explore to hilarious effect in *The Kaisers of Carnuntum* (1995). Harrison's unapologetic and resonant 'I' voice, to which we shall return in later chapters, is thus an element of his classicism.

Radical classicism

Harrison's 'classicism', therefore, consists in his constant use of Greek and Roman materials, conscious imitation of certain aspects of classical authors, sense of a continuous dialogue with earlier poets, his skilful deployment of form, metre and rhyme, sexual and scatological explicitness, secularism, commitment to a public role for poetry and strong authorial identity. But what makes this classicism radical? First, 'Classicism is evidently not a water-tight system. . . . It does not muzzle dissenters.'[46] Harrison has been consistently dissident in a class-ridden, sexist world. He has always used poetry as a public vehicle to give voice to the oppressed, whether on account of gender, race, poverty or class. He has confronted the quandary of working in a medium whose consumers are not of the same class as his birth class – to which he remains loyal – *through* his distinctive classicism. His radical treatment of Classics is aligned with his refusal to forget that the middle class's prosperity has been built on the working class's deprivation. As Lorna Hardwick has said, his classical education stands out 'as a mark of alienation, both personal and cultural, from his working-class roots'.[47] Harrison also uses classical myth to forge an inclusive public poetry rather than an exclusive curriculum. His use of that classical tradition of public poetry is class-conscious and oppositional: it is, in Patrick Deane's acute formulation, 'the deft and opportunistic annexation of classical authority by a poet not born to it'.[48]

Secondly, Harrison's poetry confronts the longstanding attempts by ruling classes, especially in Britain, to monopolize what they call 'the classical heritage' or 'classical tradition'.[49] Several poems about his childhood explore this issue. 'Me Tarzan' remembers the boy whose homework prevented him from playing in the streets with his friends: 'Ah bloody can't ah've gorra Latin prose,' he yells out of his attic window, his head protruding 'like patriarchal Cissy-bleeding-ro's'.[50] 'Still' recalls the confusion of the child getting grease on his translation of Xenophon because his father insisted the barber apply hair oil to his head.[51] 'Classics Society (Leeds Grammar School 1552–1952)' expresses the class tensions crystallized in the pedagogical exercise of Latin Prose Composition:

> We boys can take old Hansards and translate
> the British Empire into SPQR
> but nothing demotic or up-to-date,
> and not the English that I speak at home.[52]

Learning to compose in the Latin language is part of the British imperial curriculum and inimical to the working class whose language his family uses.

Recently, the term 'radical classicism' has begun to be used in relation to several media. When the eighteenth-century painter Benjamin West enlivened his precise, statue-like classical figures with a vivid colour palette derived from Titian, Jacobin political subtexts were detected; his innovation has recently been described as 'radical classicism'.[53] Harrison's use of vivid dialects within classically pulsating stanzas has parallels with West's technique. Less helpful is the atavistic neoclassical architectural style favoured by Prince Charles' favourite architect Quinlan Terry, complete with porticoes and Palladian columns. This has bafflingly been described as 'radical classicism',[54] although its similarity to its eighteenth-century models implies that there is nothing 'radical' about it. Advocates of such tame neoclassicism need to remember Young's paradox in *Conjectures on Original Composition*, 1749: 'the less we copy the renowned ancients, we shall resemble them more'.[55]

In cinema, classicism refers to stately pace, realist conventions and set-piece visual compositions, combined with certain types of master narrative. Some recent film-makers, however, have been using old-fashioned cinematography to record a quintessentially 'classicist' plot but subvert its ideological import. James Gray's *The Lost City of Z* (2016), for example, features a British explorer, Percy

Fawcett, who in the early twentieth century searched Amazonia for a fabled lost civilization. As Jake Orthwein argues, although the film feels superficially old-fashioned, it is fresh and subversive: 'A setup that at first seems like the quintessential classicism's problems (rich white male ventures into the uncivilized jungle) soon emerges as a subtle critique of colonialism'; Fawcett becomes obsessed with proving 'his fellow Europeans wrong about the supposed backwardness of Amazonian tribes'. Moreover, Gray's work 'singlehandedly falsifies the postmodern notion that classical art's problematic ideological underpinnings are best undermined by the wholesale scrapping of formal constraints'.[56] Harrison's poetry was falsifying the notion before Postmodernism was invented.

In literature, the term 'radical classicism' is intertwined with 'black classicism', which emerged in relation to African-American authors' engagements with ancient authors and with the white ruling-class invention of an American classical tradition in the cauldron of eighteenth-century slavery debates. Key figures here are Phyllis Wheatley, Ralph Waldo Ellison and Toni Morrison.[57] John Barnard's fine study *Empire of Ruin: Black Classicism and American Imperial Culture* (2018) historicizes 'black classicism' by analysing it 'in relation to the role of classicism in the dominant culture' and reading it 'within and against the discourses of national identity' that have 'served to reinforce racialized structures of power'.[58]

Harrison's 'radical classicism' has done the same for the role of classicism in the British class system. But Harrison alludes to something closer to black classicism when he calls 'On not being Milton', the sixteen lines of the first poem in *From 'The School of Eloquence'*, 'my *Cahier d'un retour au pays natal/* my growing black enough to fit my boots'.[59] One reason he is not Milton is that he identifies with the conflicted Odyssean Aimé Césaire in his prose poem *Return to My Native Land* (1939). This Martiniquean intellectual trained as a Classics teacher at the prestigious École Normale Supérieure. The poem relates his quest for identity in Paris and back home. Gregson Davis has shown how Césaire exploits the classical associations suggested by his black author-narrator, who fears that his education has led him into complicity with white people and betrayal of his race.[60] Harrison, after years in Africa, now relates to victims of racism and colonial oppression abroad as much as to the working class of England.

Poem as turning-point: 'Newcastle is Peru'

In a poem written in Newcastle upon Tyne on a cold September day in 1969, after years mostly spent in Nigeria, Senegal, Prague, the Soviet Union, Cuba and Brazil, Harrison represents himself 'as a kind of Ulysses returned to his native country in a rather desolate state'.[61] But this Ulysses has 'seen many cities inhabited by humans and become acquainted with their minds' (*Odyssey* I.3). Psychologically disoriented, trying to light a fire in an upper-storey flat, his gaze ranges over the cityscape through the window. These images are interspersed with recollections of his childhood on holiday in Blackpool and at home in Leeds, which in turn alternate with memories of Czechoslovakia, Africa and Latin America. The poem marks a pivotal moment when he recognizes that his poetic mission, as a white working-class boy from northern England, has been irrevocably altered by the humans across three continents with whose minds he has become acquainted. The British class hierarchy and the history of European colonization of the planet are fused in a dizzying semi-hallucination.

Hungover, or rather still drunk 'on nine or ten *Newcastle Brown*', he remembers swinging through the air on a fairground ride called the chair-o-plane (popular in the north of England from the 1930s). He pictures a circular tour of Leeds offering him an aerial view of its landmarks, but then the ride extends to St Vitus' Cathedral in Prague, to slaves tunnelling as they mine the Andes, and then to Africa, where he remembers watching 'a muscled woman heave/ huge headloads of dead wood'. The poem draws to a close with a confused account of a passionate sexual encounter in the Newcastle apartment and a bewildering jumble of images drawing attention to his own whiteness, his 'fingerprints lined with coal', his 'grimy fingers' smudging 'everything they touch'. The last four lines insist the reader or listener think about white skins, the northern European fashion for suntans, the disavowal of colonialism amongst black Francophone intellectuals and the idea that skin colour is implicated in the malignant 'tumour' of colonialism: he looks at a magazine full-page spread depicting

> ... aggressively fine bosoms, nude,
> and tanned almost to *négritude*,
> in the Colour Supplement's *Test*
> *Yourself for Cancer of the Breast*.[62]

The négritude movement, fostering Pan-African unity amongst Africans and their diaspora descendants, was founded in the 1930s by Césaire, along with Senegal's first president, Léopold Sédar Senghor and the politician/poet Léon Damas, born in French Guiana. Harrison's reference to '*négritude*' thus aligns him with the colonized peoples of the global south.

This intense poem is introduced by two epigraphs. The first, the source of the title, 'Newcastle is Peru', is drawn from an obscure poem attributed to John Cleveland, 'News from Newcastle; or, Newcastle Coal-Pits'. Cleveland was a seventeenth-century satirical poet, whose scathing tone (although not his Royalist politics) Harrison admires. The poem praises the coal industry of north-east England, insisting that it brings as much wealth as gold from the New World brings to the Spanish. England has its own equivalent of the remunerative Indies

> Correct your Maps, *Newcastle* is *Peru!*

For Harrison, the north of England and the colonized southern hemisphere had become interchangeable.

The second epigraph, in untranslated Latin, invites meditation on the relationship between classical literature and colonial dominion. It is the five famous lines of Seneca's *Medea* where the Corinthian chorus, after reflecting on civilization's expansion under the Roman Empire even to the Indians and the River Elbe, predict that one day in the far-off future (375–9), 'Ocean shall release the bonds of things and the vast earth shall be disclosed, and Tethys will uncover new worlds and Thule not be the most distant of lands.' The symbolic importance of this prophecy in the history of colonialism cannot be overestimated. Columbus felt he had fulfilled it when in 1492 he 'discovered' the 'Indies' thirty-three days west of the Canary Islands, and he encouraged others to believe he had done so.[63] Harrison thus introduces his poem with a reminder that the results of European imperialism he has been witnessing at first hand were foreshadowed in classical antiquity, and re-authorized in the early Renaissance by appealing to the poetry that classical antiquity had produced.

During the 'Leeds' section of the poem, the hallucinatory chair-o-plane offers Harrison an aerial view of the city's landmarks and an opportunity to contemplate classical gods, Latin mottoes and his poetic vocation:

Venus, Vulcan, Cupid stare
out vacantly on City Square,
and *Deus iuvat impigros*
above the bank where God helps those
who help themselves, declares
Leeds purposeful in its affairs.
Mercator; miles, school chapel glass
transparencies to blood and glass.[64]

Harrison imagines himself on eye-level with Leeds civic statues representing history and sex. A Victorian Vulcan, smith-god and patron of industry, does stare out from beside his forge by the dome of the old bank building (now a nightclub) on Boar Lane; the Venus made by Canova for Thomas Hope, the merchant banker and art collector, is the centrepiece of the Leeds City Art Gallery.

The images of the merchant and the soldier, however, are figures depicted in the stained glass of the chapel of Leeds Grammar School, which Harrison attended. He has described these windows in more detail in a 1971 essay. The figures were chosen to represent suitable professions for the pupils to enter. One was MILES ('soldier') and another MERCATOR ('businessman'). In one of the most scintillating prose sentences he has ever published, Harrison writes that he can't remember the figure portrayed between them; but, in adulthood,

> ...when I close my eyes now I see Poeta, the poet, sometimes as poised, saintly and acceptable as his worldly flankers, sometimes like some half-naked shaker in the throes of a virulent scribendi cacoethes, being belaboured by public school angels wielding gamma minuses like immense shillelaghs over their glossy Cherry Blossomy hairstyles, driving the poet from the Garden of Eton.[65]

The classical vocation of POETA and Harrison's working-class identity were thus indissoluble from the start. It was in the late 1960s, around this time, moreover, that he decided to do nothing for money – not even teach, as he had in Nigeria and Prague – but write poetry.

It turns out that there were two other figures in his school chapel windows: an academic, SCHOLASTICUS, and a BENEFACTOR, 'philanthropist'. These four figures were the anthropomorphic visual images which haunted his teenage years, and his fascination with classically inflected stained glass resurfaced in the portrait of Aeschylus in the window of the Westminster Abbey sequences of his original drama *Fram* nearly forty years later.[66] Harrison won his scholarship to Leeds Grammar School, and thus access to a classical education, under the terms of the 'Butler' Education Act 1944. The British educational system, in which the small proportion of under-privileged children like Harrison who performed well in the Eleven-Plus Examination could once hope for free grammar school and university tuition, has now been taken over by commercial interests. The school chapel has been turned into the Business School of Leeds University, and the windows removed. But Harrison's memory is accurate: the window figures were unveiled in 1931 and described in *The Yorkshire Post*.[67]

Nor are the two figures in the window which Harrison had forgotten irrelevant to his achievements. He is a scholar: the depth of his reading and research, in both classical and more recent literature, is staggering. He has also always wanted to be a benefactor in the true sense of the word. In the public imagination, he may be primarily associated with his most snarling poetic voice – his characteristic, embittered railing against stupidity and injustice, which made him identify with the cynical epigrammatists Palladas and Martial. In the fourth or early fifth century CE, Palladas' biting epigrams, a selection of which Harrison translated in 1975, denounce the fall of pagan culture to the narrow-minded theocrats of the new Christian regime. In 1981, he published *U. S. Martial*, a translation of some of Martial's most licentious satirical epigrams, testing the boundaries of permissible obscenity. Yet for all his bitterness, anti-clericalism and caustic sexual honesty, the fundamental outlook of Harrison's poetry is benevolent. There is a benefactor's 'charity' in the best sense, a non-judgemental, inclusive social vision, even in his most superficially harsh, profane and controversial poem, '*v.*' (1985).[68]

The two ways of earning a living that he recalls in the window and always knew he would avoid – soldier and businessman – are connected with the intertwined themes in 'Newcastle is Peru' of capitalist commerce and war – the 'military-industrial complex', a concept first made familiar by General Dwight D. Eisenhower in his farewell TV broadcast from the Oval Office in 1961. In 'Newcastle is Peru', photos of mortar-scarred villages in Onitsha, the catastrophic result of the Nigerian-Biafran War (1967–70), itself a consequence of the British colonial amalgamation of three adjacent areas in 1914, stare out at him from the newspaper he uses as kindling. He returns to this haunting image near the poem's end, where the African woman he visualizes carrying wood is located in a complex of thatched huts; 'the mortars thud/ like a migraine in the compound mud' – an early instance of Harrison's preoccupation with military weapons. He senses that his own embattled 'stronghold of love' can't last for long 'against the world's bold cannonade/ of loveless warfare and cold trade'. Even the commodification of lovemaking is crystallized in the bleak image of used condoms ferrying 'unborn semen' borne downstream by the sluggish Tyne amidst its 'swirled detritus':

> Commerce and contraceptive glide
> and circle on the turning tide;
> *Plain, Gossamer* and *Fetherlite*
> and US *Trojan*, knotted tight.

'Newcastle is Peru', written in 1969, thus marks a pivotal moment in Harrison's life. He returned to England with his first wife and two small children, and settled in Newcastle, where he still lives today. He discarded plans for a career as an academic classicist. In 1970 he published his first book-length collection, *The Loiners*, which included a republication of 'Newcastle is Peru', and leapt to national fame when it won the Geoffrey Faber Memorial Prize in 1972. It was *The Loiners* which in 1971 convinced pioneering theatre director John Dexter to commission Harrison to translate Molière's *Le Misanthrope* for the National Theatre, a version which brought him international attention and further commissions.

And the poem, with its Odyssean *nostos* (homecoming) theme, shows Harrison's enhanced understanding of world politics and the toxic legacies of colonialism in conjunction with increased awareness of self – his working-class roots, his strong sexuality, the connection between his imaginative and creative powers and the states of mind that alcohol can induce, his contempt for money and violence. It also revolves around several other constituents of his work in every poetic genre he has essayed. They include architecture, visual art and statuary; the relationship between the classical curriculum and European imperialism; poetic precursors both canonical and obscure and the interpenetration of public affairs and private experience; the division of humans by class and gender hierarchies; the physical materiality of books and writing, food and drink, the human body, detritus, and the natural and built environments; fire and the technologies of industry and war; the representation of atrocity; autobiography, sex, memory and death. These are the elements explored, largely in the linear chronological order of his major Classics-dominated works, in the remaining chapters of this book.

2

'Stone bodies': Statuary and Classicism in *The Loiners* (1970) and *Palladas* (1975)

In 2009, Harrison explained the pervasive sculptures in his poetry: 'Statues are one of the ways I try to test the traditions of European culture against the most modern destructive forces.'[1] Yet, despite general agreement that visual artworks – statues, paintings, photographs – occupy a prominent place in his poetry, critics are divided on the efficacy with which they are used. John Lyon goes so far down the road of negative assessment as to argue that Harrison's words 'are premised on, and subordinate to, the visual', his 'sentimental and domesticating verse too often [doing] a disservice to such images, blunting and blurring their capacity to disturb and challenge'.[2]

But the instrumentality of the visual artefact in Harrison's poetry illuminates the nature of his classicism. His pivotal collection *The Loiners* (1970) acquires imagistic unity from the prevalence of statuary; it establishes certain functions of the material artwork in Harrison's poetry in ways that anticipate more ambitious uses of visual artefacts in his later works. Thinking about the central image of the statue is a helpful route into Harrison's complex experiential world, since it is intricately associated with other recurring elements in his subsequent poetry – not only with his classicism, and attraction towards the ancient Greek epigrammatist Palladas in 1975, but also his political outlook, transhistorical vision (David Kennedy has called him a 'poetic time-traveller'[3]), his concept of poetry as a craft, his sense of physical embodiment as a human being with a capacity for acute sensory and sexual experiences, and attitudes to mortality and death.

Harrison the *world*-traveller always notices statues. His prose works often mention the stone figures he has visited abroad – the monumental Cervantes beneath which he dozed one hot afternoon outside a public library in Cuba, the disapproving gaze of the grand actress Mlle Mars at the Comédie-Française in Paris, contrasted with the more affable statue beside his favourite Parisian hotel of Molière.[4] He has a personal collection of statues – or rather, busts of poets – as he has described in his speech 'The Inky Digit of Defiance', delivered when he accepted the inaugural PEN/Pinter Prize in 2009:

> ...the first thing you will see in my hallway is a large eighteenth-century bust of Milton, who stares at me as I watch TV and reminds me of the grave and seriously committed role of the poet, and who, though he was blind, had one of the most unflinching and unswerving gazes of all English poets. He is one of my great heroes. I have a mini-version of this bust looking at me as I type in my attic. I have small busts of Homer, Dante, Byron and Strindberg, and framed engravings of Molière, Shakespeare, Kipling, a photo and a manuscript of Yeats.[5]

In works Harrison published later than *The Loiners*, such busts and statues sometimes feature metapoetically, as part of a self-reflexive discussion of his own role in the history of poetry and his relationship with his predecessors, both those he admires fraternally and those for whom his feelings are more conflicted. The Milton bust appears as 'a constant inspiration', to be lovingly dusted, in 'A Celebration of the Abdication of King Charles III'.[6] On the other hand, the idea of the portrait bust played an ironic role in his 1993 *Poetry or Bust*, the 'ribald verse-biography' of John Nicholson,[7] a minor nineteenth-century Saltaire poet. A working-class wool-sorter with a drinking problem, Nicholson went to London to commission a bust of himself (now in Harrison's possession) after his employer published a volume of his verse. For Harrison, the bust here symbolizes the venal moral and political 'selling out' of all artists who have ever compromised their art or acquiesced to the demands of the ruling class in return for a stipend, fleeting celebrity or an honorific title.

In the less self-conscious and less confident poetic idiom of *The Loiners*, however, before he had to negotiate the pitfalls of fame, this use of the artwork is not manifested. Nor is the link between the type of immortality which the poet can hope to achieve through song, a way of surviving death even more enduring than a monument cast in bronze or structured in stone like the pyramids, as Horace definitively expressed it in the opening stanza of his *Odes* III.30. The uses to which Harrison puts statuary in *The Loiners* are diverse;

they include the function of statue similes and metaphors in Greek tragedy – occurring in contexts dominated by eros or thanatos, or in meditations upon the nature and function of poetry.[8] But in *The Loiners*, talking to other poets about intertextuality, and mulling on poetic celebrity, are not yet amongst the obvious tasks of the textually embedded artefact.

In 1983, Harrison himself defined *The Loiners* as dealing with 'sex and history: the intimacies of the private life are a kind of earthing area for the lightning of history and of political struggles'.[9] In 'Allotments', he remembers erotic encounters, during his young manhood, in the graveyards of Leeds, where 'after love/ we'd find some epitaph/ embossed backwards on your arse and laugh' – a humorous inversion of the traditional equation of sex and death, his lover's body itself receiving the imprint of funereal verses.[10] Establishment doctors are compared in 'Manica' to 'Starchy Baptist cherubim'; medical officials disapprovingly performing tests for venereal disease become envisaged as chubby ecclesiastical sculptures.[11] And in 'The Curtain Catullus', the image of the statue is central to a vivid but disturbing sexual encounter with a Czechoslovakian woman during the Prague Spring.[12] In a taut refashioning of the poetic motif of 'Love *versus* War' beloved of the Latin poets of the first century BCE, beginning with Catullus, the monumental architecture of the city is juxtaposed with its civic statues: 'I'm not so sold/ On all this Gothic and this old Baroque.' The woman, a Communist Party tour guide, points out the monument of Jan Hus, Protestant reformer burnt at the stake in 1415, and 'Kafka's ball-less eyes caked up with snow'.

In addition to these statues of famous Czechs, the poet's voice invokes Astraea, the mythological maiden associated with the return of the Golden Age. He pleads with her to descend and make 'piecemeal' the statue of Stalin, 'chocolate-Santa-Claus-/ like'. He wants her to fill the niches once featuring images of Christian saints, but also to 'crumple' (a verb with a gently sexual overtone) a statue far away in London – one which, more than any other, represents the history of British militarism, jingoism and imperialism:

> Descend like a snow maiden from the air.
> Fill Chrysostom's or Basil's empty niche,
> Crumple stiff Nelson in Trafalgar Square

The Eastern Bloc, for Harrison, does not hold a monopoly on oppression.

The sexual encounter allows the poetic 'I' voice and his lover, briefly, to escape from the macro-political chaos surrounding them. The contrast between the tumultuous history of European conflict and the warm flesh of the lovers, 'human, young, and lustful, sick of wars', is made concrete in the contrast between statues of dead men and his 'gorgeous red bird':

I'm tired of stone bodies. I want yours.

But his lover resumes peering 'at huge saints', and 'some Church soldier launching a gold spear against the Turk'. European colonialism, inseparable from Christianity, leaves uneradicated marks on the material environment. But the poet sees sexual union – however unsatisfactory, and even overheard by sinister secret service officers – as one possible response to this gloomy history. 'The Curtain Catullus' concludes with an uneasy invitation to other Slavic women to come to his 'bugged bedroom', leaving behind 'mausoleum,/ church, museum'.

By reading his sexual encounter against a Prague cityscape in which the serial historical figures and their ideologies – the Church Fathers, the Crusades, the Reformation, the Austro-Hungarian and Soviet Empires – remain visible in buildings' material fabric, Harrison explores the contrast between the temporal dimensions of poetry and the visual arts respectively. He sometimes uses statues to establish a transhistorical frame, in which the artworks of one era can speak across the centuries to another. Material artefacts can physically transcend time, but they are not themselves fluid and subject to change in the way that languages and ideologies are. Yet individual artworks are unable to *represent* movement through time in the way that poetry can narrate diachronically. Even a statue like Myron's 'Discobolus', which gives the impression that the discus is about to be thrown, arrests the athlete's body at a single nanosecond. It was not until Lessing's seminal essay *Laocoön* (1766) that this difference between poetic and visual mimesis was understood in temporal terms: Lessing's view was that art is static but permanent, arresting its object at a particular instant in time, whereas literary mimesis (especially the transient art of theatre) represents its objects as moving through time, between presence and absence.[13]

Harrison, however, is more influenced by the key ancient Greek and Roman notions of the relationship between literature and art. First, the ancients saw the significant difference between the two as *sensory*. Visual art makes no sound, and the 'voicelessness' of the material artefact is a frequent trope in ancient poetry. Harrison knows these tropes well: he translates the famous comparison in *Agamemnon* of Iphigenia as she was sacrificed to a mute artefact,

> a painting   a sculpture   that seems to be speaking
> seeking to say things   but locked in its stone.[14]

The vacant stares and muted voices of statues, and the silent screams of figures in photographs, appear in all his work. But the ancient poets also understood that poetry, in isolation, offers nothing material to see. They responded by developing the technique known to rhetoricians as *ekphrasis*: this entails description of sights appealing to the visual imagination, especially artefacts. These begin long before the extended description of the mythical scenes embroidered on the bridal bedspread in Catullus' 'Ariadne epyllion' (poem 64) and Ovid's tale of Pygmalion and Galatea (*Metamorphoses* X). Important examples feature in the earliest surviving Greek poems, notably in the scenes of war and peace which Hephaestus/Vulcan grafted onto Achilles' new shield in *Iliad* XVIII, and the description of the gods' creation from clay and adornment of Pandora, the enticing first woman, in both Hesiod's *Theogony* and his *Works and Days*.[15] The abundance of artworks in Harrison's poetry, to which John Lyon objected, is a crucial aspect of Harrison's formal classicism.

Three of the five Petrarchan 'Curtain Sonnets' in *The Loiners*, located behind the 'Iron Curtain' in what was then called Leningrad and in Prague, develop the contrast between public artefacts and private lovemaking. 'Summer Garden' is set, ironically, in a wintry neoclassical Russian snowscape. Harrison reminds us of the devastating fatalities suffered by the Soviet Union in the Second World War, and of the military heroism of the male populace, commemorated in massive modernist statue groups, by his image of 'Leningrad's vast pool of widowhood' chipping away at the pavement ice. The same lonely women act as janitors in the city's public museums and amenities,

> who also guard the Rembrandts and rank Gents,
> who stand all day with stern unbending gaze
> haloed with Tsars' crowns and Fabergés,
> their menfolk melted down in monuments.[16]

Leningrad is presented as one vast public cemetery, where all the dead Soviet soldiers have metamorphosed from animate humanity into metallic sculpted friezes. This anticipates the fascination with inscribed gravestones and cemeteries which develops in From 'The School of Eloquence' and comes to full fruition in 'v.' and the opening in Westminster Abbey's 'Poet's Corner' of Fram.

These Leningrad monuments are grimly guarded by the dead Russian soldiers' bereaved womenfolk, themselves coupled with the metallic artefacts associated with the even older, Tsarist regime. Harrison implies that these guards do not approve of the woman with whom he's walking around the Summer Garden,

> between the statues VERITAS, HONOR,
> and PSYCHE whom strong passion made forget
> conditions of darkness and the gods' taboo.

For those who have visited the Summer Garden, its avenues, lined with baroque white statues of female personifications, are here instantly recognizable. For those who haven't, a similar scene is conjured in the mind's eye by the orthographic capitalization of the statues' names, implying the lettering on plinths on ancient inscriptions and beneath public sculptures. TRUTH and HONOR, in the poem's moral landscape, contest the judgemental attitudes of the older women, the servants of a corrupt regime. But the statue of PSYCHE, bending with her lantern to look at the sleeping body of her beloved Cupid, serves another, more surprising purpose.

This arresting statue group was created in the early eighteenth century from a design by Giovanni Lorenzo Bernini. The ancient source is Apuleius' Latin novel *Metamorphoses*. Psyche and Cupid were secretly lovers, despite the disapproval of Cupid's mother Venus. But Cupid banned Psyche from looking at his face. She broke the ban by using a lamp, and woke him when a drop of oil landed on his skin, but suffered many ordeals in reprisal. Here, in Harrison's poem, she transcends the conceptual divide between the inanimate matter of the public artefacts and Harrison's preoccupation with his lover; the 'conditions of darkness' and taboo he experiences in Cold War Leningrad suddenly make him identify with the experience of the desirous stone Psyche, suffering under diverse prohibitions.

Harrison's persona now moves inside doors. The artefacts in the fourth sonnet, 'The People's Palace', are the personifications IUSTITIA and POMONA, justice and the fruit-harvest, closed from public view.[17] They are 'wired to a U. S. import anti-theft device' and secretively stored in crates, viewable only by an academic and the ebullient man polishing the floors. The secrecy, paranoia and elitism which marked Leningrad life in the 1960s are conveyed with supreme economy in the concealment of the virtues both of moral justice and abundance of fruit – the latter being in Harrison's conceptual world always a marker of human love, generosity and the savouring of short-lived sensual pleasures which make human existence privately bearable. This trope is later developed in fullest form in 'A Kumquat for John Keats', 'The Red Lights of Plenty' (which also centres on a statue, that of Plenty with her cornucopia in Washington), 'The Pomegranates of Patmos', 'Fig on the Tyne', 'Fruitility' and 'The Gifts of Aphrodite'.

In the final sonnet of 'Curtain Sonnets', where the action shifts to a bitterly cold Prague on his birthday, 30 April 1968, the day before the traditional May Day parade, Harrison breaks new ground in his use of a sculpture. For the first time in his published poetry, in 'Prague Spring', his own perspective is almost fused with that of a stone visage.[18] It belongs to a gargoyle depicted playing a lute in a nest of carved cherries, high up on a city building, one of those Gothic cathedrals Harrison was visiting in 'The Curtain Catullus'. In the first quatrain, Harrison describes the gargoyle, high up in the clouds, who seems to have been turned into stone with his mouth wide open – whether to scream, sing or vomit:

> A silent scream? The madrigal's top note?
> Puking his wassail on the listening throng?
> Mouthfuls of cumulus, then cobalt throat.
> Medusa must have hexed him in mid-song.

The trope of petrifaction became central to Harrison's thinking about the Greek tragic mask, and unifies *The Gaze of the Gorgon*. The gaze of the masklike face of the decapitated Medusa is quite literally petrifying – it turns the viewer into rock.[19] Yet Harrison would later evolve the Nietzschean idea he found in *The Birth of Tragedy* that Dionysian art allows the masked performers and viewers of tragedy to view unbearable suffering *without* being turned into stone.[20] The singing or screaming, not-quite-human, semi-grotesque gargoyle also foreshadows Harrison's later fascination with other semi-human cast figures, such as the garden gnomes of *Prometheus* and especially the Greek satyr in *Trackers of Oxyrhynchus* – half-goat, half-man; even the brilliant stage set of that play, designed by Jocelyn Herbert, incorporated a kneeling figure modelled on the stone satyr whose back still supports the masonry of the stage where the actors played in the Athenian theatre of Dionysus. This satyr is also foregrounded in the film *A Maybe Day in Kazakhstan* and reminds Harrison of Marsyas, the satyr he came to make central to *Trackers*, the expert plebeian musician who screamed when he was flayed after rivalling the upper-class god Apollo in his song.

The poet does momentarily identify himself with the gargoyle, in the next quatrain adopting his/its own lofty visual perspective on the Prague cityscape, anticipating his/its privileged view of tomorrow's parade. The gargoyle-as-spectator thus adumbrates Harrison's use of artefacts as mouthpieces, above all in using the bust of Heine as narrator in *The Gaze of the Gorgon* (1992):

> The finest vantage point in all of Prague's
> this gagging gargoyle's with the stone-locked lute,
> leaning over cherries, blow-ups of Karl Marx
> the pioneers 'll march past and salute.

The gargoyle, simultaneously screaming, singing and feeling nauseous, is an appropriate congener of the poet surveying the absurdities and horrors of the Prague Spring.

Harrison was later to find the Czech gargoyle's 'Free World' alter ego in the stone satyr which peered into his room 'in apt. 841 of the Hotel Ansonia on 73rd and Broadway, New York' while he was translating Martial. He has written that he responded to the stare of the satyr and 'the eyes of his co-satyrs taking in the multifarious life of New York and missing nothing'; this 'combined to season these versions'.[21] The visual perspective from a high position allows the poetry of 'Prague Spring' to 'pan' like a camera fixed on a building but pointing downwards – a technique which Harrison uses in his films. But in the final six lines of 'Prague Spring', Harrison vertiginously reverses the roles of viewer and viewed, the poet's voice now expressing the political disintegration of Soviet Czechoslovakia through examining the corrosion of the gargoyle's plate surface, and the melting snow of the late thaw dribbling 'as spring saliva down his jaw'.

In 'Newcastle is Peru', Harrison's dizzying bird's-eye view veers to Prague, and the rooftop of St Vitus' Cathedral, which is topped, as he recalls here, with a weather-vane cockerel. But then the hallucinatory fairground ride swerves back to England, and this time to Newcastle upon Tyne, where Harrison imagines himself standing on the towering plinth which supports his adopted home city's most famous statue. The 'Grey Monument', which looms over the city centre at the head of Grey Street, commemorates the passing of the Great Reform Act of 1832 under the premiership of Charles Grey, the second Earl Grey. The column is forty metres high. The statue, placed atop it in 1838, shortly after the accession of Queen Victoria, was the work of Edward Hodges Baily – the same sculptor whose famous Trafalgar Statue of 'stiff Nelson' Harrison has asked Astraea, representative of utopia, to 'crumple' in 'The Curtain Catullus'. But he now pairs Earl Grey's solemn monument with one of Neptune:

> Swirled detritus and driftwood pass
> in state the 1880 *Sas-*
> *inena Cold Storage Co.*,
> and Neptune gazes at the Tyne's flow
> seawards, where the sea-winds 'boast
> and bluster' at the North East coast,
> the sluggish Tyne meandering through
> the staithes and shipyards of Peru.

The statue of Neptune, standing with his trident on two dolphins, and flanked by a pair of fishwives, was designed for the Old Fish Market in the late 1870s by a sculptor named George Burn. It is folksy and diminutive in comparison with the Earl Grey monument, but to the people of Newcastle it is just as familiar and more loved. The building was converted into a cold storage facility at the time Harrison was writing *The Loiners* (it is now a nightclub). The stony fishwives reappear, slightly modernized, as the chorus of Oceanids (transformed into female factory workers at the fish canning factory) in *Prometheus*.[22] But here, in *The Loiners*, the civic statues of Europe are markers of cartography, topography and historical change as well as of the poet's visual perspectives on his material environment.

The view downwards from atop a cathedral is once again the chief poetic visual trajectory in the penultimate poem of the collection, 'Durham'. Harrison's voice surveys the three institutions of that city, where he had held a temporary post as Poet in Residence – 'University, Cathedral, Gaol' (a line which echoes the 'mausoleum,/ church, museum' of 'The Curtain Catullus') – but now adopting 'Quasimodo's bird's-eye view'.[23] Naming the protagonist of Victor Hugo's *The Hunchback of Notre-Dame* (1831) reminds anyone familiar with the classic novel that it was from a gallery high up Notre Dame that Quasimodo watched Esmerelda, the Romany woman he loved, pray before her execution, and from which he slid down a rope trying to rescue her and persuade the Parisians to give her sanctuary. One of Harrison's personal heroes is the dissident, republican Hugo, whose *Le Roi s'amuse* he was in 1996 to translate as *The Prince's Play* for the National Theatre. But in this poem he figures himself, rather, as Quasimodo, persuading a woman to lunch and bed, to find together sanctuary from the harsh realities of the prison system and global politics.

The poem's central image is the architecture of Durham's massive Cathedral Church of Christ, Blessed Mary the Virgin and St Cuthbert, which dominates the city along every sightline. Towards the end, Harrison returns to the image of the gargoyle established in 'Prague Spring', and once again partially identifies with a grotesque stone visage:

> On the *status quo*'s huge edifice
> we're just excrescences that kiss,
> cathedral gargoyles that obtrude
> their acts of 'moral turpitude'.

These lines immediately follow the explicit emergence of the theme of sculpture, at the point when Harrison's poetic voice has asked how retreat into private intimacy can be reconciled with 'the public mess':

> At best we're medieval masons, skilled
> but anonymous within our guild,
> at worst defendants hooded in a car
> Charged with something sinister.

'Ordinary' people, if unfortunate, end up criminalized and on their way to Durham gaol. The best possible option is to live like 'medieval masons', working away cooperatively, without fame or recognition, but nevertheless skilled at our crafts – whether lovemaking or poetry. For Harrison has always insisted that poetry is a craft, which requires hard work to learn and is equivalent to any other trade or profession. This was partly his response to the working men of his family, especially his father the baker. He has said that the 'idea of becoming a master of something, of learning something, was very important to me, and partly to show off to *them* ... But I also wanted it to be real work – in the sense that my father's work was real work.'[24]

This is not, however, the whole story. Harrison found in the classical authors he read at school that the dominant language in which poets and poetry are discussed in ancient Greek authors concerns the skill or trade (*technē*), which the poet learns by hard graft and by which he earns his keep. 'Poet' (Greek *poiētēs*, Latin *poeta*) simply means 'maker' and can apply to someone who makes pots or chairs. In Homer, there is an underlying analogy between the epic bard and the smith who embosses images and actions – humans *doing things* – onto artefacts, above all in the *ekphrasis* when Hephaestus creates Achilles' shield in *Iliad* book XVIII. In the *Odyssey*, the closer analogy is between the poet and the carpenter: Odysseus, who tells much of his own story and thereby becomes a bard himself, is also an expert in woodwork: he creates boats, Trojan horses and olive-wood marriage beds. The women of Homer are experts in weaving, creating artefacts on which heroic scenes are depicted, the fabric equivalent to the stories sung by bards. The Greek lyric poets, above all Pindar and Bacchylides, develop a metaphor in which they figure themselves as craftsmen,[25] sharpening their tongues on whetstones and hammering their songs on anvils. In comparing his skilled work with that of a medieval mason, Harrison is, paradoxically, placing his own conceptualization of his craft in an unequivocally pre-medieval, classical Greek tradition.

The final poem of the collection, 'Ghosts: Some Words before Breakfast. For Jane', is perhaps the most painful and explicitly autobiographical work in Tony Harrison's whole *oeuvre*. It is a reaction to the appalling road accident his daughter Jane suffered on 5 April 1968, when a ten-ton lorry hit her, nearly destroying both her legs. The poem explores the emotions he underwent in the Royal Victoria Infirmary, Newcastle upon Tyne, waiting overnight for his little daughter to come round from surgery. It opens with the clopping sound made by the hooves of a horse drawing an 'anachronistic' beer wagon, implicitly contrasted with an enormous lorry. It is followed by the sight of the marble statue of Queen Victoria which stands outside the hospital's main doors, whitening as the daylight fades. This recalls the other 'White Queen' of the Juvenalian *Satyrae* much earlier in *The Loiners* – the Briton in Africa whose voice asserts neo-colonial rights to sexual relationships with young black men. The hospital monument also provides visual context. But the statue's prominence in the poem results from the way it sets the political compass, being cryptically addressed as 'Empress, Queen', but also symbolizing a set of restrictive Christian moral views which have played havoc with Harrison's family life. The statue is held responsible for Harrison's own mother's puritanical disapproval of sex. She interpreted the stillbirth which concluded Harrison's wife's first pregnancy as retribution for the baby being conceived before they were married: Victoria's

> clean-
> living family image drove
> my mother venomously anti love,
> and made her think the stillbirth just
> retribution for our filthy lust.

The stone statue of Victoria, lifeless, cold, and static, also serves a physical purpose as Harrison's voice describes how he willed the child to live, to breathe inside her oxygen tent,

> ... each heaved breath
> another lurch away from death,
> each exhalation like death throes ...

Her bodily struggle to breathe, along with the image of funeral flowers, is conveyed by the way he apprehends 'her pain/ through stuff like florist's cellophane'.

He shares the struggle in the waiting room, 'an airless space', and while he paces the hospital corridors, for he feels he is about to suffocate. The boundary between living, breathing organic bodies and lifeless simulacra or corpses is bizarrely reflected in the comics which litter the waiting room. The first of the interplanetary heroes he encounters is

> STONE BOY of the planet Zwen
> who turns to stone and back again.

The second is 'MATTER-EATER-LAD', whose enemy is a mad scientist called Dr MANTIS MORLO, who may 'smash/ our heroes into lunar ash'. These heroic children of the interplanetary future have superpowers. They challenge the physical laws of nature and avoid death by metamorphosing in and out of stone, or eating mineral matter. The use of classical, epigrammatic capitalization here recalls the statues of the Summer Garden in Leningrad. There is a stark antithesis between the smashed body of his own child, for whom there would be no recovery from the immobilizing coldness of death, and the fictional STONE BOY and MATTER-EATER-LAD. Yet the absurd, hyperbolic argot of sci-fi comics, far from diminishing the power of these lines, augments Harrison's expression of his incomprehension of the catastrophe and of his grief.

In the early 1970s, Harrison worked on translating French classical dramas, and by 1976 had also completed for publication the first ten poems of *From 'The School of Eloquence'*. But his first major poetic publication after *The Loiners* was his translation of a selection of poems by Palladas in 1975. Palladas is the only ancient Greek poet of whom Harrison has published an extended selection of versions. One of the attractions of Palladas to Harrison, besides the snarling, disenchanted authorial voice, was the interest in the uses to which statues could be put in poetry, which he had already demonstrated in *The Loiners*.

Palladas worked in the fourth or early fifth century CE in Alexandria. This city, like all others in the ancient Greek and Roman worlds, teemed with statues of gods, legendary heroes, civic notables and Roman emperors. Most of Palladas' poems are epigrams; they belong to a genre of short, pithy poems which originally evolved for inscribing on stone slabs, often to place beneath such statues. Three of Palladas' poems to which Harrison was attracted are explicitly concerned with statues. Palladas wrote during the death throes of the old pagan culture, disintegrating as Christianity spread; the early Christian iconoclasts systematically destroyed the statues of the pagan gods, whether by smashing them, dismantling them limb by limb or melting the metal ones down. For Palladas, statues thus symbolize the demise of the beautiful culture he loved (he was a professional teacher of classical Greek literature) and of the Olympian religion.

In one poem, three hexameter lines are imagined as being inscribed beneath some pagan statues which have avoided being melted down and turned into coins, by converting to Christianity:[26]

> 'Baptized' Olympians live here in peace,
> spared Treasury finance and coiner's mould,
> the fires of revolution and small change

These 'baptized' statues both signify and defy the revolutionary shifts in ideology that marked the triumph of Christianity – a cultural transformation on which Harrison's later work often meditates. They also mark the chasm between the world of art and the world of commerce and lucre which yawns across the entire output of this self-avowed socialist poet. The chasm is here symbolized by the coinage into which they have so far avoided being transformed. And Harrison has repeatedly returned to the image of fire, from the fire he tries to start in the semi-stupor of 'Newcastle is Peru' onwards, most memorably in the death speech delivered from his funeral pyre by the hero of his 1995 play *The Labourers of Herakles*.[27] In Harrison's poetry, the furnace or foundry cauldron is often a fiery vessel in which artefacts can be made or destroyed. He adopted from the film-maker Andrei Arsenyevich Tarkovsky the metaphor of 'smelting' a text during the creative process before it realizes its finished form.[28] In his feature film *Prometheus*, the striking miners, the subject of his art, are themselves melted down for bullion in a vast furnace; we also witness the production of the monumental golden statue of Prometheus which dominates the later sequences of the film.

The analogy between the work of the poet and the smith holds together the shortest of Palladas' 'statue' poems translated by Harrison, in Greek just one terse epigrammatic couplet:[29]

> The blacksmith's quite a logical man
> to melt an Eros down and turn
> the God of Love into a frying pan,
> something that can also burn.

The melting down of the bronze statue of Eros into a kitchen utensil again signifies the end of pagan culture and religion. But Palladas is playing with the time-honoured metaphor of sexual desire as fire (a continuous figure in Harrison's *Phaedra Britannica*), and making use of bathos. In Harrison's own poetry and above all in almost every line of *The Trackers of Oxyrhynchus*, the juxtaposition of an 'elevated' aesthetic image, of which statues of the Olympians are emblematic, with an unglamorous, everyday object, signifies the harsh divisions between social classes and their different claims on art.

The final 'statue' poem by Palladas which Harrison chose is formally more complex, involving direct speech from both Palladas and the hero Herakles.[30] Palladas, appalled to find a statue of Herakles toppled from his plinth, addresses his shock to the demigod. But in the final two lines, Herakles appears to Palladas in a dream, saying even gods must bend with the times:

> That night he stood at my bed-end
> and smiled and said: *I can't complain.*
> *The winds of change are blowing, friend,*
> *your god's a weather-vane.*

The short fragments of direct speech, the dream and the conceit whereby an elevated cultural figure chats colloquially – these techniques recur in Harrison's subsequent poetry. What is less easy for all the readers of Harrison who do not read ancient Greek to appreciate is how he has absorbed the key features of the epigrammatic genre – a sardonic, often gnomic tone, lapidary precision, austere economy with the number of words, syntactical run-on over line-end, disciplined yet intricate use of aural echoes both internal to the line and at verse-end, along with alliteration, assonance and rhythm manipulated to pack as emphatic a punch as possible in the shortest possible time. In his own poems, these qualities are reproduced in his colloquial English, the tension between his formal control and exuberant demoticism creating his distinctive voice and soundscape. Harrison, after creative experiments with statues in *The Loiners*, thus immersed himself in the most disciplined, haiku-like ancient Greek poetic genre he could find, and one which itself reflects its own 'classicizing' drive for formal precision in its consistent engagement with the poetry/artefact analogy.

3

'Frontiers of appetite': *Phaedra Britannica* (1975)

Introduction

Harrison made the leading character in his 1975 *Phaedra Britannica* 'after Racine' associate her aberrant sexual passion with the rhythms, heat and oppressive idleness experienced by ruling-class British women in India under the Raj:

> Heart beat like a tom-tom, punkah flapped
> backwards and forwards and my strength was sapped.
> I felt you mocking, India, you brewed
> strange potions out of lust and lassitude.[1]

She echoes words Harrison found in the memoir of an Indian Civil Service wife: 'the throbbing tom-toms became almost like our heartbeats'.[2] The play broke new ground in the public portrayal of British imperial activities in India and in the adaptation of French neoclassical rewritings of classical Greek and Roman drama; it also prefigured the emergence of 'Reception Studies' within academic Classics by its pioneering comparison of ways in which the classical world has been used more recently.

Literary historians often group Harrison with other 'committed' poets associated with Leeds in the 1950s–1960s, especially Jon Silkin, Geoffrey Hill and Wole Soyinka, who was a student at Leeds University at the same time as Harrison; they collaborated on performances at the Empire Theatre on Briggate.[3] In the public imagination, Harrison is usually seen as one of the triumvirate of famous post-war poets who spoke in non-metropolitan dialects of English, and whose surnames begin with 'H', alongside Ted Hughes and

Seamus Heaney. Despite Heaney's exploration of the darker consequences of British rule in Ireland,[4] none of these comparisons, however, does justice to Harrison's international horizons. They obscure both his fascination with the seedy underbelly of European colonialism and his engagement with Continental literature.[5] His fascination with French culture culminated in 1996 with his provocative version of Victor Hugo's play *Le Roi s'amuse* as *The Prince's Play*, which he persuaded Richard Eyre to stage at the National Theatre (Harrison refuses to call it the Royal National Theatre). His reading of Hugo's riotous anti-monarchical satire, banned after one performance in 1832, relocated the plot from sixteenth-century France to Victorian London. It identified the philandering rapist Crown Prince with the future Edward VII, drawing an implicit parallel with Prince Charles, whose relationship with Camilla Parker Bowles had come under scrutiny since he had divorced Princess Diana.[6]

Harrison's engagement with French theatre had begun twenty-five years before, in 1971, when the ground-breaking director John Dexter commissioned a new translation of Molière's *Le Misanthrope*. Dexter had asked the poet Adrian Mitchell if he knew of any writer 'who enjoyed the classical restraints of a rigid verse form, who had wit, humour, and above all whose language was dramatic and not literary'.[7] Mitchell suggested Harrison, who, alongside another old friend from Leeds University, the Ulsterman James Simmons, had produced an English-language version of an ancient drama when teaching in West Africa. In *Aikin Mata*, they had transposed the sexual politics of Aristophanes' *Lysistrata* from Athens in 411 BCE to contemporary northern Nigeria, in voices, performance styles and society.[8]

The production was years ahead of its time. Globally, it anticipated the explosion of performances of Greek drama, now in professional repertoires in every continent, a development which has been traced to the late 1960s.[9] But in grafting the Aristophanic situation of a war between Athens and Sparta onto contemporary tribal rivalry between Yoruba and Ibo peoples, and utilizing their indigenous rituals, *Aikin Mata* was innovative. It anticipated by a decade the 'intercultural' or 'transcultural' trend in world theatre, which saw directors abandoning narrow national or ethnic theatre traditions to mingle 'Eastern' and 'Western' repertoires, performance styles and ethnology: the Japanese director Tadashi Suzuki used Noh conventions to realize Euripides from the late 1970s, and the Russian-French-English Ariane Mnouchkine harnessed

Kathakali, Kabuki and Balinese traditions to Aeschylean tragedy in her *Les Atrides* (1990). Harrison's production was far less well funded and widely reported, but he was one of the earliest pioneers of 'intercultural' Greek theatre.

In *Aikin Mata*, Harrison required some male actors to perform female roles. A mixed group of Yoruba and Ibo men needed to forget their tribal rivalries and merge identities as a chorus of old Hausa women. Such gender-role-inverting or 'gender-blind' practices are familiar in serious theatre today, but in the 1960s to 1970s they were regarded as shockingly avant-garde. This was a bold response to a much-loved classical comedy, which traditionally invited productions with elaborate pseudo-authentic 'Grecian' costumes and reconstructions of the pillared Athenian Acropolis. In his letter to Dexter, Mitchell described Harrison thus:

> Knows French, most of his translation's been from Greek, including a black Aristophanes which he wrote for Africa with immense success, using the tribal warfare thing. And for my money he's the best man for couplets in England, can make them rough or smooth, but they sound like people talking.[10]

Dexter read Harrison's prizewinning poetry collection *The Loiners* out loud and decided that he 'had found a voice for Molière'.[11]

The two men clicked, although Dexter teased Harrison by referring to him as 'Northern Gloom'.[12] Harrison's gift for identifying a revelatory new context into which to transpose a challenging 'classical' drama manifested itself again when moving *The Misanthrope* three centuries forward from Louis XIVth's *ancien régime* of 1666 to 1966 and the authoritarian presidency of Charles de Gaulle. Harrison was soon launched into prominence when the Molière production opened on 22 February 1973 at the Old Vic (the National Theatre was still housed there) and was chosen for the twelve-year-old British National Theatre's New York première at St. James' Theater in 1975. The transposition to 1966 was felt to illuminate both Moliere's verse form and witty satire on hypocrisy and the anxieties of France just before the civil unrest and barricades of May 1968.[13] These insights were reinforced by Tanya Moiseiwitsch's design, representing an elegant drawing room in a Parisian official building, and the stellar performances of Diana Rigg and Alec McCowen, who delivered Harrison's 'oddly slangy' couplets with dazzling acerbity.[14]

Dexter, delighted by the success of Harrison's translation of classical French verse drama, commissioned him again for Racine's *Phèdre* (1677). In 1975, *Phaedra Britannica*, performed by the National Theatre Company, also premiered at the Old Vic (founded in 1818), which had the advantage, as Dexter saw, of being 'a perfect home for a Victorian melodrama'.[15] Billed as 'after Racine', the text also drew on other responses to the myth of Phaedra and Hippolytus, including Euripides' *Hippolytus* of 428 BCE and Seneca's Neronian *Phaedra*, dating from around 60 CE.[16] On the first page of the first of the four dense notebooks which Harrison compiled while he worked on this text, he instructed himself, 'Do extracts of Euripides and Seneca as exercise in control.'[17] On the same page are two quotations, carefully typed, from experts on French classicism: Martin Turnell, 'Racine remains one of the few great masters who is absolutely untranslatable', and François Mauriac, 'Of all our authors, Racine is one of the least accessible to people of other countries.'[18]

Harrison has also written here, 'the couplet a custom-built treadmill'. Scholarly discussion of *Phaedra Britannica* has been confined almost exclusively to form and language, exploring the rhyming couplets which Harrison, as predicted by Mitchell, skilfully crafted, welding Racinian verse to often colloquial English which sounded 'like people talking'.[19] But his most significant decision was analogous to the transposition in *Aikin Mata* of the context of Aristophanes' *Lysistrata* to modern Nigeria. Racine's version of the ancient story of Phaedra and Hippolytus was relocated from the Bronze-Age city of Troezen in the Greek Peloponnese to British India under the Raj.

Wole Soyinka remained close to his friend Harrison, both while he taught at Ahmadu Bello University in Zaria, Kaduna State, in the mid-1960s, and after his return to England. Soyinka had discussed with Harrison his adaption of Euripides, *The Bacchae of Euripides: A Communion Rite*, set during the postcolonial African Wars. Daringly commissioned by the new Director of the National Theatre, Peter Hall, it opened on 1 August 1973.[20] Harrison had suggested setting *Phèdre* in colonial India to Dexter by 14 June of the same summer, when Soyinka's African *Bacchae* was in rehearsal. Dexter wrote to him,

> You are a tempting bugger; the idea of *Phèdre* in the Raj is almost irresistible. She is a neurasthenic English lady; the trouble is she also a queen and how you bring those two things together I don't know.[21]

Dexter's fear that Harrison might make Racine's play incoherent by not embracing Phèdre's status as a woman whose husband wielded power proved unfounded. As wife of the Governor of India, she stood at the apex not only of the vast territories then under the control of the East India Company, but the increasing areas of the global atlas that had recently come under British rule. The process of British imperial acquisition of the planet had shifted up several gears in the 1840s. Between 1842 and 1849, at breakneck speed, Britain annexed Sind, the Punjab, Hong Kong, Labuan in Indonesia, and, in Africa, Natal, River, and Gambia.[22]

Harrison's *Phaedra Britannica* is one of his least discussed works today. I suspect this is because it used white actors whose complexions were darkened by make-up. White actors took the roles of the minor Indian characters and two major ones; Lilimani (the Indian daughter of a rebel chief killed by the British) was played by Diana Quick; in her 2009 memoir, she expresses no embarrassment about taking the role, instead saying that she felt affinity with Lilimani because her own ancestors had worked in India, and her great-great-grandmother Lucky may have been an Indian called Lakshmi.[23] Thomas Theophilus (the mixed-race Rajput/English Hippolytus figure) was played by David Yelland, and named after Sir Thomas Theophilus Metcalfe (1795–1853), an East India Company civil servant. Such use of 'blackface' in theatre is now rightly condemned as a racist act for which there is no excuse.

The director was aware of the issue: Dexter asked the NT's casting director to find 'coloured' actresses of 'Indian' appearance for both Ayah and Lilimani.[24] In Harrison's defence, while Dexter and Peter Hall subsequently chose Diana Quick without consulting Harrison, Dexter's request to the casting director was prompted by the poet. Harrison had pasted into his notebook an article in *The Times* about the problems facing black actors trying to find work.[25] Alaknanda Samarth, who played Ayah, was proud to be the first Indian actress to play a classical leading role at the National Theatre.[26]

But retrospective embarrassment about the blackface and the National Theatre's failure to find appropriate actors, beside Samarth, of south-east Asian heritage should not prevent us from appreciating that *Phaedra Britannica* was more influential than has been acknowledged. This was a result of the bold transposition of the story – the tragic love of a stepmother for her mixed-race stepson – to India just before the 1857 'Indian Mutiny'. First, the production encouraged the insertion of those quotation marks around the word 'Mutiny' if not to replace the noun altogether with 'revolt' or 'rebellion'. The majority of Britons had always agreed with the journalists who in the late 1850s used that term, with all its treacherous connotations, to incite zeal for brutal retribution against the Indians who had challenged British colonial control.[27] But there had always been a few commentators like Karl Marx, who insisted in the *New York Daily Tribune* that 'by and by there will ooze out other facts able to convince even John Bull himself that what he considers a military mutiny is in truth a national revolt.'[28] Advocates of Indian Independence had criticized the term 'mutiny' before V. D. Savarkar's *The Indian War of Independence* (1909). But when *Phaedra Britannica* was first performed, many Britons and other Westerners persisted in unquestioningly calling it the 'Indian Mutiny'; some still do so today.

The second way in which *Phaedra Britannica* was directly influential was on theatre practice, since it was pioneering in the history of radical adaptation of canonical tragedy. And thirdly, it proved visionary in the sphere of Classical Reception Studies, prefiguring by many years both the emergence of Performance Reception as a distinct area of research and the field of Postcolonial Classics.

Harrison's Anglo-Indian tragic household

In the opening scene of Racine's play, Hippolyte tells his tutor, Théramène, that he must seek his father, absent now for six months; Théramène responds that he has personally scoured both sides of the Gulf of Corinth, and the Aegean sea towards Crete with no results.[29] Harrison uses the rejoinder to his Hippolyte character, made by his well-informed schoolmasterly tutor, Burleigh, to establish the Indian geographical location and the precise historical context:

> The company's had sepoys scour as far
> as Jalalabad and Peshawar
> north to the very outposts where its *raj*
> is constantly beset by sabotage.[30]

The stage directions specify that the scene is the Durbar Hall of the British Residency in Hyderabad in west central India, an opulent Palladian villa with a classical portico; Harrison had studied its architecture.[31] This edifice, a tourist hotspot today, was built at the beginning of the nineteenth century by an East India Company colonel, James Achilles Kirkpatrick (in a notebook Harrison underlines 'Achilles' when discussing Kirkpatrick).[32] After promotion to the post of Resident Minister in Hyderabad (1798), he married a local noblewoman, by whom he had two children.

The inter-racial marriage and the mixed-race offspring were prompts to Harrison's imagination.[33] But he was most interested in the four tense years between the Government of India Act 1853, when British India remained under the administration of the East India Company in trust for the Crown, and the momentous conflict of 1857–8, during which British attitudes to Indians and the manner of imposing imperial control were hardened irrevocably. Before the rebellion, Britons were inclined to see India as a 'fairy-tale land where sultans sat on ivory thrones', fanned by opulently dressed attendants waving peacocks' wings.[34] But the reports of rapes, mutilations and murders allegedly committed by the sepoys (middle-ranking officers in disaffected Indian regiments within the East India Company's army) repainted India as a terrifying slaughterhouse lethal to all white Christendom.[35]

The measures taken after the revolt were swift and draconian. The proportion of European soldiers was drastically increased; native Indians were forced to disarm; British army officers were granted far more power to dictate punishments; above all, the British Parliament passed the Government of India Act on 2 August 1858, transferring British power over India from the East India Company to the Crown.[36] A new government post was created – Secretary of State for India – and the Governor-General was now to be known as Viceroy of India, implying that he was the personal representative of Queen Victoria as well as 'ruler of one sixth of the human race'.[37]

The post became one of the best-paid and most coveted in the British Empire; being appointed Viceroy of India was the ambition of the Enoch Powell, a brilliant English classical scholar of far-right political views, loathed by Harrison; Powell became notorious in April 1968 after misrepresenting lines from Virgil's *Aeneid* to foment fears about levels of non-white immigration to Britain.[38] He had been appointed to the Chair of Greek at Sydney University in 1937; he was so distressed by Indian Independence in 1947 that he stayed up all night, walking the streets of London.[39]

During the years preceding the 1857 rebellion, the real-life Governor-General of India was a workaholic, authoritarian and bellicose Scottish aristocrat named James Broun-Ramsay, committed to consolidating British control of India by any means possible and expanding its territories. The references in *Phaedra Britannica* to the troublesome areas beyond Jalalabad (now in Pakistan) and Peshawar (Afghanistan) locate the action in a British colonial territory which was constantly growing and witness to shocking levels of violence daily.

Broun-Ramsay's frail Scottish wife did not cope with the Indian climate and tense political atmosphere; she died in 1853 in what was then called Ceylon. Broun-Ramsay did not remarry. But the governor's wife ('Memsahib') in Harrison's version, like Racine's *Phèdre*, kills herself. This is after the catastrophic breakdown of the relationships between herself, her husband, who is the Governor of Bengal (and equivalent to Theseus/Thésée), her mixed-race stepson Thomas Theophilus and Mehmsahib's Indian nurse ('Ayah' rather than the classical unnamed 'nurses' and Racine's Oenone). This family breakdown symbolizes the violence underlying the British exploitation of India on the social, political and economic planes, especially in the years just before and including the brutal suppression of the 1857–8 uprising. And the political dimension of his play is related more intimately to the classical precedents, especially the Senecan tragedy, than to Racine. Even the details of British rule in India resemble the ferocious Roman imperial vision of the world at Seneca's time more than the cultured absolutism of the court of the Sun King: the infamously brutal Bengal Horse Artillery charged into combat like Roman cavalrymen, wearing armoured headgear which ostentatiously imitated Graeco-Roman helmets, with gaudy, encrusted metal visors, high crest-holders and bristling scarlet plumes.[40]

Harrison's notebooks document his research into every detail of life and death under British rule in India, allowing him to add vivid local details which contribute to the picture of the strange, decadent, deracinated life lived by the governing class in the heyday of the Raj: where Racine's Phèdre says she's unlike '*ces femmes hardies*' who can stay calm while committing crimes, Memsahib elaborates that these women are 'frequenters of mess balls and evening shows'.[41] The background reading evident from the notebooks also reveals that Harrison wanted to draw parallels between colonial India in the

1850s and classical civilization that bypassed Racine's version altogether. The heat of ancient Greece and India led him to make references to punkah fans, for example, fascinated by their rhythmic stirring of the fetid air, but these fans are not in Racine: he envisaged them as equivalents of fans he found illustrated in ancient Greek vase-painting.[42] Intrigued by the problem of rendering intelligible the passion of Phaedra's mother Pasiphae for a bull, he investigated the motif of sex with beasts in Indian temple art, pasting both a disturbing neoclassical painting of the classical myth and Indian erotic sculpted friezes from Rajasthan in a notebook and writing for extra information to P. S. Rawson, Curator of the Gulbenkian Museum of Oriental Art in Durham, and author of *The Erotic Art of the East* (1968).[43]

The enigmatic figure of Captain (later Colonel) James Skinner (1778–1841) was seminal. Skinner was the mixed-race son of Colonel Hercules Skinner, a Scottish officer in the East India Company Army, and an Indian mother. She was a royal member of a Rajput clan. This remains a high-caste clan of hereditary aristocrats in northern India. Its members had a reputation for a warrior ethos, 'honour' values, militant opposition to their Muslim would-be conquerors and equestrian skills even amongst their women, suggestive of the Amazons. Skinner's mother had been taken captive at the age of just fourteen. Skinner had seven children by her (two of James' brothers were given the resonantly classical names of Hercules and Alexander), but she committed suicide when James was twelve.

James received an English education at prestigious schools in Calcutta; he advanced to a distinguished military career, raising two cavalry regiments for the British ('Skinner's Horse', later renamed 'Bengal Lancers'), which remain a part of the Indian army. He became known as 'Sikander Sahib', when the Indian compliment was bestowed upon him that he bore a resemblance to the great Sikander, or 'Alexander the Great', a mighty leader.[44] Skinner's life was recorded by a Scottish travel writer, James Baillie Fraser, a coeval with access to Skinner's papers.[45] The exotic story had been brought to the British public in 1961 with Dennis Holman's biography, read by Harrison.[46] Although loyal to the British, Skinner was proud of his Rajput ancestry, and, along with imitation classical helmets, his cavalry regiments wore the long yellow kurtas (coats) that his maternal ancestors had worn to ride into battle.[47] He was the perfect model for Harrison's Thomas Theophilus, cruelly contrasted as a 'half-breed Rajput colt' with Memsahib's own 'pukka sons' by Mehmsahib's own Baluchistani Ayah.[48]

Harrison exposes the brutality of the British Raj. When the death of the Governor is announced by his aide-de-camp, the tension mounts. A rebellion is feared, with Lilimani, the daughter of a rebel chief named Ranjit, as focus for unrest. The ADC fears that Thomas may decide to join the rebels, staying loyal to his mother's Rajput lineage.[49] Just two lines of Aricie's description of her past to Ismene in the Racine are expanded and lent vivid new colour:

> J'ai perdu dans la fleur de leur jeune saison
> Six frères, quel espoir d'une illustre maison ![50]

This translates literally as 'I lost in the flower of their youth / six brothers – what a hope for an illustrious household!', but in Harrison it becomes this:

> I, last of Ranjit's royal household, forced
> to watch my brothers face the holocaust!
> My father bayonetted! The redcoat guns
> killed my six brothers. All my father's sons.
> The eldest, proud and strong, a bloody mess
> blown from a cannon into nothingness.
> Smoking smithereens! India's red mud
> churned even redder with her children's blood.[51]

This passage has been cross-fertilized by another ancient text, the *Iliad*, from a renowned passage where Andromache laments that Achilles slew her father Eetion and seven brothers when he flattened her city (VI.414–24). Andromache's lament implanted the idea in Harrison's mind that her father was killed by the British, as well as her brothers. A spectator of *Phaedra Britannica* familiar with the *Iliad* will feel the contrast, however, between the respect Achilles showed towards Eetion's cadaver and the bayonetting of Ranjit.

The pastoral vision of the young men amidst their livestock contrasts equally with the gruesome detail about Lilimani's eldest brother. 'Blowing from the gun' was a mode of capital punishment associated with British rule in India from its first recorded instance in Lakhipur in 1761,[52] to at least the 1870s. In 1764, Hector Munro executed twenty-four 'ring leaders' who were accused of encouraging a battalion to desert.[53] Incidents of the punishment reached an appalling climax during the 1857–8 'Mutiny'; hundreds were executed in this way.⁵⁴ Harrison returns to the image of the Indian rebel body being blown from a cannon when Thomas expresses his loyalty to the cause of Lilimani's people, having seen her country

> ... gagged on blood. Blood, so much blood
> even the sun-baked earth was turned to mud,
> your brother's bloody gobbets and splashed gore
> Spattered like catsup from the cannon's jaw.⁵⁵

Classical antiquity and India

The reverberations of ancient Rome and of Latinity were implied by the play's title. 'Britannia' was the name the Romans gave to the province consisting of modern England, Wales and the parts of lowland Scotland they had conquered. 'Britannicus' was the cognomen given to the son of the Emperor, Claudius, who in 43 CE put the seal on the conquest of Britannia. Racine's Roman history tragedy of 1669, about Claudius' unfortunate son, was entitled *Britannicus*. Two of the nouns the adjectival *Britannicus* qualifies in Latin are *legiones*, military regions, and *lingua*, or language (e.g. Tacitus, *Germania* 45). Having decided to set the play in Hyderabad, Harrison considered calling the play *Phaedrabad*.⁵⁶ But the Latinate title conveys the classical (Senecan) ancestry of Racine's text, the theme of imperialism, and the act of translation not only between languages (those of India, Greek, Latin, French and English) but between entire civilizations.

Harrison's *Phaedra Britannica* notebooks reveal him reading other Latin poetry – Ovid's version of the Hippolytus story in *Metamorphoses* XV.497–546 and Horace's famous lines in *Odes* I.19, '*in me tota ruens Venus/ Cyprum deseruit*' ('Venus in her entirety, charging against me, has deserted Cyprus').⁵⁷ Harrison intuitively drew a connection between Horace's description of the effect of love on him as a lyric poet, and the famous French director Jean-Louis Barrault's remark that at the end of Racine's tragedy, Phèdre is '*entirement consumée*'.⁵⁸

Sheridan Morley saw how the setting had solved problems which English-language productions have always encountered when attempting Racine's masterpiece:

> Phaedra lies behind closed doors and her passionate love for her stepson, the barbaric horror of his death, the prolonged absence of her husband and even her eventual suicide all acquire a relentless, terrible logic......the subcontinent can be made to stand for everything untranslatable in the original, from *Venus tout entière à sa proie attachée* through to the concept of fate itself. India...comes to represent antiquity, guilt, empire, mythology and virtually all the abstract ideas which are needed for an understanding of the play.[59]

Morley also praised the monsoon breaking at the end, to beat against the sultry residence building.[60] The suffocating heat was emphasized both by the verse and by the actors' laboured gait.[61] Thunderclaps were used metaphorically to describe psychological trauma, but Memsahib first hears the 'rain, cool rain/ giving the blood-red earth new life again' only when the poison takes effect and she cathartically confesses her crime to the Governor. The text ends with this stage direction, relating the sudden outpouring of grief in the formal dirge to the arrival of the monsoon: the servants 'kneel and begin a chant which gradually becomes dominant. The sound of rain like slow applause.'[62] This suggests of an un-Racinian ritual chorus like those in the Greek and Roman tragedies,[63] and those in India which reminded classically trained British administrators of the choruses in ancient drama.[64] Harrison's pathetic fallacy is pure Seneca, reminiscent of the eclipse of the sun at the climax of *Thyestes*.[65]

Other departures from Racine show Harrison turning to his ancient prototypes and away from the innovations of the French adaptation. The important part played in the Racinian plot by the political rivalry between Phèdre's adult son and Hippolyte over the Athenian throne has been deleted, restoring the play's cleaner classical plotline. Some phrases reveal Harrison's immersion in Greek tragedy: in an un-Racinian moment, when Thomas loses control in front of Lilimani, he says she can 'watch iron bend, and adamantine break', words suggestive of famous lines in both the Aeschylean *Prometheus Bound* and Sophocles' *Antigone*.[66] Harrison has also studied Robert Browning's monologues, several of which are immersed in Euripidean tragedy; Browning's 'Artemis Prologuizes' was originally intended to open a sequel to Euripides' *Hippolytus*. When translating Hippolyte's appeal to his father in Racine, Harrison imitated Browning's use of 'disjointed syntax', since he decided it was 'the only way of emphasising natural rhythms of speech'.[67]

Harrison said he was substituting 'mythical Britishness', for 'French classicism', in response to Katherine Wheatley's *Racine and English Classicism* (1956).[68] He listened to the voices of British people living in India, and to their 'mythologization' of its enormous, frightening, incomprehensible natural world and human culture.[69] The idea of mythologization of personalities is discussed when Lilimani's attendant, Tara, says that it's only the 'myth' of Thomas that paints him as 'ascetic, cold, severe': the reality she has observed is otherwise. He is in love with Lilimani.[70]

The character most 'mythologized' is His Excellency, the Governor, always away on mysterious campaigns, surrounded by secrecy; his courageous feats are elaborated, in the constant retelling, to reach near-supernatural levels of heroism. As Burleigh puts it in the opening dialogue, in a significant expansion on Théramène's equivalent speech in Racine,

> Besides, perhaps for reasons of his own
> H.E. prefers his whereabouts unknown.
> One knows his nature, ready to pursue
> anything that's savage, strange, or new,
> his 'curiosity' how wild tribes live
> his 'scholar's' passion for the primitive.[71]

Burleigh, says Thomas, painted a picture of his father's heroic derring-do against native 'savages' when he was a child, in semi-mythical language which makes him sound like Heracles – or Theseus – amassing a whole CV of labours:

> ... a giant cannibal fought hand to hand,
> the cripplers grappled with, mutilation banned,
> dacoits encountered, and suppressed by law,
> rebellions put down, and so much more.
> Like hunting tigers!

Some Indian words, like 'dacoit' (an armed robber) may have been unfamiliar, and thus exotic or mythical-sounding, to Harrison's London audience.

In the Indian context, even the most supernatural of the Greek hero Theseus' exploits circulate as plausible rumours. Tara repeats reports of his death: he had helped another British ruler violate a native queen, before they had both descended, mysteriously, into the land of the dead: 'beyond/ the forbidden river, Indus, into Khond', they disappeared 'into the place where ghosts and dead souls are'; Thomas thinks his father may not be dead, after all: 'India's dark gods won't have him harmed./ I've often felt that Siva and his crew/ favoured my father.'[72]

Hunting, lust and empire

Racine was not much interested in the classical Hippolytus' passion for hunting. Harrison bypassed the French tragedy to mine the ancient texts for hunting imagery; he studied classical statuary depicting the slaughter by muscular heroes of hybrid beasts such as centaurs.[73] In Euripides, after Aphrodite's prologue, Hippolytus makes his first grand appearance returning from the hunt with a chorus of huntsmen, bearing spoils from the chase, sings a hymn to Artemis and holds a dialogue with one of the huntsmen (52–120). Seneca opens his *Phaedra* with Hippolytus at the head of a corps of hunters holding whips and dogs on the leash; as they head into the woods, he barks orders laden with violent metaphors: they must range over all Attica casting nets, laying snares, terrorizing deer, hurling spears, dismembering and skinning dead beasts (lines 1–84). In both Greek and Latin texts, these vivid hunting scenes lay the groundwork for many subsequent images of hunting, to express both sexual pursuit and political conquest.

When her love has turned to hatred, Memsahib says that her stepson's 'head should be mounted along with all/ the monsters on the Sahib's study wall'.[74] Harrison has revived this ancient image, and made the hunting of the beasts of India so intimately associated with the British Raj a conceptual vehicle. He describes them as his 'images of the hunter, the Victorian type, projecting his inner repressed desires onto the fauna of India, amassing tiger pelts, covering his walls with animal heads. The Governor himself is renowned as a great hunter, naturally, often scorning the rifle with its distant, rationally controlled despatch for closer gladiatorial combat with a bayonet'.[75] The term 'gladiatorial' insinuates a parallel with the bloody Roman entertainments of the amphitheatre, where in *venationes*, or hunting shows, wild animals would be stalked and slaughtered: it was perhaps in developing the hunting motif of *Phaedra Britannica* that Harrison's idea for the caged beasts beneath the amphitheatre of *Kaisers of Carnuntum* two decades later (1995) was born. Another stimulus was the aural similarity of the words 'minotaur' and 'man-eater',[76] leading Harrison to replace the man-bull hybrid of the ancient legend with a man-eating tiger. Vivid photographs of tigers roaring and leaping are pasted into the notebooks.[77]

In other differences between *Phèdre* and *Phaedra Britannica*, Harrison edges closer to his Senecan prototype even than to Euripides, an atypical move for a dramatist who prefers all forms of Greek theatre and entertainment to Roman.[78] He pointed out in his own reflections on *Phaedra Britannica* that Pasiphae's crime of bestiality is never referred to so specifically in Racine, but it is in Seneca and in his own play (see below).[79] In his characterization of Memsahib, he downplays the notion in both Euripides and Racine that Phaedra/Phèdre is torn between desire and a sense of social obligation, bringing her more into line with the harsh psychological contours of Seneca's protagonist, and indeed of the other fragmentary play on the theme by Euripides, which Harrison had investigated.[80] The rhetoric, for all its English colloquialism, often owes more to Seneca's diction than to Racine's. When Memsahib declares her love to Thomas, she fantasizes that it was he, not his father, who had first come to her attention when he dealt with a man-eating tiger terrorizing their locality. This is a substitution for Phèdre's fantasy that Hippolyte had killed the minotaur, not Thésée, and had done it with her help, not Ariadne's:

> C'est moi, Prince, c'est moi dont l'utile secours
> Vous eût du Labyrinthe enseigné les détours.
> Que de soins m'eût coûté cette tête charmante!
> Un fil n'eût point assez rassuré votre amante.
> Compagne du péril qu'il vous fallait chercher,
> Moi-même devant vous j'aurais voulu marcher;
> Et Phèdre, au Labyrinthe avec vous descendue,
> Se serait avec vous retrouvée ou perdue.[81]

It would have been mine, my lord, my useful aid that would have instructed you about the mazes of the labyrinth. What careful precautions would that charming head of yours have cost me! One thread would not have been sufficient to give confidence to your lover; a companion in the danger which you were going to seek. I would myself have chosen to walk before you, and Phaedra, having descended into the labyrinth along with you, along with you would have been found again at last.[82]

Harrison has put the classical back in different ways. First, Memsahib explicitly likens his fame as a hunter of wild animals and achiever of heroic exploits to that of a mythic ancient warrior:

> He'd taken on so many beasts like these
> he seemed like Theseus or like Hercules.[83]

Secondly, the oratory becomes more formal. Harrison uses more exaggerated anaphora than Racine does, in imitation of the most Senecan of rhetorical structures, during Memsahib's fantasy of taking her sister's place in the monster hunt:

>   I would have taken the initiative.
> Everything she gave, I too would give.
> I would have led you to exactly where
> the monstrous tiger had its tangled lair.
> I would have shown you every little twist
> to where the jungle's deep and gloomiest.
> I sense your shots sink home with a soft thud!
> The stillness of the beast! The smell of blood![84]

Emphatic anaphoric repetition of a pronoun in the same grammatical case (here nominative singular), and in the same position in the metrical line, is typical of Senecan tragic character's elevated monologues.[85]

Harrison had also researched traditions of English translation of Seneca, especially the landmark sixteenth-century *Tenne Tragedies of Seneca* by a team including Jasper Heywood and John Studley, even though it did not include *Phaedra*.[86] His search for English verse to imitate also took him back to the Elizabethan and Jacobean dramatists influenced by Seneca; the Governor echoes another power-hungry ruler, Shakespeare's Macbeth, whose opening line is 'So foul and fair a day I have not yet seen.' The Governor's first words on arrival are 'Fortune relenting has turned foul to fair.'[87] Harrison also read widely in English Augustan poetry, which was influenced by Latin examples more than by Greek; he relished Thomas Otway's translation of Ovid's letter from Phaedra to Hippolytus (*Heroides* IV.129–32) while noting that Otway was a near-coeval of Racine. He studied Otway's translation, published the same year as the première of *Phèdre* (1677), of Racine's *Bérénice*, into English heroic couplets.[88]

The Stoic beliefs underlying Senecan tragedy, but downplayed in Racine's, reappear in *Phaedra Britannica*, where they map with ease onto the 'muscular Christianity' of the British in India (the term appeared in the mid-1850s at the time when the play is set). This valued the physical toughness of white men across the Empire, whether missionaries, businessmen or bureaucrats, and an idea of masculinity which tolerated physical hardship 'stoically', accepted the vicissitudes of fortune, and suppressed passion as the Roman Stoics dictated the Stoic sage must do.[89] Three decades after the tense period in which *Phaedra Britannica* is set, a man who had achieved a First Class in Greats at Balliol College Oxford, and was placed first in the Classics-dominated entrance examinations for the Indian Civil Service, described the ICS as 'a corps of men specially selected, brought up in a rigour of bodily hardship to which no other modern people have subjected their ruling class, trained by cold baths, cricket, and the history of Greece and Rome'.[90]

An extreme psychological dualism, in which the psyche needed to use reason and self-control to master 'animal instincts', marked both ancient Stoicism and Victorian attitudes to sexual morality;[91] Harrison has welded the two in the Governor's terrified policing of the boundary between human and beast in others, despite his own predilections for bloody violence and rapine.[92] Stoics, moreover, pessimistically saw humans as possessing little power to intervene in the workings of the cosmic principle of *Fatum*, and there is a fatalistic streak in Harrison's Hyderabad household: Burleigh says to Thomas, who is trying to deny the strength of his passion for Lilimani,

> You may protest. I fear it makes no odds
> once your fate's been settled by the gods.[93]

Thomas insists it was 'fate, not folly' that killed his father; declaring his love for Lilimani, he says that 'Reason's unseated. Nobody can rein/ runaway passions into line again.'[94]

The Olympian gods retained by Racine are replaced by Indian deities, with Harrison exploiting the affinity between ancient Mediterranean and Hindu anthropomorphic polytheism which the scholars of British India documented from the late eighteenth century onwards (see below). Just as Soyinka identified the Dionysus of Euripides' *Bacchae* with the Yoruba god Ogun, the functions of both Aphrodite/Venus and Poseidon/Neptune are in *Phaedra Britannica* performed by avatars of Siva. His name dominates the play's theology and soundscape: 'Siva's avatars subdue sahibs' (masters).[95] Memsahib senses that her erotic fixation is the work of this Hindu 'Lord of the Universe' and master of both destruction and reproduction. She first became infatuated at her wedding to the Governor: 'I felt flesh scorch/ as Siva smoked me out with flaming torch.'[96] She tried to cure her passion by experimenting with Indian religion:

> Besought a Hindoo priest
> to placate his deities. But nothing ceased.
> I saw that sacrifice was offered at the shrine
> of every god you Hindoos hold divine—
> Siva, Kali, Krishna...[97]

But both fate and Olympian deities are sometimes equated by Harrison with the whole overwhelming British experience of a semi-personified India, where sexual pleasure is even celebrated – as it was in ancient Greek religious art – in temple carvings. This helps Harrison make sense of the bizarre backstory of the equivalent to Pasiphae, Memsahib's mother, and her bestial tastes in sex:

> Mother! Driven by the dark gods' spite
> Beyond the frontiers of appetite.
> A *judge's* wife! Obscene! Bestialities
> Hindoos might sculpture on a temple frieze![98]

Where Racine's Phèdre prays to *Implacable Vénus* to help make Hippolyte love her as revenge for spurning her as a goddess, Harrison makes her invoke India, whose 'sensual nature' Thomas has ignored.[99]

In Harrison's play, as in Seneca, there is an association between the hunting motif, sexual predation and the drive for imperial expansion. This even affects aesthetic form, with Harrison advising himself to use 'whiplash couplets' for the furious and bitter exchanges between the Governor and Thomas.[100] The equation of burning sexual appetite with brutal colonialism is made explicit by Burleigh, who asks Thomas, 'Are you still/ fighting off love's *raj* with iron will?'[101] The Governor's expansion of the empire is symbolized by his portrayal as a sexual predator of near-legendary repute. Burleigh wonders whether Theseus may be 'absorbed, preoccupied both day *and* night,/ let's say, "researching" some strange new marriage rite'.[102] He has a history of sexual assault against women in India, both native and British, including, we hear, advances made towards both Memsahib and her now deceased sister. There had been, Burleigh catalogues,

> Scores of 'incidents' throughout Bengal,
> O far too many to recall them all—
> the purdahs plundered, the zenanas [segregated female apartments]
> many an infamously flagrant act—
> the young girl daubed with kohl and henna dye
> snatched from a Parsee caravanserai.
> The Judge's daughters! Both! The sister's mind,
> After her heart was broken, soon declined.
> Disowned. A drunkard. Died. And then the other
> became the Memsahib and my stepmother!

This may sound extreme. Yet it reflects the atrocity of the sexual violence suffered – at least by indigenous Indian women – at the hands of British soldiers of all ranks. The Anglo-Irish radical Thomas Russell abandoned serving in the army in the 1780s, disgusted by 'the unjust and rapacious conduct pursued by the authorities in the case of two native women'.[103] In the 1880s, despite the repeal of the Contagious Diseases Acts in Britain and the colonies, passed under pressure from feminist campaigner Josephine Butler, the enforced confinement of women in prostitution camps for the use of soldiers continued under the new Cantonment Acts. Lord Roberts, Commander-in-Chief of the British army in India, ordered 'a sufficient number' of 'sufficiently attractive women to be supplied to the regimental bazaars'. Procurement of women was thus officially institutionalized across all British-ruled South-East Asia.[104]

American missionary Katharine Bushnell met a prostitute in Calcutta who had been taken as the mistress of an Englishman at the age of eleven, and then abandoned in a brothel; others had been forced by near-starvation to submit to conditions akin to sexual slavery. Hundreds of Indian women who believed themselves married to British men were routinely abandoned, with their children, when their husbands returned home.[105] Twelve British soldiers raped a woman in broad daylight in Rangoon, in front of thirty more men who did nothing to stop them. She died of her injuries, yet no legal action was taken.[106]

Phaedra with consequences

Harrison knew that adapting the uniquely French style of theatre represented by *Phèdre* into an intelligible English idiom presented challenges. His quest led him to study adaptations and translations in both French and English. He researched previous performances, especially Barrault's 1943 production at the Comédie-Française (wittily analysed by Barrault himself in a book in which Harrison immersed himself since it is 'unlike any description of a production ever written'[107]), and the famous realization of the role by Marie Bell in 1960.[108] He attended every performance he could discover during the creative process: in Richmond, Yorkshire and Derby Playhouse in 1973 and at the Théâtre Essaïon in Paris on 21 June 1974.[109]

These experiences increased his commitment to radical adaptation of a drama with triply 'classical' Greek/Latin/French credentials, of which there is no true equivalent. The only other myths dramatized by both a Greek tragedian and Seneca are *Hercules Furens*, *Medea*, *Troades*, *Agamemnon*, *Oedipus*, *Phoenissae*, and *Hercules Oetaeus*. Of these, only two have major French neoclassical adaptations, Corneille's *Médée* and Voltaire's *Oedipe*, and few would claim that either holds the same position in cultural history as Racine's *Phèdre*.[110] In *Phaedra Britannica*, Harrison blazed a trail with the reimagining of an exemplar of French classicism, based on famous ancient tragedies, in a completely new context. His example proved immediately influential, beginning with a relocation by the Royal Shakespeare Company of *Much Ado about Nothing* to India just a year later, in 1976.[111]

Phaedra Britannica was revived in New York in 1988, by the Off-Broadway Classic Stage Company, directed by Carey Perloff. It was the fourth play this Classics graduate had directed at the CSC since becoming its director in 1986. The first two had both been verse dramas by 'classic' Modernists based on a Greek tragedy: T. S. Eliot's *The Cocktail Party* (informed by Euripides' *Alcestis*) and Ezra Pound's *Elektra*, a translation of Sophocles: Harrison's new play, in the context of this repertoire, must have seemed to Perloff an obvious choice. This production benefited from a stand-out performance by actor Bob Gunton, later renowned for his realization of authoritarian roles such as Warden Samuel Norton in the 1994 prison film *The Shawshank Redemption*. He brought the Governor to vivid life as 'a paragon of British paternalism, a scourge to anything that challenges his power',[112] in a menacing way that convinced audiences more than Michael Gough's performance at the Old Vic. Perhaps an actor from a former British colony was at a psychological advantage.

More than a decade on, the Indian characters were all played by actors of Indian heritage; the dancer Rajika Puri receiving highest praise as Ayah. The casting was welcomed in *India Today Magazine*: 'Minorities have traditionally found it hard to break into American theatre because it was difficult to even audition for non-Equity actors. The powerful Actors' Equity Association scrutinizes all casting to ensure its members are well served. But Equity's new non-Traditional Casting Project has enabled ethnic actors to become its members.'[113]

Phaedra Britannica also anticipated by many years the turn in classical scholarship's attitudes to what used to be called the 'Classical Tradition' and is now usually called 'Classical Reception' – the ways in which classical antiquity has been reused, recycled and appropriated in and since the Renaissance. Harrison had himself, in the late 1960s, contemplated the possibility of an academic career with a research specialism in the Augustan and eighteenth-century reception of Virgil; he published two academic articles on this topic.[114] But in *Phaedra Britannica* he was 'doing' Classical Reception through the creative media of both verse and live theatre performance. It was not until the 1990s that 'Performance Reception' – the study of the realizations of ancient Greek and Roman texts in performance in theatre, ballet, opera and musical drama, cinema, circus acts and stand-up comedy, for example, rather than in media designed for reading – became an established sub-discipline.[115] The two foundational books, both published in 1991, were Hellmut Flashar's *Inszenierung der Antike: das griechische Drama auf der Biihne der Neuzeit* and Marianne McDonald's *Ancient Sun, Modern Light*, more than a quarter of which is devoted to Harrison.[116] His work lies at the centre of the academic study of ancient drama in performance, along with his relationships with myself from the early 1990s and with Professor Oliver Taplin from ten years earlier, in 1981, when Harrison invited him to attend National Theatre rehearsals for Peter Hall's production of Harrison's translation of the *Oresteia*.[117]

It was partly Harrison's sustained engagement with ancient plays that inspired my idea for a permanent Archive of Performances of Greek & Roman Drama, which I co-founded with Taplin at Oxford in 1996; it has since convened numerous events and produced many books on various aspects of

Performance Reception.[118] The influence on the methodologies of Performance Reception exerted by the intense research into earlier versions of the myth, past performances and translations which Harrison later conducted while working on *Medea: A Sex-War Opera* has been described in a fine essay by Fiona Macintosh.[119] But Harrison was even more prescient in 'receiving' antiquity against the grain of colonial ideology, focusing unflinchingly on its darker role as the curriculum of European imperialism.

Most Classical Reception research exploring the British experience in the eighteenth, nineteenth and early twentieth centuries used to focus on elite culture: *belles lettres*, fine art and Oxbridge curriculums.[120] Over the last two decades, however, several studies have appeared of ethnicity, slavery, imperialism and colonialism in relation to Classical Reception in Britain and her territories abroad.[121] But Harrison was doing such research as early as the 1970s. For *Phaedra Britannica*, he read dozens of nineteenth- and early twentieth-century books about and by the British in India, scouring them, always from a position critical of British imperialism, not only for atmospheric language and imagery but for references to classical antiquity. Thirty years later, when I was researching the classical parallels with Indian civilization drawn by early Victorian Britons for a conference I held with Phiroze Vasunia to mark sixty years since Indian Independence,[122] Harrison's 1976 essay on the composition of *Phaedra Britannica* proved more useful than any work of scholarship both in leads to documentation and in analysis.[123]

As Vasunia observes, 'classical Greek and Roman exempla served colonial British ideology' in several discrete contexts in relation to India. Harrison had read a path-breaking study published in 1968 of architectural styles, by Sten Nilsson, who showed that the elegant neoclassical cities then called Madras, Bombay and Calcutta (now Chennai, Mumbai and Kolkata) were motivated by an appetite for parallels between classical models of empire and the British Raj.[124] The English private garden became an arena in which the British wives of East Indiamen and government could display their 'Grecian taste'; Arcadian vistas were framed by white colonnades and porticoes.[125]

British Classicists confronted with another ancient culture in India had developed comparative linguistics and the emergence of comparative theology and anthropology. Sir William Jones, a judge in Calcutta in the late eighteenth century, used his classical scholarship to elaborate the affinity between

Greek, Latin and Sanskrit; his pioneering essay, 'the Gods of Greece, Italy and India' (1784),[126] outlines features shared by the divinities in the classical Mediterranean and Indian religions. In 1850, a Scottish judge assisted Dalpatram, a prominent local intellectual and poet, on a Gujarati version of Aristophanes' *Plutus* set in the colonial world of mercantile Ahmedabad, so convinced was he of parallels between Greek comedy and indigenous Indian performance forms.[127] The interest shown by the Governor and Burleigh in Indian rituals is Harrison's response to this form of intellectual imperialism. Men like these were trained to assert their supremacy in India by education in the Greek and Latin Classics.

Vasunia and others have shown that the Indian Civil Service exams in the mid- and later nineteenth century disproportionately rewarded performance in classical languages relative to Sanskrit and languages spoken in modern India. This helped to keep the percentage of native administrators down to below five per cent. When an Indian candidate, Satyendranath Tagore, passed the competitive examination in 1864, his examiners promptly lowered the maximum weight given to Sanskrit and Arabic.[128] Most administrators of south-east Asia, from 1806 onwards, had been trained at the East India Company's neoclassically designed training college at Haileybury in Hertfordshire. Candidates were chosen from young men who presented themselves via patronage, friendship networks and nepotism; the qualifying entrance exam, however, was dominated by Classics and theology. By the 1830s, students were asked to translate the Greek New Testament, some of Homer, Herodotus, Xenophon, Thucydides, Sophocles or Euripides, and some of Virgil or Horace. They also needed to answer questions in 'ancient history, geography, and philosophy'.[129] Vasunia, who has led the new twenty-first-century postcolonial studies of Classics and India, has documented how these students' 'facility with Greek and Roman material can be appreciated from the numerous allusions, references, and translations that appear in the articles of *The Haileybury Observer*'.[130]

But it was *Phaedra Britannica* that first gave British cultural and intellectual life a richly researched and vibrant picture of the fascination of the nineteenth-century British administrative class in India with ancient Greece and Rome. He gave us 'Postcolonial Classics' decades before it became a respectable field within the discipline. And he gave it to us in a play which still reads with searing power, and – with properly considered casting, preferably altogether race-blind – would richly reward a twenty-first-century revival.

4

'Shaggermemnon': Aeschylus' *Oresteia* and *Continuous* (1981)

Dying mothers and fathers

The success of his *Misanthrope*, followed by *Phaedra Britannica*, meant that Harrison had succeeded in achieving what many critics thought impossible – the revival of verse drama. On 8 May 1956, the première of John Osborne's *Look Back in Anger* at the Royal Court had heralded a revolution in British theatre. The urbane, romantic, witty verse dramas of Christopher Fry, such as the (much-revived) *The Lady's Not for Burning* (1948), were ousted by blisteringly immediate, intense and angry prose plays about social alienation, sex and the suffocating power of the establishment. Simultaneously, the growing presence of television drama and early soap operas bolstered the supposition that drama and its diction should aim at verisimilitude, at representing a reality in which people do not normally speak verse. But Harrison's conversion of canonical French verse plays into blazing couplets that still sounded something like natural English speech was game-changing. He became 'the de facto writer-in-residence at the National Theatre through the whole of the Seventies and Eighties',[1] and was able to influence decisions about the repertoire.

His response was to conceive ambitious plans for turning two foundational texts in world drama – the English Mystery Plays and Aeschylus' *Oresteia* – into a vital form of non-realist modern, contemporary theatre addressing political and controversial themes.[2] Essential to this project was the sheer 'artifice of the verse...brandished as a means of engaging and delighting the audience'.[3] Harrison's enthusiasm for Aeschylus found a sympathizer in Peter Hall, who had wanted to stage the *Oresteia* ever since he had performed in the Cambridge Greek Play's 1953 production of *Agamemnon*.[4]

Hall knew that Harrison read Greek, and could produce a faithful but speakable English verse version that would work on stage. Harrison began to think about translating it in 1973, when Hall was appointed director of the National Theatre. And work it did. Some of its demotic vigour resulted from the response of both men to a 1976 production of *Agamemnon* in the Greek Theatre at Bradfield College, where respectful 'heritage' performances in false beards and tasteful tunics have delighted the parents of expensively educated boys since 1882. Hall remembered a bishop in the audience, 'gravely following his Greek text, while the story of cannibalism, murder, and corruption was enacted before us'; he decided to take inspiration from the Renaissance when 'the classics were subversive – almost revolutionary' rather than what they became later in British education – 'pillars of conformity'.[5]

The Harrison/Hall production was a triumph, even though it appalled conservative critics, as we shall see. It set a new and much higher bar for the quality of performance translations of ancient texts. It inspired other creative people, including the novelist Barry Unsworth, to use the Atridae myth.[6] It proved that ancient plays were commercially viable and was the first English-language production staged at Epidauros in the ancient theatre. The intense engagement with Greece which marks many of Harrison's subsequent works began with that Epidaurean adventure in 1982. The National Theatre holds extensive archives on the *Oresteia*, which premiered in the Olivier at the National Theatre on 28 November 1981, and in 2012 the British Film Institute re-mastered a recording, thought to have been lost, of a 1983 live broadcast for Channel Four Television.

The entire linguistic and performance idiom of *The Oresteia* was shaped by four interactive factors: Harrison's ongoing work on the English Mystery plays and engagement with Anglo-Saxon poetry, his self-education in feminist theory and politics, his reflections on mothers and fathers caused by the deaths of his parents, Florrie and Harry Harrison, on 13 December 1978 and 21 February 1980, respectively, and his increasingly sophisticated, Marxism-informed appreciation of how the class system had cramped their lives and sabotaged his relationship with them. These factors fed both the implicit politics of the *Oresteia* and his explicit exploration of the class war in his second full-length book of poetry, *From 'The School of Eloquence' and Other Poems* (1978), and its much expanded version of 1981, the year of the première of the *Oresteia*, entitled *Continuous: 50 Sonnets from The School of Eloquence*.

Anglo-Saxon meets Greek

The English Mystery Plays enterprise began in earnest in 1977 when Harrison's version of a selection of the York plays under the title *The Passion*, directed by Bill Bryden, was performed on the terrace outside the National Theatre. Bryden's experimental ensemble, based at the Cottesloe, continued to work with Harrison on *The Passion*, and develop the accompanying *Nativity* and *Doomsday*. The three parts were performed together in a nascent state at the Edinburgh Festival in 1980 and eventually went into the repertoire of the Cottesloe, where in 1985 the production was filmed for Channel Four Television.

Along with Bryden, music director John Tams and designer/actor Bill Dudley, in the years before and while he translated the *Oresteia*, Harrison was (re)creating the lost art of Yorkshire's medieval Mystery actors. They delivered exhaustingly alliterative verse, designedly and energetically consonantal so that it could not die, like vowels, in performance in front of large audiences at huge religious festivals in outdoor spaces. An important factor was Harrison's evolving relationship with the actor Barrie Rutter, who joined the cast of *The Mysteries*, and whose powerful presence, voice and Hull accent Harrison had in mind when translating the *Oresteia*.[7] The process led him back to the earlier Anglo-Saxon four-stressed line, with its strong caesura and consonantal alliteration of the first three stressed syllables, exemplified in *The Battle of Maldon* (110–12):

Bogan wǣron **by**siġe;   **b**ord ord onfēng.
Biter wæs se **b**eadurǣs.   Beornas fēollon
on ġe**h**wæðere **h**and,   hyssas lāgon.

Bows were busy;   shields received spears.
Bitter was that onslaught.   Warriors fell in battle
on both sides,   young men lay slain.

The four stresses, caesura and alliteration provide the metrical structure of most of Harrison's *Oresteia*, for example:

> Calchas the clanseer cunning in seercraft
> when he saw before him the armed sons of Atreus
> knew what menfolk were meant by the preybirds.[8]

Greek, like Anglo-Saxon, permits clustering of consonants; Harrison meditates in a notebook,

> Both Browning and Hopkins had an instinct for the density of Greek with its (agglutinative) syntax and it has always been my impression of it not vowelled, as melodious as Gilbert Murray made him [Aeschylus] seem, but craggy as mocked by Euripides in Aristophanes' FROGS.[9]

Consonontal alliteration was paired with short, Northern vowels. This was inseparable from the decision to use masks and integrate the poetry with the musical score, by Harrison Birtwhistle, with whom Harrison had previously collaborated on European ballad forms in *Bow Down* (1977). That work had already shown the impact of Harrison's interest in the ancient theatrical chorus.[10] Harrison knew that vowels easily get lost in masked performances and that the diction needed to be as viscerally percussive as the music. He wrote to Hall, 'We don't want Barnsley Working Men's on a Saturday night knees up but I have written SHORT vowels. It matters because unless the vowels stay short the consonants don't register.'[11] The beautiful masks, created by acclaimed theatre designer Jocelyn Herbert, with whom Harrison now established a fruitful collaboration that extended until her death in 2003, appalled traditional critics accustomed to hyper-realism.[12]

Just as distinctive as the rhythmic form are the compound nouns, whether an altogether new coining ('clanseer'), rare ('preybird'), obsolescent ('seercraft') or standard modern English but derived from Germanic roots ('menfolk'). German, Anglo-Saxon and ancient Greek form compounds with more ease and frequency than modern English; amongst ancient authors, Aeschylus was notorious for his cragginess and ear-battering neologistic compounds (Aristophanes, *Frogs* 814, 818–25, 929). Harrison has said,

> As a Northerner I am drawn to the physicality of Aeschylus's language. I relish its cragginess and momentum. At school I was never allowed to read verse out loud because of my Yorkshire accent. They said I was a barbarian, not fit to recite the treasures of our culture. And while my translation of

Aeschylus isn't what you could call a deliberate revenge, it is most emphatically a rediscovery of the dignity of the accent.[13]

But he also suggests a more rarified inspiration behind his substitution of Anglo-Saxon-style compounds for those of Aeschylus:

> Two of my Anglo-Saxon-style neologising inventions – namely 'yokestrap' and 'hackblock', I recalled suddenly, at a later stage, I had lifted from Robert Browning's much maligned *Agamemnon* of 1877... I think it might be true to say that the seeds of my principal choices were lurking there in Browning from the beginning without my fully realising it.[14]

The Anglo-Saxon dimension of his chosen verse form, prompted by Browning's experimental, semi-literal version, allowed Harrison to exploit the sense of a performance which draws on its culture's earliest ancestors, creating a collective act of memory, just as Aeschylus' audience were watching a play set many centuries before their own day in a period of civilization poetically indissociable from the archaic diction of Homeric epic. It also allowed him to explore societal affinities between the clan structure of the pre-classical Greece staged in the *Oresteia* and pre-Norman England.[15]

Oliver Taplin was invited by Harrison to attend rehearsals, and his intimate acquaintance with the translation has helped him write the best available analysis. Taplin argues that the insistent compounds 'foreignize' the language, drawing attention to its craftedness. The compounds do not appear in precise correspondence to compounds in Aeschylus' Greek, and they have various functions:

> At one extreme of the sliding scale there are the unique formations (more often than not hapax legomena in English) which are generally of the kind that is closest to the Aeschylean lexicon: words like 'galesqualls', 'bloodstorm', 'lootlust', 'whore-war', 'oar-spoor', 'childstew', 'grieftrills', 'woecups', 'flesh-chef', 'lootpearl', 'loose flow', 'shrewgrudge'. At the other extreme, there are recurrent formations, words which become part of the basic vocabulary of the plays, and integral to their whole thematic texture. These would include, for example, 'he-child' and 'she-child', 'he-god' and 'she-god', 'bed-bond', 'blood-bond', 'man-lord', 'blood-grudge'.[16]

As Taplin points out, another effect of these coinages is to distance the Bronze-Age Greeks' language from the contemporary-world connotations of our everyday speech. They are 'part of Harrison's anthropological foreignizing. Thus, "he-child" and "she-child" avoid "son" and "daughter"; "clan-chief" avoids "general" or "king" or "prime minister" – all with notions of hierarchy or of national unity that should be avoided.'[17]

This is broadly true. There is no attempt to topicalize or update the plays, or transplant them to a new context, as in *Aikin Mata* and *Phaedra Britannica*. But the notebooks reveal that the intellectual cauldron from which Harrison's translation emerged also contained a vast amount of reading about contemporary political events, which affected his evocation of the tense atmosphere of Argos under the tyranny of Aegisthus and Clytemnestra: the chorus says 'the whole space of Argos whispers with spies./ It only takes one to report to our rulers.'[18] He has pasted in cuttings on Irish political funerals,[19] on the trial on charges of torture and murder of Luís Cabral, deposed first president of Guinea,[20] on the imprisoned members of the Bader-Meinhof gang and the continuing activities of the Red Army Faction, which he saw as illuminating Aeschylus' Erinyes.[21]

Infrequently, Harrison reminds his audience of their specific 1980s anxieties about warfare, especially nuclear weapons. Sometimes this is done with a light hand: corpses return from Troy 'in army-issue urns' with 'dogtags on the amphorae'.[22] When the herald recalls his terror the morning after the storm at sea, the audience is first invited to think of a familiar northern British scene with a reference to the collie rounding up sheep, where the Greek refers to a gust of wind 'like a bad shepherd' (Aeschylus, *Agamemnon* 657):

> Blackness. Waveforce. Sea heaving and swelling.
> Fierce thrashing galesqualls whistling from Thrace,
> hurricanes blasting, rain lashing and pelting,
> ship-prow smashing ship-prow, horned beast goring beast,
> beasts with their horns locked butting each other.
> You know when a collie not used to its charges
> scatters the daft sheep every direction,
> colliding, collapsing, that kind of chaos…
> well that's how the waves were. Next morning
> the Aegean had mushroomed with corpses and shipwreck.[23]

The verb 'mushroomed' is a dazzling choice (the Greek says 'flowered', 659), prompting comparisons with nuclear clouds over Hiroshima and Nagasaki.[24]

Other terms are even more insistently contemporary: the Greek contingents are 'the Allies', and injustice leads to 'bloodright' being 'shattered to atoms of nothing'.[25] Athena in *Eumenides* talks like a five-star US General. She tells the Erinyes not to let their 'dewfalls of acid shrivel the seedpods', and that she alone of the gods has access

> to Zeus's munitions,
> the mighty he-god's missiles of thunder.
> But this isn't a case for desperate deterrents.[26]

The noisy use of the nouns 'munitions', 'missiles' and 'deterrents' reveals Harrison's engagement at the time with campaigners for nuclear disarmament, which would have repercussions in his later work, including versions of *Trojan Women* and *Lysistrata* designed to be staged at Greenham Common,[27] and the theme of the dehumanizing technologization of warfare in *Square Rounds* (1992), *The Shadow of Hiroshima* (1995) and *Prometheus* (1998).

The unrhymed, four-stressed alliterative line is capacious enough to allow variety in syntactical form, length and rhetorical polish of sentence, and in individual characters' own style of speaking – their idiolects. In stichomythia, where characters engage in intense question-and response dialogue, with the speaker exchanged line by line, Harrison decided to emphasize the strange formality of this poetic form by introducing rhyme.[28] The text separates the couplets to stimulate the actors into delivering them as such, and even numbers them in a series, as in the tense dialogue between Clytemnestra and Agamemnon in the carpet scene:

> 4. **Clyt.** Are you afraid of what the people might say?
> **Ag.** The voice of the people exerts its own sway.
>
> 5. **Clyt.** Mangrudge is proof that a man's reached great heights.
> **Ag.** And only he-women go looking for fights.[29]

At the time of the *Oresteia* he used the metaphor of 'kabukified ping-pong' for the stichomythia sections, which Simon Goldhill describes as 'absolutely formalized and antirealist', an effect created 'by slowing down the delivery and putting a crash of music between each line'.[30] This put weight on the semantic significance of each line, as the argument unfurled. But by 2012, Harrison had revised this metaphor and encouraged actors to treat stichomythia as a game, rather, of squash, with actors hurling their lines frontally to bounce off the audience and back again to their interlocutor to return.[31]

The core metre, in speeches or stichomythia, rhymed or unrhymed, is also alternated with other verse forms. Harrison was aware that the ancient Greeks held the moments of change between one metre and style of delivery in tragedy particularly emotive: the Aristotelian *Problems* 19.6 asks why shifting between types of delivery creates the sense of tragedy. The answer is *anōmalia* or 'contrast', 'for in a serious situation, whether happy or afflicting, contrast produces pathos, while uniformity is less moving'.[32] So Harrison uses diverse rhythms, paces and affective gear-shifts, for example in the first stasimon of *Agamemnon* where he imagines the lament of the bereaved women of Argos, in *Cheophori* with a short trochaic line at the commencement of the formal dirge, at the moment when Aegisthus is about to be murdered, and for the choral responses when Orestes begins to lose his sanity.[33]

She-gods and wolf mothers against the patriarchy

Harrison's sympathy with nuclear disarmament was inextricable from the interest in feminism which informs every word of his *Oresteia*. Harrison's gender-polarized noun pairs such as 'she-child'/'he-child' or 'she-god'/'he-god' do more than 'foreignize' his ancient Greeks. Benedict Nightingale saw exactly what Harrison was doing, even if he disliked it: by these neologisms, 'Harrison does much more than he should to emphasise the trilogy's sexual implications. . . Thus what's implicit in Aeschylus is made excessively and sometimes speciously explicit, presumably to suggest that the trilogy dramatizes a turning-point in the relative power of the sexes.'[34] For these nouns show Harrison responding to recent work by feminists on the ideological work done by language. He observes that 'he-god and she-god rather than god and goddess' produce 'a noun confrontation', appropriate since 'the polarity of male and female is a basic thematic pulse of the whole trilogy', whereas 'the scales [are] already tipped by the feminine diminutive'.[35] Harrison's insistence that only an all-male cast was appropriate to a text of such influence in the history of misogyny thus anticipated by several years, and was probably an inspiration behind, Sue-Ellen

Case's much-cited article arguing that feminists should avoid ancient Greek theatre altogether.[36]

Harrison has always been bemused when censured for his poems' allegedly hyper-masculine, heteronormative poetic voice, obsession with semen, male libido and objectification of women;[37] he was criticized for admitting in 'Changing at York' that he slept with other women while still married to his first wife.[38] He was hounded by the press for supposedly mistreating women when conducting a fairly public affair with actor Sian Thomas while still married to his second wife, opera singer Teresa Stratas, in the late 1980s, and for unashamedly referring to them both in the poem 'Laureate's Block'.[39] In 1994, Luke Spencer complained, without much evidence, that Harrison's theatre shows women as 'at their best…recalcitrant and irrational, at their worst masochistic and murderous'.[40] By insisting on an all-male cast for the *Oresteia*, when such 'gender-blind' practices were still regarded by advocates of realism in theatre as scandalous, he made himself vulnerable to attacks from feminists. Some women objected to female actors being deprived, as they saw it, of the opportunity to star in an important production, and some assumed that he somehow approved of the unmitigated misogyny of Aeschylus' trilogy. Marina Warner said the casting was an 'enormity' in which the actors played 'as men, with deep, undisguised voices, and jock straps showing through their chitons'.[41]

These views were mistaken. Harrison was convinced that the misogyny of the trilogy could only be realized by having the female roles delivered by male actors, as in the ancient theatre. In an interview, he said that using women actors would imply that the National Theatre was 'smugly assuming that the sex war was over and that the oppression of the patriarchal code existed only in past times. The maleness of the piece is like a vacuum-sealed container keeping this ancient issue fresh.'[42] Harrison was keen to heighten the tension between female and male spectators by separating them. He saw the excitement this would create as a substitute for the religious power of the trilogy in its original performance context. He wrote in a notebook opposite the vicious gynaecophobic tirade of Apollo (*Eumenides* 657–73): 'We can't make it holy [or special in that Greek sense] but segregating the audience into m. and f. would electrify the auditorium.'[43] Unfortunately, the National Theatre refused.[44]

Harrison's interpretation informed his choices as a translator everywhere. He wrote women into the memorable choral passage, beginning with the image of the war-god Ares as the 'gold-exchanger of bodies', where the old men of Argos lament the number of war dead whose ashes were brought back from Troy. Aeschylus' text speaks of the grief of 'loved ones' in the (masculine) plural crying out for their men; Harrison has amplified this to mean women wholly unmentioned in the Greek, 'wives mothers sisters', who are given the direct speech:

> which grey ashes are my man's?
> they sift the jumbled names and cry
> *my husband sacrificed his life*
> *my brother's a battle-martyr.*[45]

Harrison has forced his audience to acknowledge that war bereaves women even more than men.

The *Oresteia* brims with statements about the respective roles of women and men, especially concentrated in Clytemnestra's speech and others' comments upon her.[46] Harrison often expands or heightens the poetry in these passages, from the watchman's opening speech onwards. One and a half lines in Greek, which literally translate 'Thus orders the expectant mind of the woman who thinks like a man', become the emphatic anaphoric triplet,

> The woman says watch so here I am watching.
> That woman's not one who's all wan and woeful.
> That woman's a man the way she gets moving.[47]

The watchman's speech heightens the disrespect for the queen implicit in the Greek.[48] When Clytemnestra confronts the chorus over the corpses, the Greek can be translated literally: 'Do you claim the deed is mine? Do not deem that I am Agamemnon's wife. A phantom resembling that corpse's wife, the ancient bitter evil spirit of Atreus, that grim banqueter, has offered him as payback, sacrificing an adult in return for young ones'; Harrison's Clytemnestra asks at greater length, with heightened rhetorical emphasis,

> Spouse? No! Wife? No! What swung the swordblade's
> the semblance, the shape of the corpse's wife only.
> Wielding the weapon was no wife and no woman

but the family's phantom, Atreus the flesh-chief
offering flayed these fully fledged victims,
one for each butchered and barbecued babe.[49]

Aeschylus' diction is also elaborated to make Orestes say that Aegisthus is a 'she-man/ who queens it beside the real clan-chief, his consort'.[50]

As translator, Harrison takes sides with Clytemnestra and the Erinyes in *Eumenides*. When translating 566–81, the opening of the trial, where Orestes speaks, he writes in the notebook, 'it is all shit!', and repeats the word 'shit' when the Erinyes finally capitulate.[51] His use of stress in the songs of this threatened female collective highlights their strength, unity and opposition to men:

She-kin, show our force. Join hands!
Dance the doom-dance steps, display
through our grim music that our band's
a power over men that gets its way...[52]

His notebooks, moreover, consistently connect the sexism of the Greek text with the contemporary position of women. There are cuttings about the Yorkshire Ripper, arrested and convicted in 1981 for multiple sexualized murders of women across West Yorkshire,[53] but the ones Harrison has selected are by women and focus on women's shock and disappointment at the police's incompetence and advice to keep off the streets after dark. Jean Stead's article includes a poem by a Leeds woman entitled 'Poem for Jacqueline Hill', in honour of one of his victims. The poem includes direct speech by men, telling women to

fear the dark, stay at home,
We cannot answer for the consequences
If you get on buses;
Leave us the hunting paths in the city jungle –
Be good: be stupid: never, never be free.[54]

By 1979, coincidentally or not just after his mother's death, Harrison began a self-education in feminism, researching early matriarchies, and reading classics such as Simone de Beauvoir's *The Second Sex*, Kate Millett's *Sexual Politics* and Mary Daly's *Gyn/Ecology*. He collected feminist posters, misogynist cartoons and cuttings about male violence, including one about a Japanese student who ate his girlfriend after murdering her.[55] He investigated *The Daughters' Cycle Trilogy* (1977–80), the Women's Experimental Theatre's rewriting of the Atridae myth from a feminist perspective in New York, especially *Electra Speaks*, which focused 'on the struggle against male dominance embodied by the father, the son and the phallologocentric language that traps women in dominant discourse'.[56]

By late 1980, he was attending a Matriarchy Study Group and researching the connection between male hormones and aggression.[57] Most surprising of all, he has pasted in and read the entirety of Froma Zeitlin's landmark in feminist (and structuralist) Classics, 'The dynamics of misogyny: myth and mythmaking in the *Oresteia*', which I was told at exactly the same time, as an undergraduate at Oxford University, was 'not to be read' since it was 'feminist gibberish'.[58] Here was a man of the theatre speeding ahead of mainstream classical scholarship in his grasp of pioneering hermeneutic theory.

Ad Patrem and the class struggle

The emphasis on the theme of sex war in the *Oresteia* that Harrison's lexical choices created upset some critics, including Nightingale, as we have seen. The same theme has also dominated subsequent critical discussion of the script and production.[59] Nightingale had an acute ear for Harrison's agenda, and was just as irritated by what he sensed was a subversively working-class perspective on the ancient script, delivered in consonantal plebeian Yorkshire accents, as by its insistent feminism. Nightingale fulminated in the *New York Times* that it sounded 'like a collaboration between the author of *Beowulf* and some street-cafe poetaster in jeans'.[60]

While the theme of gender conflict may have been Peter Hall's priority, Harrison's feminism was grounded in his class-conscious, materialist conception of human history; he intuitively related to Marxism, and in 'A Good Read' cites Marx as one of the authors he had read as an undergraduate and who had increased the alienation between himself and his father: 'That summer it was Ibsen, Marx and Gide.'[61] That poem came from the third (1984) version of his continuously evolving *From 'The School of Eloquence' and Other Poems* (the first of its poems were published in 1978[62]), which contained far more explicit consideration of social class than anything in *The Loiners*.[63]

For most readers, Harrison's second epigraph needs decoding. It is in untranslated Latin. It combines the opening and conclusion of Milton's poem *Ad Patrem*, probably composed in 1637, in which the young poet defends his vocation to his father. Harrison wanted to provoke discomfort in his readers by confronting them with a text they did not understand, in a language 'owned by' the elite;[64] once they had tracked down a translation, he hoped that they would both politically relate Harrison to Milton's republicanism and understand that his alienation from his father, whom he came to appreciate more after his mother's death, was caused by his disorienting classical education. Yet that same classical education had given Harrison the training in a school of eloquence that might rescue this elderly baker from Leeds from the voicelessness and oblivion which were normal for his class.

Translations of Milton's Latin poems are not easily accessible, so here is my version of the lines quoted by Harrison:

> Now I wish the Pierian springs would roll their refreshing streams through my heart, and pour through my mouth all the water that flows from the double summit, so that my Muse, forgetting inconsequential songs, might ascend on vigorous wings in the service of my esteemed father. This poem may please you, excellent father, but it is a minor work that she muses over for you. I do not myself know what more fitting gift I can give you in return for what you have given me, although even my greatest gift could not recompense you, and the arid thanks returned in empty words can never equal your gifts ...
>
> If you [my youthful poems], dare to hope for perpetual life, to outlive your master and gaze on the light, and if black oblivion does not seize you into crowded Orcus, may you conserve these praises, and the name of my father celebrated here, as an example far into the future.

And the 'minor work' that follows does indeed bring Harrison's father's personality, language and views to vivid life.

In an interview, Harrison said, 'I came from a loving, rooted upbringing which was disrupted by Education and Poetry. And I've been trying to create new wholes out of that disruption ever since.'[65] The grief he underwent during the three years in which both his parents died must have informed the intense representation of psychological agony in his *Oresteia*. It is palpable in 'Blocks', the account of his mother's funeral when he can't make a speech, 'For all my years of Latin and of Greek'; 'Book Ends' portrays him and his father just after Florrie's funeral, when they'd eaten the last apple pie she had cooked: they sit in devastated silence, separated by a vast of gulf of 'not the thirty or so years, but books, books, books'.[66]

Harrison's love-songs to his father, mostly composed while he was translating Aeschylus, convey the rich gifts Harry Harrison had bestowed on his son: the examples of musical speech, strong principles, pride in appearance, dignity, deep love of a woman, and aversion to swearing, gambling, debt or begging. Harrison's sonnets explore memories of his father's working-class parenting style and recreational activities: his conscientious tending of his front garden, making and installing its wooden gate, accompaniment of his little son to the barber's and to the cinema to watch gangster movies, building sandcastles on holiday, and his final, if grudging, acceptance that his son was a professional poet. In 'A Good Read', Harrison contrasts his own reading of Ibsen, Marx and Gide with his father's 'programme at United!/ The labels on your whisky or your beer!' Yet he shares his father's class position on elite culture:

> I've come round to your position on 'the Arts'
> but put it down in poems, that's the bind.

The problem is that in order to further the cause of his natal class, Harrison can only use poetry – a medium which is often, though it need not be – associated with the upper classes.

Harrison the Marxist is aware of the harshness of his father's life ('fifty weeks of ovens and six years of war'[67]), and endless early risings on cold days to work at the bakery. He also acknowledges the ideological prejudices held by such white working-class Leeds inhabitants against foreign immigrants. While writing the earlier poems to his father he was translating the *Oresteia*, but also pasting into his notebooks quotations from Trotsky's *Literature and Revolution* and photographs of both Trotsky and Brecht.[68] Rather than the canonical commentary on *Agamemnon* by Eduard Fraenkel (1950), he used the anthropologically inflected edition by communist Greek scholar George Thomson.[69]

References to physical work and humble labour in the trilogy are translated with love and attention to detail, from the watchman's physical misery to the herald's memories of the terrible conditions the regular soldiers experienced at

Troy, and the plight of the chorus of *Libation-Bearers*, 'palace work-slaves', 'hauled from our homeland, dragged here as drudges' and 'brought into bondage'; 'Serfwomen, freeborn', 'fettered to fate' and 'Shackled to shame'. Orestes says that it was the ordinary men of Argos 'who braved long war boldly and battered down Troy', and the nurse remembers the efforts she expended to look after Orestes as a baby: 'That lad gave me trouble in tonloads.'[70]

The chorus of *Choephori* liken the joy that will result from the delivery of the house of Atreus to the joy of simple fisherfolk, but from the perspective of women:

Like the women of fishermen who wail
until they glimpse the first white sail.

The wind drops, the dark sky clears,
the women's wailing turns to cheers.

Cheers as the laden ships reach shore
and loved ones suffer storm no more.[71]

Harrison laid the groundwork for his feminist self-education by studying the nineteenth-century theory favoured by Marx, in his annotations on Lewis H. Morgan's *Ancient Society* (1877), that women had only been subordinated at a particular point in human history which coincided with the development of private property and subsequently the state; before that, there had been equality between the sexes and even 'primitive matriarchies'. The idea was first mooted in J. J. Bachofen's *Das Mutterrecht* (1861), but its evolutionary economic explanation of patriarchy obviously suited both Marx and Engels; Engels expounded the thesis in detail in *The Origin of the Family, Private Property, and the State* (1877). Harrison's interest in this theory also led him to read the lesser-known work on the topic by Marx's revolutionary son-in-law Paul Lafargue, *The Evolution of Property from Savagery to Civilization* (1890).[72]

The demotic model of theatre he encountered in the Mystery Plays lies behind his vision of a public, democratic rendering of Greek theatre as much as do his readings of Brecht, Marx and Trotsky. The English plays were created by and for working people via the trade and merchant guilds and were integral to the calendar and lives of medieval towns. Harrison had previously recorded his identification with craft guild members in 'Durham', the penultimate poem of *The Loiners* (see above pp. 28–9). In his version of *The Mysteries*, the biblical tales were presented metatheatrically as plays-within-plays, by actors representing craftsmen and guild members, who welcomed the audience into the theatre and mingled throughout with them.

Harrison realized that the verse form was part of this central contract with the audience – just as it is established in a children's pantomime when the Good Fairy delivers the rhyming prologue. This meant that the words were always the priority and that the poetry needed to be of a quality that could keep listeners engrossed for hours. He knew that he was in an unusual position as both a classical scholar who could hear every resonance in Aeschylus' lexical choices and as an increasingly confident poet himself with a command of the roughest vernacular as well as the most revered canonical authors. When he was first working on *Eumenides*, he inscribed in his notebook a remark made by D. S. Carne-Ross, which forms part of his own implicit manifesto:

> Only a poet can translate poetry. A poet perhaps in some way *manqué*, but still a poet. It is plain impertinence for a man who has written no good verse of his own to offer the public a verse translation of a great poet.[73]

He painstakingly crafted verses which are never less than exciting, and sometimes rise to spine-tingling. Peter Levi described the watchman's line 'Put down your palliasse. Dew-drenched by daybreak' as 'invading the mind'.[74] Yet Harrison never lost sight of the problems his modern audiences without degrees in Classics might experience when hearing allusions to arcane myths, so he sometimes deletes proper names or expands by several lines an important reference, such as the Pythia's description of the harpies' persecution of Phineus at the opening of *Eumenides*; he also expands where the image is particularly significant, for example the references to Clytemnestra's 'oriental' prostration before Agamemnon in the carpet scene.[75]

Lee Hall points out that Harrison's famous off-the-cuff remark, that his insistence on the primacy of poetic rhythm meant that he was like the man who came to 'read the metre/meter', was made at the same time as *The Mysteries* and *The Oresteia* were being created at the National Theatre. This was also 'a time when the train you sat on to get there, the water you got at the bar, the electricity that provided the illumination was all publicly owned. Was all held in common.'[76] And the people controlling the nation's theatre were not from elite backgrounds. Peter Hall was a stationmaster's son from Suffolk, Harrison Birtwistle a baker's son from Lancashire and Bill Bryden a shipyard worker's son from Greenock. None assumed that metropolitan Received Pronunciation was the correct vehicle for drama. All were committed to creating a public form of theatre that bypasses the ruling-class stranglehold on 'the Arts' to address people directly, and is communally consumed. Part of that project was the radical commitment to performing canonical theatre scripts in northern English accents, which irrevocably appropriated elite cultural property for Everyman.

Clytemnestra's language becomes much coarser immediately after she has murdered her husband and gloats over his corpse:

Look at him, Shaggermemnon, shameless, shaft-happy,
Ogler and grinder of Troy's golden girlhood.[77]

This is not only aggressively masculine in its sexual violence and riotous alliteration of 'sh' and a hard 'g', reinforcing the key-word 'shag', but it has class implications. Slang verbs like 'shag' and 'shaft' are not quite swear-words, but they are regarded as tasteless, foul-mouthed and 'low'; when pronounced with a northern short 'a', 'shaft' can sound threatening in addition.

Such trenchant slang is used from the watchman's prologue to *Agamemnon* onwards. There are frequent, guttural hard 'g' consonants, partly informed by Harrison's experiments with Agamemnon's name and with the English word 'gag'. These prompted the cluster of g-sounds at the climax of the chorus' account of the sacrifice of Iphigenia, 'like a goat to the godstone/ a gag in her mouth' in front of 'that gang round the godstone'.[78] A similar monosyllable to 'gag' is the word 'gob', used by the watchman. Harrison translates the colloquial Greek proverb, 'a great ox has stepped on my tongue', meaning that the watchman intends to keep silent about something, with heightened alliteration and assonance, as 'Say that an ox ground my gob into silence'.[79]

Caroline Latham shows that Harrison had been thinking about the power of the blunt slang word 'gob' for years. In his response to Brecht, 'The Ballad of Babelabour', Harrison had described the speech of labourers throughout history, 'the hang-cur ur-grunt of the weak/ the unrecorded urs of gobless workers'.[80] In his manifesto poem 'Them & (uz)' (1978), where he announces to the ruling class his intention to 'occupy/ your lousy leasehold Poetry', he describes Demosthenes, his 'gob full of pebbles'.[81] The word recurs in another 1978 poem, 'Working', about Patience Kershaw, a nineteenth-century mineworker, and there Harrison adds a note: 'Gob: an old Northern coal-mining word for the space left after the coal has been extracted. Also, of course, the mouth, and speech.'[82] As Latham says, the watchman's use of the word 'resonates with class and cultural connotations'.[83]

There are many other jarringly crude and uncouth words: the chorus of *Agamemnon* use the words 'cretin', 'gut' and 'guts', and 'blood-bog', call Helen a 'Troy-knacker' and describe 'foodpots and grain jars crapping their contents' and a lion-cub 'whimpering for the tit'. They describe themselves as 'doddering about on sticks' without 'juice enough to serve the Wargod' and as 'Argos geezers'. The messenger says that the Greeks had suffered 'god-aggro enough on the banks of Scamander'. Clytemnestra, for all her early formal rhetorical arias when she is dissembling, can be colloquial ('catnap', 'yanking'); she calls Cassandra a 'sparrowbrain', 'a maniac, more like' and 'champing her chops on the chainbit'. Cassandra can equal her coarseness, saying that Apollo 'got me flat on my back', calling Helen 'hell-bitch' and 'shark-hag', and complaining that the palace 'stinks like an abattoir drain'.

In the confrontation between the chorus and Aegisthus the language becomes increasingly colloquial and savage, reflecting the harshness of the Greek dialogue. Aegisthus calls the chorus 'dodderers', and says, 'You're pushing your luck you old foulmouths.' They respond by telling him to 'Grow fat on injustice. Shit on the state!', and call him 'a dungheap lord'. The choruses favour the noun 'gullet'; the one in *Choephori* says that Clytemnestra 'hacked off' Agamemnon's 'cock, his hands, his feet', and call Skylla 'a bitch on heat'. Electra refers to 'slop-pails'. Orestes says that he has felt as though he is being 'gobbled alive'; Electra declares, 'I'll bare my wolf-fangs when she smiles./ Wolf mothers breed wolf daughters.' Orestes calls his mother a 'wolf-bitch' and refers to her and Aegisthus 'tupping'. The nurse Cilissa remembers how baby Orestes used to 'piddle' and 'crap'.[84]

Even the solemn proceedings depicted in *Eumenides* illustrate Harrison's conviction 'that verse could be foul mouthed and outspoken without compromising a jot of its seriousness'.[85] The Pythia coins a Germanic-sounding participle, 'beshitten', when describing the effect when the Harpies, attacking Phineus, 'splattered their bat-bowels over his platters'. The ghostly Clytemnestra says that the Erinyes are 'fagged out by sleep' and urges them to attack Orestes, to 'fart fire through your flues till he flops like a fruitrind'. Apollo says the Erinyes should live in places 'larded with shit and chewed gristle'. Athena uses the verb 'spew'.[86] Conservative critics were appalled at the coarseness of the language into which Harrison had translated a revered classical pillar of high culture, and they derided it as undignified, ugly and cacophonous.[87] As so often with criticism of Harrison, unease with his class politics masqueraded as aesthetic derision. The real problem was that Olympian gods and the Argive Royal Family sounded like dockers from Hull.

5

'All the versuses of life': '*v.*' and *Medea: A Sex-War Opera* (1985)

'No more Greek'

Harrison's most famous work, '*v.*', was written during the National Union of Miners' strike which began in 1984, in protest against the closures planned by National Coal Board chief Ian MacGregor. It was published in 1985.[1] This long quatrain poem is now regarded as a classic of late twentieth-century literature, often studied by British teenagers taking Advanced-Level English exams. The V-sign draws together football and the Second Wold War victory sign; it symbolizes 'divisions of class, gender, religion, [and] language' and the conflict within Harrison's consciousness between the class of his birth and the cultural circles in which he now moved.[2] He has said that 'versuses are very important to creating the verse…this rather awful pun of course in that title' gives him the 'dialectic' he needs if he is to create.[3] But '*v.*' did not explode into the national consciousness until November 1987, when Channel 4 Television broadcast a film of Harrison reciting it, directed by Richard Eyre.[4] The broadcast created public uproar, mostly focused on its four-letter words, which Sean O'Brien calls its 'spraycan discourse'.[5]

The programme involved the longest and densest cluster of sexually explicit words that had ever been broadcast in Britain at the time. It made Harrison headline news. Mary Whitehouse protested in *The Times*. The *Daily Mail* was horrified, denouncing it as a 'torrent of filth'. Gerald Howarth, a Conservative MP, had tried to have the broadcast proscribed (although he had not even read most of the poem) by tabling an Early Day Motion in Parliament entitled 'Television Obscenity'.[6] The parliamentary rumpus ensured that a much larger audience tuned in. But the scandal obscured the reality that the aspect of '*v.*' to which the right wing really objected was its resolute sympathy with the working class.

A modern response to Thomas Gray's 'Elegy Written in a Country Churchyard' (1751), 'v.' recounts a trip made by Harrison to a cemetery in Beeston, Leeds, to visit his parents' grave. In the poem, the graveyard, now a haunt of local football fan skinheads, has been defaced by obscene racist graffiti. This prompts meditation on the divisions (as in *v.* for 'versus') caused by class, racial and other conflicts in his society:

> These Vs are all the versuses of life
> from LEEDS v. DERBY, Black/White
> and (as I've known to my cost) man v. wife,
> Communist v. Fascists, Left v. Right,
>
> class v. class as bitter as before,
> the unending violence of US and THEM,
> personified in 1984
> by Coal Board MacGregor and the NUM.

There follows a ferocious dialogue on education, life chances and the purpose of poetry with a skinhead who speaks in Leeds vernacular. He turns out to be an 'alter ego' of the poet himself.

The quotation from then NUM President Arthur Scargill that introduces 'v.' reads: 'My father still reads the dictionary every day. He says your life depends on your power to master words.'[7] Poetry helps to compensate for inarticulacy. Harrison had earlier memorialized two uncles who struggled to speak in his signature poem 'Heredity' – Joe and Harry – 'one was a stammerer, the other dumb'. He has written that these 'early experiences of family inarticulacy were what drove me, I see now in retrospect, into a passion for language and languages, and for what is still for me the supreme articulacy and eloquence of poetry'.[8] The poem 'v.' releases the voice of the poor youths of Leeds, in contrast with Gray's poem, in which the underclasses who might have had poetic talent, but remained agricultural labourers, lie buried, 'mute' and 'inglorious'.[9]

In the sixth quatrain of 'v.', where Harrison reflects that this cemetery may be his own last resting-place, the memory of his classical education at Leeds Grammar School and Leeds University provides the first wide-angle frame for the cemetery:

> If buried ashes saw then I'd survey
> the places I'd learned Latin, and learned Greek,
> and left, the places where Leeds United play
> but disappoint their fans week after week/. . .[10]

The classical languages distinguish Harrison from the football fans; their youth is spent on the football terraces rather than in educational institutions.

Latin plays its part in class alienation again in quatrain 11, where a former Mayor is honoured by an inscription 'in a bit of Latin'. Harrison contrasts himself as a 'classical' poet with the beer-swilling underclass by capitalizing the brand name of their favourite lager, HARP. But the next reference to Classics is kept for the dramatic moment when the skinhead's voice irrupts into the poem. Harrison sends himself up when the poet here pompously asks himself, using a Greek term rather than its obvious English equivalent 'racist', and an unnecessary French one, why the vandals write what they do. Are they 'Giving the dead their xenophobic feeling, / or just a *cri-de-coeur* because man dies?' The skinhead snarls in response,

> So what's a *cri-de-coeur*, cunt? Can't you speak
> the language that yer man spoke. Think of 'er!
> Can you only get yer tongue round fucking Greek?
> Go and fuck yourself with *cri-de-coeur*.[11]

The skinhead can't tell the difference between ancient Greek and French, and the poem prompts us both to realize this and to acknowledge our own intellectual snobbery in judging him for his ignorance. But the French is important.

The classicism of '*v.*' lies predominantly in its dialogue with canonical poets – Gray, Wordsworth and Byron, but especially with Rimbaud, as Christine Regan has shown. Rimbaud was a Communard, and poet of the commune; Harrison presents himself in '*v.*' as 'an unlikely union of high cultural poet and dispossessed vandal, an idiosyncratic loner who finds his ghostly twin in a nineteenth-century French poet'.[12] Harrison is jolted out of his elegiac reminiscing by a youth who tells him that 'A book, yer stupid cunt's, not worth a fuck!' The poet responds in the skinhead's own language,

> You piss-artist skinhead cunt, you wouldn't know
> and it doesn't fucking matter if you do,

> the skin and poet united fucking Rimbaud
> but the *autre* that *je est* is fucking you.

The poet thus embeds, in the obscene Leeds patois he is increasingly using himself, the alien French of Rimbaud's celebrated dictum '*Je est un autre*' ('I is someone else');[13] the poem subsequently acts the dictum out, when the cultured poet Harrison 'metamorphoses into an illiterate neo-Nazi vandal':[14] the spray-can-wielding *Doppelgänger* 'aerosolled his name. And it was mine.'[15] But first, the skinhead forbids the poet to use languages he can't understand, which are collectively subsumed, twice in one quatrain, under the label 'Greek':

> Ah've told yer, no more Greek...That's yer last warning!
> Ah'll boot yer fucking balls to Kingdom Come.
> They'll find yer cold on t'grave tomorrer morning.
> So don't speak Greek. Don't treat me like I'm dumb.

The poet makes no further classical references, but gradually morphs into the skinhead himself.

In the opening quatrain, the authorial voice of '*v.*' had addressed future readers with a meditation on Harrison's paternal ancestors and their trades:

> Next millennium you'll have to search quite hard
> to find my slab behind the family dead.
> butcher, publican, and baker, now me, bard
> adding poetry to their beef, beer and bread.[16]

As Sandie Byrne has suggested, rather than call himself 'poet' here, as he does on his passport, Harrison chooses the resonant term 'bard', with its Homeric and medieval associations. This is not solely for aural and alliterative reasons.[17] Antony Rowland, while noting that Harrison does not often refer to the *Odyssey*, has suggested that there is 'an Odyssean sensibility behind '*v.*', which tracks the poet's journey from his Beeston youth to exile in the geographical specificities of north Leeds, and in which the skinhead appears as a kind of ghost in a libation that ironically invokes the spirit of the living poet'.[18]

The parallels between Homer's Odysseus could be developed – Odysseus of the far-flung travels, the increasing isolation, the wordless encounter with his own mother in the Underworld, the sense of the Leeds ghosts haunting the Underworld maze of disused mining corridors, and the return to the hearth and bed of a much-loved woman from whom he fears he may be parted again. But ultimately, the poem is about Harrison's problems with reconciling his vocation with his class origins and political position. Harrison describes the vandalism described and enacted in 'v.' as 'that act of vandalism that I would like to commit on English literature',[19] and desire to break out from the esoteric, closed world of poetry.[20] Yet he has still come no nearer to finding an answer to his own self-doubt, expressed in the vandal's assertion, 'it's not poetry we need in this class war'.[21]

'The old male-concocted curse': *Medea: A sex-war opera*

In the same year as the publication of 'v.', Harrison was commissioned by the Metropolitan Opera in New York to write a libretto for a new work about Medea. He had remained in touch with director John Dexter after *Phaedra Britannica* and Dexter's move to New York. He had provided the translation of Smetana's *The Bartered Bride* for Dexter's production at the Met in 1978, and had fallen in love with its soprano star, Teresa Stratas, with whom he contracted his second marriage in 1984 (he had previously divorced his first wife, the mother of his children, Rosemarie). He was spending long periods living with Stratas in the USA, and learning about the history and practice of opera; this influenced both his treatment of the choruses of the *Oresteia* and the televised musical drama on the theme of Herod, *H.* (1984).[22]

Now he was asked to write a new libretto about one of the most prominent of classical heroines in the opera house and theatre for centuries, from Calderon (1636, in *Los Tres Mayores Prodigios*), Cavalli (1649) and Charpentier (1693) to Cherubini (1797), Grillparzer (1821), Mayr (1826), Legouvé (1856) and Mendès (1898).[23] He even drew on a translation into Czech (1878).[24] He responded with a libretto which refers to all of these, either musically or verbally, but in demotic tone resembles more the startlingly feminist Victorian burlesque in rhyming English verse by Robert Brough, *Medea; or, the Best of Mothers with a Brute of a Husband* (1856), to which it also refers. Harrison presents the version of the story told in the high operas, which Brough was parodying, as one big misogynist male fabrication, in an 'ingenious, witty, hard-hitting piece of social intervention'.[25]

When Harrison had wanted to separate the audience of the *Oresteia* on gender grounds, he had not been permitted. Four years later, he decided that the new opera was to be fundamentally structured, like Aristophanes' *Lysistrata*, around two hostile choruses of women and men, but, unlike in the ancient comedy, they were never to be reconciled. The chorus sing,

> As the sex-war's still being fought
> which sex does a myth support?
> you should be asking.
> [...]
> Beneath *all* Greek mythology
> Are struggles between HE and SHE
> That we're still waging.
> In every quiet suburban wife
> Dissatisfied with married life
> Is MEDEA, raging.[26]

The work was never performed at the Met because there were what the *New York Times* called 'creative disputes' between Harrison and the composer, Jacob Druckman;[27] the American had shifted during his career from musical neoclassicism to modernism, but was not known to be ideologically adventurous in his treatment of storylines or partial to libretti including near-obscene and colloquial diction. The Argonauts refer unmistakeably to performing cunnilingus on the women of Lemnos.[28] It is interesting to speculate on Druckman's reaction when he was asked to compose music to accompany the following choral lines, in which women sarcastically expand Jason's wish in Euripides for a world where men could procure children without the involvement of women:

> They could dispense with Motherhood
> and 9 month pregnancies and blood
> and breast feeding.
> Euripides makes Jason say
> if only men could find a way of
> wombless breeding,
>
> and omit that childish phase
> those far too formative first days
> of nipple sucking

and, in fact dispense with all desires,
find reproduction that requires
no fucking!²⁹

The Met cancelled the commission in 1986 and plans for a Bonn production collapsed. A version of this text did finally achieve theatrical realization, although not in operatic form, in 1991. The Volcano Theatre Company's *Medea: Sex War*, performed in London and Edinburgh, combined parts of Harrison's libretto with extracts from Valerie Solanas's notorious 1960s radical feminist text, *The S. C. U. M. Manifesto* (Society for Cutting Up Men). Fern Smith played Medea and was later to play mam/Io in Harrison's *Prometheus*.

The erudition feeding the work's multiple sources makes it, as Fiona Macintosh has said in a penetrating article, 'a revolutionary piece of writing', and not only because it assumed an 'uncompromisingly feminist stance on the conventional storylines of theatre and opera'. Like *Phaedra Britannica*, it exemplifies Harrison's foundational role in the foundation of Classical Reception Studies, an entire new field of scholarship within the Academy, but here the main emphasis is on the history of sexism in art rather than on the history of imperialism and racism.[30]

Harrison's immersion in feminist literature paid off in the opera's insistence that not only has the story of Medea been fabricated by patriarchs, but also the very concept of 'the feminine' is a construction. In conversation, Harrison is trenchantly and sometimes hilariously disrespectful about psychoanalysis, but in the case of universal male fear and hatred of women he made an exception. He had studied George Devereux's ultra-Freudian *Dreams in Greek Tragedy* (1976), with its emphasis on ancient Athenian males' Oedipus complex,[31] but it is the Jungian idea of archetypes, mediated by the *Ur*-matriarchal divinity proposed in Robert Graves' *The White Goddess* (1948), which informs Harrison's tripartite goddess. She unites Virgin (young Medea/Creusa), Mother (Medea) and Crone (Nurse/Arete); she is 'the archetypal feminine/ that fills men's dreams'.[32] The opera's overture accompanies enactments representing 'the misogynist myths that Harrison is writing against',[33] including a hideous effigy of a 'vast female figure' who attacks her children, 'the archetypal Mother, whose act of murderous betrayal confirms the castration fear embedded in this configuration of her "power"...a collective projection of the psychoanalytical fear of separation from the mother'.[34]

The two epigraphs Harrison gave to this text, perhaps originally destined for the programme essay, rather innocuously assert the plural nature of the production of myths and narratives. They are Lévi-Strauss's contention that 'we define the myth as consisting of all its versions', and William Irwin Thompson's description of myth as 'a polyphonic fugue for many voices'.[35] But the first scene shows that this polyphony may be not be harmonious. Myths have plural versions, but they viciously compete under pressure from ideologies and rival subject-positions within society. A male chorus deliver a misogynist tirade (the first of several) fusing extracts from previous versions of Medea's story, in their original languages, including those by Euripides and Seneca, and George Buchanan's Latin version of Euripides (1544). The women's chorus, on the other hand, patiently examine the connection between the social oppression of women and the stories society tells, disclosing many layers of 'male mythologising'.[36]

Harrison had read the French philosopher Catherine Clément's *Opera, or the Undoing of Women* (1979), which exposed the centrality of female death to the plots of canonical opera. Its argument is wittily summarized in an aria by 'Downstage Woman', who shifts between functioning as a more knowing avatar of Medea and the women's chorus leader:

> When the mother's pain's the maximum
> you want pure, pear-shaped tones to come
> and not a screech.
> No matter if she's got TB
> so long as air for the high C
> gets through one lung.
> She dies of stabwounds, fever, pox
> and all you care, up in your box,
> is how it's sung.
> Tosca, Carmen, Butterfly,
> it seems all women do is die
> in music drama.
> A woman is what men desert;
> in opera (as in life!) men hurt
> and harm her.[37]

But he was ahead of the curve in the academic dissection of the patriarchal values structuring ancient myth. He was working on *Medea* at the same time as Carolyn Heilbrun, a Columbia University Professor, was writing her seminal and incendiary essay, 'What Was Penelope Unweaving?' She first delivered it to a conference in 1985. It argued that women are trapped by the narratives in which their roles had been defined. They did not include the role of quest hero, or indeed of anything much other than object of desire, or (dis)obedient mother. Heilbrun urged that women needed to produce new narratives which, independent of love and marriage, gave them role models with agency, a variety of experiences, intellectual range and adventures equivalent to male quest narratives. They needed to 'unweave' the old stories which underpinned patriarchy and reweave them to reveal and counter male violence.[38]

Heilbrun's lecture caused a furore even within the liberal academic audience who first heard it. In 1985, Harrison's opera would have tested New York opera aficionados' tolerance levels to the limit, especially in the way 'Downstage Man', an avatar of Jason who functions as male chorus-leader, articulated their potential response:

> We don't put in a hard day's work
> and pay good dough to hear some jerk
> preach women's rights.
> Politics are not the thing
> we pay sopranos to sing
> on gala nights.[39]

Some were still shocked by the similar retelling of Medea's story, as a plot invented by a malicious Corinthian PR team working for the palace, in Christa Wolf's famed novel *Medea: Stimmen* more than a decade later (1996).

Euripidean Medea

The phrase in this section's subheading, 'the old male-concocted curse', comes from the penultimate passage delivered by Harrison's Downstage Woman. The curse is the slur on Medea's reputation which has framed her as a child-killer. In a manner recalling Medea's address from the chariot in Euripides, Downstage Woman addresses Jason, standing under the prow of the Argo. His Medea predicts that Jason will be killed by a plank from the ship (1386–8), but in this opera, the death is consummated:

>We claim back Pelion's trees
>that helped you once to cross the seas
>and now's this wreck.
>We make that prick, the ARGO's prow
>wilt and fall on your head *now*
>and break your neck!⁴⁰

This stanza also refers back to the first sentence of Euripides' tragedy, where the nurse wishes that 'the pine tree had never been cut down to fall in the woodlands of Mount Pelion to make oars for the hands of the heroic men who went to fetch the golden fleece' (3–5). This is a typical example of the complex reuse of the Greek text in the opera.

It opens with two words in Greek, both meaning 'child-murderer', accusations levelled at Medea by the male chorus, but originally by Jason at the end of Euripides' play, παιδολέτορ (1393) and παιδοφόνου (1407). After the overture's scene with the filicidal mother effigy, two parallel enactments take place, one with Medea sitting in an electric chair awaiting execution, and one with Creusa, as Jason's new wife is sometimes called (she is not named in Euripides), sitting on a throne after receiving Medea's gifts. Deliberate parallels are drawn visually between the seats and headgear, Medea's execution cap mirroring Creusa's golden coronet. Just as the State Executioner (Jason) is about to pull the lever on the electric chair, attention is shifted to Creusa who, Harrison's stage direction instructs, is portrayed by the singer and the music '*in the extremest agony. The music is electrocution, every brain cell alive with electrical pain, an 'Aureole' whose dynamic is agony*'. He wanted the audience to feel similar pain taking place in Medea's brain, '*fragmented by high-voltage and momentous shock*'. As Macintosh argues, in Harrison's *Medea*, 'women are united in the pain they suffer at the hands of the patriarchy.'⁴¹ But for all his political purpose, he has found this pain in Euripides' *Medea*, when the messenger reports the lingering death of the Corinthian princess (1156–1203), in a foretaste of his later engagement with the convention of the tragic messenger speech (see Chapter 8).

Both Medea and Creusa now disappear into a pit, from which the triple goddess, a feminine rival of the Christian Trinity, emerges singing. She is performed together by a soprano, a mezzo and a contralto; in harmony, and in Greek, they sing the great chorus from Euripides about how women's stories have hitherto only been framed by male poets, or otherwise they would have a counter-myth to relate about the abuses men inflict upon them (421–45). They follow this with Buchanan's Latin translation of these stanzas, and Mendès' much compressed French version. Harrison has seen, before any feminist classicist had fully appreciated it, that Euripides was presciently aware that the content of myths depended, under patriarchy, on whether their creators were male or female. The same trilingual sequence is repeated near the end, just after the dying Jason has destroyed the triune goddess, but it is sung now by the full chorus of women. They have altogether superseded the male chorus, long since driven from the stage. Harrison specified that for this final sequence the chorus women should wear their own clothes, as if returning to their New York City homes from work, to emphasize the continuing relevance of the opera's feminist message.[42]

Simultaneously with this final, triumphant chorale, Harrison specified that Downstage Woman would finally explain the passage's importance. She twice sings, through the chorus, the following explanation and translation, quoted from David Talboys' stately late Georgian prose translation, of the first of the two Greek stanzas:

> Did you know that what you hear
> is from Euripides' *Medea*?
> of 431
> that 431 BC?
> The breaking of male monopoly
> has just begun!

> These words from a women's chorus
> at least 2,000 years before us
> weren't much heeded, but since what they sang then
> should still be listened to by men
> a translation's needed.

> 'The waters of the hallowed streams flow upwards to their sources, and justice and everything is reversed. The counsels of men are treacherous, and no longer is the faith of heaven firm. But fame changes, so that my sex may have the glory. Honour cometh to the female race; no longer shall opprobrious fame oppress the women.'[43]

The women's chorus, with this grave translation heard through it as a solo, are the last sounds the audience hears; the last things they see are headlines referring to filicidal mothers projected on a screen, culminating in one about a filicidal father instead: A FATHER CUTS HIS 4 KIDS' THROATS (*The Sun*, 9 October 1983). For society's vilification of women criminals, especially infanticidal mothers, in comparison with the way it depicts violent men, is a theme of the libretto. Harrison had in mind the malicious press denigration of Myra Hindley, convicted of the murder of children in the south Pennines. The language of the newspapers was extreme even in comparison with that of her fellow 'Moors murderer' Ian Brady.[44]

Although dispensing with Aegeus and Medea's Athenian escape route, Harrison has also used parts of Euripides' *Medea* as a basis for the second of the two acts, the action of which begins at Corinth with the marriage of Jason and Creusa. Medea's first aria regrets that she left her homeland, echoing several of her speeches in Euripides.[45] She slightly changes the emphasis of the Euripidean Medea's assertion that she would rather stand three times 'beside her shield' than bear a single child:

> Though I'd prefer to face ten men with spears
> or a phalanx of bowmen in war yet I *would*
> have gone through the pain, have gone through the fears
> and endured all the birthpangs and blood.[46]

There are three passages of quickfire rhyming and largely stichomythic dialogue between Medea and Jason, echoing their confrontations in the Greek tragedy,[47] notably this paraphrase of Euripides' *Medea* 536–8 and 1339–40:

> M. You speak about your feelings. Think of mine.
> J. You're not a Greek. Your feelings aren't so fine!
> Barbarians are all passion and no mind![48]

There is a short scene with her sons in which Medea gives them the gifts for Creusa, as she does in Euripides (956–75).[49]

Act II's gruesome description of Creusa's protracted death is derived from Euripides' messenger speech (1156–1203), but transferred to a vindictive aria sung by the gloating Medea.[50] It also informs the intervention of some satisfied Furies, whom Harrison imports, perhaps inspired by *Eumenides* or the Furies of the Senecan stage – one certainly appeared in his *Thyestes* (23–121) and both Seneca's Medea and his Juno in *Hercules Furens* have visions of Furies, even if in Neronian Rome they were not physically impersonated by actors.⁵¹ But Medea's celebration segues into a recurring lament in which she expresses her regret, taken from her 'vacillating speech' in Euripides' play (1021–80), for never being able to see her boys as adults and attend their weddings.⁵² In both the two scenes of child-killing which the libretto specifies, Harrison exploits Euripides' heartbreaking and innovative use of the offstage voices of the boys, begging their attackers to stop and let them stay alive (1271–9).

Misogynist Hercules

To point out the misogyny that lies behind the longevity and resilience of Euripides' version of Medea's story, Harrison introduces Herakles/Hercules into the opera. This is the first time this hero and his reputation in ancient Greece and Rome came to preoccupy Harrison; we shall see in the next chapter that Hercules/Herakles was to play vital roles in both plays Harrison staged a decade later, in 1995. In Act I of the libretto, Hercules is an Argonaut (see below), but in Act II he is modelled on the protagonist of Euripides' *Herakles*, in which the Panhellenic Superhero, whom the chorus call 'arch-enemy of "cunt" and "cow"',⁵³ kills his wife and three sons. As 'Downstage Woman' wryly comments, the filicidal Herakles has never achieved notoriety remotely equivalent to that of the filicidal Medea:

> He killed his children! I don't hear you
> give even a *sotto voce* boo.
> He killed his children. So where
> is Hercules's electric chair?
> A children slayer? Or is Medea
> the one child-murderer you fear?⁵⁴

There is also a Senecan version, *Hercules Furens*, which may have suggested the chorus of Furies in Harrison's *Medea* (see above).

When Hercules first barges into Act II, looking for the wedding party of Jason and Creusa, he is drunk and buffoon-like, as in yet another play by Euripides, his *Alcestis*.⁵⁵ *Alcestis* combined comedy with tragedy, taking the final position, like a satyr play, in its tetralogy; through Hercules, Harrison introduces laughter into this otherwise bleak work. He intercepts Medea's nurse and sons on their way to the palace with the gifts, and tries to get the boys to feel his muscles and drink with him. There then follows the terrifying sequence in which the opera stages what it asserts 'really' happened to Medea's children in ancient Corinth before men set to work to distort her story.

Harrison the scholar knew Pat Easterling's brilliant 1977 article in which she showed that Euripides almost certainly invented the idea that Medea had murdered her own children, in full consciousness of what she was doing.[56] So he turned to the alternative version reported by Pausanias (2.3.6–7). In this travel writer's account, the boys were stoned to death by the Corinthians 'on account of the gifts which myth says they brought to Glauce'. Harrison fuses this with the ancient tradition that Jason and Medea had fourteen children rather than two. A scholion on Euripides' *Medea* (Schol. B 264) reports another tradition in which their seven sons and seven daughters were killed by the Corinthians in the sanctuary of Hera Akraia, where they had taken refuge as suppliants. A similar tradition lies behind the assertion of Seneca's Medea that she would have borne Jason 'twice seven' sons if he had so desired (954–6), an assertion which Harrison's Medea repeats in English and her nurse quotes both in Seneca's own Latin and John Studeley's English translation of it.[57] In the middle of Act II, when the audience has reason to believe that Medea may have killed her sons, not two but fourteen boys, in pairs, are pursued onto the stage by the men of Corinth. They stone the children to death, one by one, in front of Medea's eyes.

The horror is supplemented by yet another ancient variant tradition, also reported in a scholion on the ancient text (Schol. B 9): 'Euripides changed the murder of the children to Medea because he accepted five talents from the Korinthians...[who] were angry that she was ruling the city.' She was ruling it on the ground of some claim 'based on her paternal lineage'. Here Harrison has found the evidence that Medea was framed for the filicide, when it was actually Corinthian patriarchal men, terrified of women in power, who had butchered the children. Moreover, the first man to spin the misogynist yarn was the tragedian Euripides himself. When Downstage Man objects to the unfamiliar way in which the opera's plot has developed, Downstage Woman retorts that Euripides had forged

> Another male plot to demean
> women's fertility. Fourteen! Fourteen!

Euripides blackened her in his play.
These MEN bribed him. He was in their pay.[58]

Going back behind the canonical ancient Medea sources to arcane Hellenistic scholiasts yet again shows the depth of Harrison's learning.

In Hercules' second scene, Harrison fuses three myths. The first enacts the Greek hero's submission to the Lydian queen Omphale, when he was required to do woolwork and wear female clothing. This echoes the scene in Euripides' *Bacchae* where Pentheus dresses up as a maenad on stage. In the second, the chorus turn once again into Furies and drive Hercules mad; he butchers his own sons (played by the same singers as Medea's first two sons). This draws on both the Euripidean and Senecan plays about his crime of filicide. In the third, Harrison draws on Sophocles' *Trachiniae* and its Latinized Senecan *Hercules Oetaeus*; his Hercules puts on a poisoned robe sent by his last wife, Deianeira, and dies a lingering death, cursing the entire female sex, past, present and future: world power, he sings as he expires,

> always should belong
> with the male sex, with the strong.
> And not the smallest rabbit hole
> left in the Earth Mother's control.
> In every sex-war that will be fought
> you'll find Hercules the Argonaut.[59]

Hercules represents the most boorish and hyper-masculine misogynist in the libretto. Much of this characterization is drawn from his configurations in ancient Greek and Latin tragedy. But in one respect, which would make the coruscating libretto today unperformable, at least without substantial editing, Harrison draws on Hercules' characterization as gay pursuer of his young squire Hylas in Apollonius' *Argonautica*.

Apollonian Argonauts

The story of the Argonauts' journey to Colchis, told in Pindar's *Pythian* 4 and in greater detail in Apollonius' *Argonautica*, forms the bulk of Act I and returns intermittently in Act II. This begins with a long sequence in Lemnos, the Argo's first port of call as narrated in Apollonius' first book. The female chorus take on the identity of the women of Lemnos, who killed their husbands because they had adulterous relationships with Thracian slave women. The label 'Lemnian Women' was, for the ancient Greeks, proverbial shorthand for women's depravity, as Harrison knew well from a strophe in Aeschylus' *Choephori* (631–8).

There is an altercation between Downstage Man and Downstage Woman about the Lemnian women's culpability; Downstage Man claims that they were goaded by the obsolete Goddess, who has not yet accepted that 'natural male supremacy' and that male gods have replaced her,[60] an idea Harrison discovered when researching Engels on primitive matriarchies for the *Oresteia*. At this point Jason enters, carrying the lever from the electric chair which will soon become the tiller of the Argo. He is followed by the Argonauts, who build the ship onstage, and sail off singing heartily, in a scene reminiscent of Wagner's *The Flying Dutchman*, to enjoy

> The truly manly heroic life
> a man couldn't share with any wife
> and only a man understands,
> the open sea, adventures and strange lands.[61]

The prominent Argonauts in the libretto personify three models of sexuality. Jason is a highly sexed but faithless womanizer. Hercules is gay. Butes, the simple bee-keeper, according to the other Argonauts, is a lonely widower: 'He's the only one of us loves his wife/ and she died on him, and he's sick of life.'[62] But, as Harrison would now readily admit, the characterization of Hercules is irredeemable.

As the most boorish and misogynist of the male characters in the libretto, it now seems deeply inappropriate that Hercules is also the only gay character and the most comically pilloried. The same complaint could be directed against Harrison's choice of a gay man to explore the relationship between sexual and colonial exploitation in some of the poems of 'The White Queen', with their echoes of the sexual imagery of Juvenal VI, written in the 1960s, although they need to be read alongside his pillorying of Cuban homophobia in his 1970 essay 'Shango the Shaky Fairy'.[63] Hylas, the young Argonaut with whom Hercules is infatuated, and calls his 'little friend',[64] wants sex with a Lemnian woman. Earlier on, Downstage Woman has accused male audiences of enjoying the deaths of women in opera, eliciting 'male fans' bravos/ and fags' applause',[65] thus not only using an abusive term for gay men, but articulating the stereotype of the opera-loving male homosexual. Harrison made no room in this libretto for the reality that many gay men have secure romantic relationships, women friends and feminist goals. It would be possible to include a more positive homoerotic Hercules in this opera, rather than make male homosexuality part of the problem of misogyny.

Both Hylas and Hercules go missing, as they do at the end of Apollonius' first book (I.1172–1357). Hylas is seduced by the water-nymphs' singing in Mysia, Asia Minor. Hercules does not reappear until the murderous climax of the next and final act. The remainder of Act I dramatizes parts of the Black Sea and homebound voyage sections of the *Argonautica*, from the arrival of the Greeks at Colchis in Apollonius' Book III to the island wedding night of Jason and Medea in Apollonius' Book IV. Another type of male misogyny is embodied in the figure of Medea's father, Aeetes, who in a long aria berates his daughter for displaying 'feminine' tenderness and sympathy with victims which he thought he had trained her out of, making her more acceptably manly, by forcing her to watch scenes of torture and execution. In contrast, Harrison presents Alcinous and Arete as a loving and mutually respectful married couple in counterpoint to the disastrous erotic relationships suffered by every other character in the opera besides Butes. But he omits Medea's crimes in the ancient Greek epic, especially her murder of her brother Aspyrtus. Act II begins with Jason's next wedding, in Corinth, to draw attention to his cynical careerism and casual attitude to adultery, and then dramatizes the scenes of child-murder in which Euripides and Seneca, as we have seen, are the dominant classical sources.

Harrison the staunch feminist, Harrison the challenger of boundaries of permissible references to sex and swear words, and Harrison the expert historian of stage plays and opera on ancient themes – the 'Reception' of classical literature – are all demonstrated in this published libretto. So, too, is Harrison, especially in the Hylas episode, as a writer sometimes insensitive to the influence that art might exert on perceptions of gay men. But Harrison the classical scholar, master of recondite ancient sources, is also in evidence on every page.

Alongside Hellenistic scholia, Pausanias, Euripides, Seneca and Apollonius, the work draws on Ovid's *Heroides* and *Metamorphoses*, Valerius Flaccus'

Argonautica and the long, learned Virgilian cento *Medea* by Tertullian's contemporary, Hosidius Geta. One excerpt from Harrison's stage direction when the triple goddess first arises gives a sense of the density of classical scholarship – as well as the 'spraycan discourse' – with which Harrison presented the contracted composer. The goddess, played by three women, emerges on a revolving platform,

> and sings as though the three had one voice as some of their ancient names were *Nete, Mese* and *Hypate* which signify the low, middle and high tones of the Greek system of scales...*Diva Triformis* [Ovid *Met.* 7.177]... They sing in round and in three different languages [v. Valerius Flaccus, *cantuque trilingui*, vii.184].[66]

If only the right composer could have been found, a Harrison Birtwhistle as in the *Oresteia*, or Richard Blackford, who became Harrison's regular musical collaborator in the 1990s, the example of this scene alone might have enlivened operas on classical themes fundamentally and forever.

6

'Bookworm excreta':
The Trackers of Oxyrhynchus (1988) and Other Plays and Poems

A theatre of matter

After translating Aeschylus, and writing a libretto rooted in Euripides, Harrison turned to the third great Athenian tragedian, Sophocles. *The Trackers of Oxyrhynchus* embedded a version of the long surviving fragment of Sophocles' satyr play, *Ichneutae*, or *Trackers*, in a frame-drama exploring the discovery of the papyrus on which it was preserved in a garbage tip at Oxyrhynchus, and the mythological personality of the satyrs. It was designed for a single performance in the ancient theatre of Delphi on 12 July 1988, but a new version was performed first at Salt's Mill at Saltaire in Bradford, then at the National Theatre, premiering on 27 March 1990, at the Carnuntum amphitheatre near Vienna, at the Wharf Theatre in Sydney, Australia in 1992 and the West Yorkshire Playhouse in 1998.[1] It was a resounding critical and commercial success.

In the early 1990s, Harrison returned to Herakles/Hercules, who had fascinated him since *Medea: A Sex-War Opera*, and included him in two further new plays embedding fragments or quotations from ancient texts for site-specific performances. *The Kaisers of Carnuntum* was performed twice in the Roman amphitheatre at Petronell-Carnuntum, Austria, on 2–3 June 1995, and *The Labourers of Herakles* on an excavated site intended for the New Theatre of the European Cultural Centre of Delphi, Greece, later in the same summer, on 23 August 1995.[2]

All three plays were written with the voice of actor Barrie Rutter in mind.[3] They were created in collaboration with Harrison's favourite designer, Jocelyn Herbert,[4] who shared his commitment to giving voice to the voiceless – here the working class, the victims of Roman, Austrian or German imperialism and xenophobia, and Muslims massacred in the Balkans by Bosnian Serbs, respectively. Their register veers between tragedy and comedy. They all exhibit Harrison the bookworm's joy in obscure ancient literary culture, and a transhistorical vision of the role ancient texts have played in creating the physical, cultural and psychological landscapes of the modern world.

They also share a Lucretian and Epicurean philosophical fascination with cyclical processes of material production, consumption, digestion and waste disposal, in relation not only to the recycling of literary texts but also to the archaeologically and industrially shaped physical environment and above all to the human body. The discussion of the plays here follows an introductory section exploring Harrison's distinctive brand of scatology, in other poems too, in order to illuminate *The Trackers of Oxyrhynchus*, the most ambitious of these plays, as well as some key images in the others.

Harrison's classical scatology

Amongst the verses by Palladas Harrison had chosen to translate in the 1970s is this succinct assault on another poet:

> Where's the public good in what you write,
> raking it in from all that shameless shite,
> hawking iambics like so much *Betterbrite*?[5]

Bad poetry, composed for money, is 'shameless shite', which rhymes with *Betterbrite*. The poet whom Palladas is attacking is compared with someone selling lamp oil. Harrison has here invented a new product, inspired by the famous British 'direct sales' company Betterware, whose inexpensive range of household products was (and still is) sold by door-to-door salesmen and is culturally associated with aspirational, petit-bourgeois housewives. If the Betterware Company were to have made a lighting product, it would have been called Betterbrite.

This apparently facetious little translation reveals Harrison's struggles to define his own role as a literary figure. The poet whose shameless shite has failed to impress Palladas is criticized on the remarkable ground that there is no 'public good' in what he writes. For Palladas, this idea is an unusually responsible one, but it has always been central to Harrison's own project. In Palladas' Greek, as Harrison knew, the question 'where's the public good?' – more literally, 'how have you been useful for the polis?' – harks back to the earliest extended discussion of the social role of poetry, Aeschylus' debate with Euripides in Aristophanes' *Frogs*. But the phrase 'useful for the polis' also resonates with the passage in Plato's *Republic* where Socrates declares that the poets will be turned away from the city until someone can prove that what they compose is useful to the community as well as pleasurable (X.607d6–9).

This brief translated poem contains three other ideas that repeatedly intertwine with expressions of poetry's public role throughout Harrison's *oeuvre*. The first is the remuneration of poets. The second is the comparison of composing poetry with the material production involved in working-class trades, since for Harrison, whose father was a baker, the poet is a 'maker', a *poiētēs* in the Greek sense. Both strands are especially prominent in *Poetry or Bust* (1993), the play about the early nineteenth-century wool-sorter and 'Airedale poet', John Nicholson. But the third idea introduced in the Palladas translation is the relationship between the production of poetry and the production of 'shite', waste matter, by the human body. Harrison did find the idea of using a swear word to describe the socially useless poet's output in Palladas, who calls it *blasphēmias* (approximately equivalent to the English term 'profanities'). But it is Harrison who chose an English-language equivalent with a scatological overtone not to be heard in the Greek.

Scatology, or coprology, has proved generative in Harrison's quest for imagery for the painful tension created in his work by his 'dual' class identity, and by his own ambivalence towards elite culture.[6] In his earlier poetry, as we have seen, this tension was often focused on his relationship with his father.[7] It is expressed most concisely in 'Turns', in *From 'The School of Eloquence'*. Here he proclaims his class solidarity in calling his father's cloth hat not 'his cap' but 'our cap'. But he also acknowledges that he survives by writing poetry that is read only by the higher classes in whose service, as a worker in an industry with an arduous daily routine, his father had ruined his health:

> I'm opening my trap
> to busk the class that broke him for the pence
> that splash like brackish tears into our cap.[8]

That father worked in the food industry, and the digestive function of the human body became increasingly important to Harrison. Three decades after the Palladas collection, in 2005, two poems in *Under the Clock* display precisely the Classics-class-cloaca cluster of ideas, now developed in arresting directions. The first is 'The Ode Not Taken', subtitled 'C. T. Thackrah (1799–1833)'; it is Charles Turner Thackrah whom the poetic voice celebrates. A controversial Leeds surgeon, Thackrah had trained at Guy's Hospital alongside a famous poet:

> Dissecting corpses with Keats at Guy's,
> Leeds-born Thackrah shared the poet's TB.
> Cadavers that made Keats poeticize
> made Thackrah scorn the call of poetry.

Harrison is interested in Thackrah because he became a pioneering researcher into occupational disease. From 1817, he was Leeds Town Surgeon, with responsibility for the city's paupers. His commitment to the improvement of his fellow citizens' lot led to his 1831 treatise, *The Effects of the Principal Arts, Trades, and Professions . . . on Health and Longevity*. The standard textbook on the subject for six decades, this detailed the diseases associated with more than 150 occupations, especially work in textile factories and by children, and ways in which they could be prevented by modifications in diet, posture, exercise and ventilation. Thackrah campaigned to reform factories and reduce working hours. Yet he had originally been destined for a career as a clergyman, and received a classical education. Harrison muses on his preference for medicine over a more cerebral profession. Thackrah

> Could write hexameters by Virgil's rules,
> and parrot Latin epics but he chose
> flax-hecklers' fluxes with their 'gruelly' stools,
> the shit of Yorkshire operatives, in prose.

Medical research on the digestive system of the late Georgian Yorkshire proletariat, necessary to the improvement of their lot, was the achievement of this trenchant native of Leeds. In celebrating it, Harrison reflects on both the parallels and contrasts between the production of Latin verses (part of the elite education of the Georgian gentleman) and the production of polemical, campaigning medical prose. Furthermore, the movement in this sentence from the neutral reference to the hexameters of Virgil through the less respectful allusion to being able 'to parrot' Latin epics, to the hardcore realism of quotation from Thackrah himself on the flax-worker's 'gruelly' stools, concisely evokes a man with a mission and no time to waste on cultural irrelevancies. (His time really was curtailed because he only undertook his medical training at the cost of acquiring the tuberculosis that killed him.) The workers' own shit in this poem thus functions as nothing less profound and political than a permanent reproach to the British class system.

This is virtually without precedent. A few recent writers of prose fiction, including Salman Rushdie in *Midnight's Children* and some novelists discussed by Reinhold Kramer in his study of scatology in English-Canadian literature, have recently used excrement to mark class structures.[9] But in poetry, shit has almost always characterized things which are perceived as unpleasant. Scatological satire, in which it is never advantageous to be represented by shit, has been around for a long time, as anyone versed in Aristophanes or Martial (as Harrison is) knows.[10] Scatological vituperation has played a time-honoured role in attacks on artistic or intellectual efforts, ever since Aristophanes' *Clouds* and Catullus' assault on Volusius' *Annals* as *cacata carta*, 'shit-smeared sheets' (36.1).[11] Characters in Jonson's dramas echo these ancient models in sharing what has been called 'the copious and ubiquitous scatological rhetoric of Early Modern Europe' when they imagine putting the paper on which the works of rivals were written to the use of cleansing the 'posterior'.[12] But in the English language, the filthiest and most vituperative scatology is probably provided by the 'high heroic Games' held by the dunces in the second book of Pope's *Dunciad* (2.18); the excrement on which they slip and in which they dive and swim stands for the inferiority of their writings and their morals (see 2.69–108, 272, 276–8).

Harrison once turns such scatological invective on his own poetry – or at least on the potential insult to working-class suffering involved in composing sonnets to be read by the bourgeoisie. One of the embedded voices in 'Working', the sonnet for Patience Kershaw, the teenaged mine-worker whose testimony was recorded by the 1842 Children's Employment Commission, says, 'this wordshift and inwit's a load of crap/ for dumping on a slagheap.'[13] For Dante, it is moral sins – flattery and fraud – which find a metaphor in excrement.[14] Scatology that is politically rather than aesthetically or morally engaged also has a history. One of Juvenal's illustrations of the instability of fortune is the chamber pots made from Sejanus' statue, once melted down (X.61–4). During the English Civil War, excremental imagery was used by poets on both sides to characterize the repellent nature of their opponents' agendas, although the Royalist anti-Parliamentarians had the advantage because the term 'Rump Parliament' was so suggestive.[15] In France, the doctors of the absolute monarch Louis XIV were gratified to discover that his inoffensive bowel movements reflected his unique status and perfection and therefore that of the monarchical body politic; they were rarely loose, because 'nobody in the whole world has been as much a master of himself as the King'.[16]

In the late nineteenth and early twentieth centuries, the shock factor in the public, theatrical use of scatological language had a social and political impact, above all in the first, famous 'merdre' of Alfred Jarry's *Ubu Roi* that caused the audience to riot at the première on 10 December 1896.[17] Modern dramatists and poets contemporary with Harrison have used derisive scatology for political effect, as John Osborne in his *Luther* (1961) makes his dissident hero describe his notice of excommunication as a piece of latrine paper from the devil's own latrine in Rome – 'papal decretals are the devil's excretals'.[18]

But Harrison's use of shit is different. For him, shit represents not the oppressor but the oppressed. He has thought about the repugnance that is the customary response to faecal matter in both classical sources and more recent ones, and inverted the way it operates. He has reformulated the conventional trope of literary revulsion as symbolic of the privileged classes' barbarous response to the indigent. If there is a precedent for this it is Thomas Carlyle's description of the British underclass, reduced to beggary, as 'the scandalous poison-tank of drainage' and 'that tremendous Cloaca of Pauperism'.[19] Although, in marked contrast to Harrison's ubiquitous sympathy for the dispossessed, the physical disgust Carlyle felt towards the London poor is palpable in such rhetoric, the target of his scatology was at least not the noisome poor but the social and economic system that produced them in the first place.

Aristophanes, Catullus, Martial, Pope, Carlyle, Jarry, Osborne (and, as we shall see below, Rabelais, Swift and Nietzsche) – it seems that Harrison's scatology has, if not a literary pedigree, then a tradition against which he is reacting. Yet defecation is not an aspect of his innovatory literary art that has received much attention. This is not surprising. Although the Indo-European etymological root from which 'scatology' derives may ultimately be the same as the root of *scire*, 'to know',[20] scatology in literature is often regarded as 'the last taboo', or 'the last veil' clouding our vision of truth, as Victor Hugo describes it in *Les Misérables*.[21] Breaking the last taboo in order to attack class inequity, as Harrison does, is risky, since writers who use coprology have always made themselves vulnerable to reactions of intense disgust in their readers, and at best reductive Freudian analysis in their critics.

Excoriation or psychological speculation has certainly been the fate of the coprological imagery produced by Jonathan Swift, regarded as the most scatological author in the English language to date.[22] Most of Swift's scatology is in the same Augustan tradition of vituperation, derived from Latin poetry, that Pope and many of that literary generation practised. But something of Harrison's more humane treatment of human effluvia is occasionally anticipated by Swift. One of his riddles in the *Thesaurus Aenigmaticus* (1725–6) uses the universal human need for elimination of waste products in order to cast class-based notions of hierarchy in a compellingly absurd light that burlesques Graeco-Roman epic conventions. The answer to the riddle, which is entitled 'The Gulph of all human Possessions', is a privy; the setting is Olympus, and the speaker is Jove: Necessity, the Tyrant's Law,

> All human race must hither draw:
> All prompted by the same Desire,
> The vig'rous Youth, the aged Sire.
> Behold, the Coward and the Brave,
> The haughty Prince, the humble Slave,
> Physician, Lawyer, and Divine,
> All make Oblations at this Shrine.[23]

Yet with the exceptions of Swift and Rabelais (see below), it has universally been taken for granted by authors in the Western tradition, even those whose political views are not dissimilar to Harrison's, that bodily waste products are symbolic of what is properly repugnant in society.

However, recuperating bodily functions in the cause of intellectual endeavour is something that Harrison has in common with Nietzsche, a thinker whom he has elsewhere used (albeit selectively) to brilliant effect.[24] Nietzsche, like Harrison, clarifies the connection between human consciousness and the interior of the body by repudiating the longstanding Platonic and Christian negation of the flesh and insistence on the priority of a transcendental world of ideas, or disincarnate spirit. Like Harrison, Nietzsche used the ancient Greeks to kick-start all his thinking about human experience: Nietzsche's work reinstates entrails and their contents to a place of philosophical significance and sees them as a locus for truth. Entrails were one of his favourite symbols for the process of 'undercutting metaphysical and transcendent aspirations: going into the body lies at the opposite pole from going beyond it'.[25] Nietzsche uses the innards to make people see what he thinks is the truth, however abominable, beneath surfaces.[26] Yet Harrison's inner man is not monstrous like Nietzsche's, nor are his truth-telling excreta abominable. Harrison treats bodily evacuation equally fearlessly, but also with a most un-Nietzschean humanity, even the 'charity' that the visual artist Tom Phillips saw was integral to the inclusive social vision projected in 'v.' in 1985.[27] In that poem, the non-judgemental and charitable attitude is extended even to the 'peeved' and 'pissed' football supporter who has vandalized the cemetery by spraying the word 'SHIT' on an obelisk.

Tracking Oxyrhynchus excreta

Humour is the means by which the shock factor of Harrison's scatology is alleviated, a lesson he perhaps learned from the traditional limerick verse of his hometown which had appeared as the epigraph to *The Loiners* (1970):[28]

> There was a young man of Leeds
> Who swallowed a packet of seeds.
> A pure white rose grew out of his nose
> And his arse was covered with weeds.

The papyrus containing Sophocles' *Trackers*, Oxyrhynchus Papyrus no. 1174, was refuse. The location of poetry within the Epicurean cycle whereby matter, including the materials on which poetry is recorded, constantly circulates in the world and through the food chain, is introduced in the opening speech of papyrologist Bernard Grenfell. He complains that the Egyptian workers, the fellaheen, do not appreciate the cultural value of the papyrus texts:

> We ship back papyri to decipher them at Queen's
> but they'd use them, if we let them, as compost for their greens.

Bits of Sappho, Sophocles and Plato
used as compost for the carrot and potato.[29]

In the next speech, delivered by Grenfell's fellow papyrologist Arthur Hunt, ancient writings are brought closer to actual excrement in the scholar's fears:

If one of our backs were turned our fellaheen
would be sloshing Bacchylides on their aubergine.
If we're not double-quick the local folk
will mix Homer and camel dung to grow their artichoke.[30]

Hunt is using scatology in a derisive way: Homer should *not* be contaminated by camel dung. The gulf between art and bodily refuse should be impermeable. As soon as Grenfell is transformed into Apollo, this theme is reasserted; Apollo is appalled at the fate of the papyri. His verses have been

Converted into dust and bookworm excreta,
riddled lines with just ghost of their metre.
All my speeches, all my precious words
mounting mounds of dust and millipede turds.[31]

The excremental image, thus established through camel dung, bookworm excreta and millipede turds, brings new life to an old term of abuse when Apollo describes the felon who has stolen his herd as a 'dissembling cattle-rustling shit'. For elite scholars Grenfell and Hunt, and for Apollo, excrement is to be derided. It represents philistine members of the Egyptian working class, the physical destruction by idiots of high classical art, and the criminal who challenges the elite's rights by stealing their property.

What a different note is struck from the thrilling moment that the satyrs leap out of their Egypt Exploration Fund crates and begin their clog-dancing chorus, directed by Silenus (Barrie Rutter) to track down 'each missing Greek word/ then sniff out the trail of Apollo's lost herd'. The act of recovering the lost poetry of Sophocles is equated here with locating a herd of cows by olfactory means – tracking them down by smelling their dung. 'Seek cow-clap... (track it...track it...),' sings one group of satyrs; as they parody the Furies in the stage production of Harrison' own translation of the *Oresteia* sniffing for the blood of Orestes, the Yorkshire-dialect speaking chorus of satyrs warm to their excremental theme:

> Sniff, sniff
> sniff at the dung
> t'devil who did this is gonna get 'ung.
> Snffi, sniff
> sniff every turd
> t' droppings'll lead us t' god's 'erd.
> Snif, sniff
> sniff left and right
> sniff every tincture
> of cattle shite.
> Sniff, sniff
> sniff every clue
> sniff every sort of numero two.
> Sniff, sniff
> sniff without stopping
> sniff every turd, sniff every dropping.[32]

In this hilarious parodos, Harrison luxuriates in alternative words for dung (turd, droppings, shite, numero two) and in contriving rhymes to match them. But he did not find much support for this in the papyrus. The Sophoclean 'tracking' sequence is indeed introduced by Silenus instructing the satyrs as follows:

> Come, everyone ... nosing the scent ... somewhere, perhaps a breath of wind ... squatting double ... follow the scent closely.[33]

In the Greek there is no surviving word for excrement; the terms for 'scent' and 'nosing' and 'wind' are anodyne and unspecific; they could be used of looking for roses. The satyrs are said to be searching for hoofprints.[34] Harrison has made his play explicitly coprological when his Sophoclean prototype was not.[35]

The personality of the satyr offered Harrison a vehicle through which to explore the animal aspect as well as the divine spark in the human being. But Joe Kelleher has pointed out that Harrison had previously chosen, for the cover of his translations from Martial, a photograph of a carved stone satyr. The satyr serves as a kind of mask for Harrison's persona as a translator. This persona is neither neutral nor self-effacing, but has 'a diabolically gleeful grin', suggesting that the transformation of poetry from the ancient language to modern vernacular is the work of a personality with 'an inscrutable agenda' of his own.[36] The same applies to the satyrs in *Trackers*. The audience realizes that the inscrutable Harrison is gleefully concentrating on excrement, but is not yet clear why. The excrement equated with poetry at last becomes, if not human, then at least anthropomorphic with the arrival of the still incontinent baby Hermes from the nymph Cyllene's cave; now papyrus serves as a diaper. But Hermes is also the first individual ever to play the lyre – the very icon in antiquity of poetic art. Hermes produces music simultaneously with faeces:

> *Apollo* Let me have your gadget or you'll get a good slap.
> That papyrus you're wearing. It's full of warm crap.
> *Hermes* That nymph's too snooty to change a kid's nappy.
> I can't help it, can I, if I'm all crappy.
> *Apollo* There, there, little fellow, but you're scarcely fit
> to give lyre recitals with pants full of shit.
> You're frankly disgusting. I think that the lyre
> requires a performer in formal attire.
> Change your crappy papyrus while I serenade
> these lowly satyrs with the lyre you made.[37]

The one place where human excrement is visible in our culture is when it is produced by small babies. Harrison, here in the part of his reconstruction of *Trackers* that is his own invention, gives the audience striking images about art – its producers and consumers and class orientation – through contrasting figures on stage. The appealing baby-cum-musical-genius, with his dirty nappy, contrasts with the envious, snobbish adult god who decrees that music should only be performed in formal clothes, and with the 'lowly satyrs' who have tracked down art as they have tracked down cattle by their dung. It is to miss the *political* clout of this scenario to see it primarily in psychoanalytical terms.[38] As Richard Eyre has put it in a different context, 'Tony wants the whole body of society, not just its head, to be involved in art.'[39]

Apollo's serenade evolves into a statement on the cosmic order and the satyrs' place within it. He fears that the audience will find the start of the play 'unpromising', with its 'trail of turds', but he reassures them that what has resulted, in the lyre, is Art. Apollo describes the hierarchical scale of creation in which all creatures are allotted their place. Being half-animal, goatish and foul-smelling, the satyrs are nearly at the bottom of this scale, but not quite:

> Below the beasts, all beasts, come beetles and the mite
> whose mandibles make meals of Sophocles
> and leave gaping holes in such lost plays as these.
> This little mite, the lowest in creation
> turns Sophocles to dust and defecation,
> and turns manuscripts of Mankind's masterpieces
> to little microbe meals and microbe faeces,
> letters, then a line, a page of words
> make minutest mincemeat and the tiniest of turds.[40]

The lowest stratum in the cosmic order manufactures faeces and turds.

Harrison's satyr play is a manifesto on the gulf that separates elite art from popular culture, and on social stratification that has always silenced the poor, the hungry, and the oppressed. This is represented above all in the flayed body of Marsyas, who was punished by Apollo for daring to play the music of the elite, producing Harrison's much-quoted lines:

> Wherever in the world there is torture and pain
> the powerful are playing the Marsyas refrain.
> In every dark dungeon where blood has flowed
> the lyre accompanies the Marsyas Ode.[41]

But he is equally sympathetic to the voices of those who have accepted their exclusion from the privileges enjoyed higher up the class system, represented by Silenus:

>   I don't rock the boat./
> I add up the pluses of being man/goat.
> Unlike my poor flayed brother, Marsyas,
> I've never yearned to move out of my class.
> In short, I suppose, I'm not really averse
> to being a satyr. I could do a lot worse,
> I just have to find the best way to exist
> and I've found, to be frank, I exist best pissed.[42]

The circulation of matter in the food chain, all the way through the body until it is expelled to the refuse dump, or peeled off a torture victim's body, at the Delphi première of *Trackers* became a commanding image for both cultural and social exclusion.

This was made even more explicit in the new ending that Harrison wrote for the National Theatre production that opened in London in the Olivier auditorium in March 1990. Here the satyrs underwent a transformation into the homeless who sleep rough on the South Bank of the Thames, near the National Theatre. Since they are freezing, they shred the papyrus of the *Trackers*, from which they sprang as satyrs, to use as bedding, and Silenus distributes small bits to use as toilet paper:

> Here, take this little bit
> it'll come in handy after a shit ...
> And here it's poda ba and apapap
> take it and use it after a crap.[43]

Silenus says that he will be Apollo's spokesman,

> ... and say that I don't mind
> if you use my papyrus to wipe your behind.
> I am happy that my long-lost Satyr Play's
> divided up into Andrex and dossers' duvets.[44]

No amount of great art matters if people are freezing cold and lack even the most basic physical necessities of life, symbolized in the papyrus bedding and papyrus-toilet-roll (Andrex).

Epicurean arse verse

The collection with the poem on Thackrah, a decade and a half after *Trackers*, concludes with a longer poem that explores further than ever before the illumination of both Classics and class that Harrison has found is made possible by faecal imagery. 'Reading the Rolls: An Arse Verse', first published in 2004, is also his strongest statement of his materialist conception of the world and the position of words within it.[45] Its fundamental symbol is the human being sitting on the toilet, engaged in producing or consuming verse as s/he processes foodstuffs through the body and ejects them as faecal matter. The poem is introduced by an epigraph quotation, in the original Latin, of Lucretius' *De rerum natura* I.823–7, which asks whether all words are simply the same sounds, or letters of the alphabet that signify sounds, rearranged in different ways, just as the world is constructed of particles of the same elements in constant flux (my translation):

> Indeed, throughout these very verses of mine you can see many elements common to many words, although you must admit that lines and words differ from one another both in meaning and in the sound that they produce.

Harrison has repeated that he is not a religious man. If his world view can be affiliated with any particular philosophical tradition, it is the atheistic and materialist one founded by the ancient Greek atomists and Epicureans. Another writer drawn to these ideas was Marx, whose 1841 doctorate was entitled *The Difference Between the Democritean and Epicurean Philosophy of Nature*.[46] That matter and idea are dialectically inter-related – the fundamental premise of Marx's dialectical materialist philosophical method – is a view underpinning all Harrison's work.

'Reading the Rolls' consists of three sections that explore the relationship borne by words to the material elements from which they are produced and the materials on which they are recorded. In the first section, the predominant trope compares poetic inspiration with gaseous vapours that morph into language – whether from beneath the Pythian priestess' seat or from gas pipes or rotting rats beneath the floorboards of Harrison's childhood. But in the second, the matter that is paired with poetry is the 'war-time infant turds' that, as a small boy, he had deposited in his family toilet.

> I'm aware today the earliest verse
> I ever mumbled wiped my arse,
> enjoyed for what they were, not judged,
> torn off the roll, and used, and flushed.[47]

Patriotic verses were then printed on Izal toilet paper. This picture was partly presaged by 'The Excursion' in *The Loiners*, where he says that his 'earliest reminiscences' were of the bombardment of Leeds, of 'explosions like flushing a closet'.[48] Harrison's scatology here is anticipated by Rabelais, in whose five-book novel *Gargantua and Pantagruel* coprology looms large.[49]

The image of the four-year-old Leeds boy's experience of bodily evacuation, and its association with the recitation of rhyming verse, is foreshadowed in book I, ch. 13 of the old French novel. As Gargantua approaches his fifth birthday, he reveals his intelligence to his father when describing how he has devised different ways for wiping his bottom after defecation – he has used items of his mother's clothing, a cat, the leaves of various plants, different leaves, flax, wool and paper. As Gargantua explains how paper was not wholly effective at removing his turds, he suddenly bursts into rhyme, to his father's delight. In the 1653 translation of Thomas Urquhart,

> Yes, yes, my lord the king, answered Gargantua, I can rhyme gallantly, and rhyme till I become hoarse with rheum. Hark, what our privy says to the skiters:
>
> Shittard,
> Squirtard,
> Crackard,
> Turdous,
> Thy bung
> Hath flung
> Some dung
> On us.[50]

Rabelais' hilarious episode, combining a child's delight in rhyme with his early experiences of defecating in the 'privy' (as well as the father-son relationship prominent in Harrison's earlier poems), has resurfaced in 'Reading the Rolls'. But after expanding this account of his own juvenile versification in the lavatory, including lines attacking Hitler, Harrison displays his wide reading by summarizing a passage in a letter written to a son by another father, the eighteenth-century Earl of Chesterfield:

> Lord Chesterfield's advice
> to his son was Latin verse,
> not lengthy epics like Lucretius
> dangerous and irreligious,
> but shorter poems like Horace *Odes*
> construed while extruding turds,
> a page per shit for the beginner
> before consigned to Cloacina.[51]

An investigation of the Earl's patrician letters reveals the astonishing recommendation to his son that good time management meant taking two sheets of an edition of Horace to 'the necessary-house', where they could furnish both edifying reading matter and disposable toilet roll, which could subsequently be sent down as a sacrifice to 'Cloacina'.[52] Harrison is delighted with the Earl's reference to this goddess, the benign divinity who in the less squeamish ancient world presided over the Roman Cloaca Maxima and whose shrine in the forum is attested from as early as Plautus (*Curculio* 471; see also Livy III.48 and Pliny, *NH* XV.119). She was sometimes identified with Venus as Venus Cloacina.

As Harrison's poem develops, the word-matter relationship is reconceived in terms of the Epicurean philosophical texts elucidated through coprological imagery; the individual imagined in the process of defecating is transformed from the figures of the four-year-old working-class Harrison and the aristocratic son of the Earl of Chesterfield to the ungendered reader whom the grown-up Harrison now addresses: this reader should feel at liberty to shred the pages on which the poem is written into paper snow,

> Or feel free in need to use these verses,
> if not too rough, to wipe your arses ...[53]

In section 3, after humorously wondering whether his reader is still reading because s/he is captivated by the verse or, alternatively, constipated, the poem moves on to the related image of poetry that emerges from papyrus rolls of Epicurean philosophy carbonized at Herculaneum, philosophy that 'iridesces' because it

> aims to free the mind from fear
> and put the old gods out to grass
> and live life in the moment's grace.[54]

If any world view is advocated by Tony Harrison, it is surely this. But it is yet again Harrison's coprology that is used in order to characterize the Epicurean philosopher who has been rescued from these papyri, Philodemus of Gadara – or, rather, it is used to characterize the hierarchy constituted by Philodemus' client relationship with his aristocratic patron Piso. His fawning poetry as he 'brown-nosed' Piso was 'crap', at least according to Cicero's *In Pisonem*. Here we come almost full circle back to the epigram of Palladas with the complaint that a poet who sold bad poetry for a living was hawking 'shite'.

These days we are able to read Philodemus' epigrams in conjunction with the fine commentary of David Sider, as well as the fragments of his Epicurean theory as it emerges from the cinders of Herculaneum, and to decide whether they are really 'crap'.⁵⁵ But we can also read Harrison's poem. His ensuing fantasia on the themes of vowel sounds, love poetry, the dance of words in the never-ceasing entropy of the cosmos, and the recovery of ancient texts through modern technology is concluded with a renewed address to his reader in the toilet:

> The soul goes with cloacal matters
> as much as tragedy with satyrs,
> so, if you're sitting on the loo
> where your ω fits in an O,
> peruse these prosodics from my pen,
> then use, and flush them down the pan.
> [Though perhaps for average shits
> I've given you too many sheets.]⁵⁶

In de-alienating excrement from the human body, Harrison has forged one of his most challenging and innovative poetic figures. Scatology is a pronounced feature of ancient and much more recent satire, but it has almost always been used in a way that preserves and affirms the notion that it is inherently disgusting and needs to be excluded. What Harrison has done is put the digestive system back into the imagery of human experience, but without the fear and hateful derision that conventionally attends it. Effluvia, like human consciousness, is just part of the Lucretian atomic cycle, after all: for Harrison, effluvia can stand not only for class struggle and the correction of false consciousness, but also for such elevated forms of mental work as philosophy or art, the Epicurean doctrine of living for the moment, or the relationship of tragedy to satyr play.

Harrison's cloacal imagery is, however, not dispassionate. It is actively sympathetic to his fellow humans in its portrayal of our undignified digestive functions: it is humane. Little in earlier poetry in English quite shares this quality, except perhaps Swift's socially levelling privy riddle and the lyrical description by Swift's friend John Gay of London's sewage system as Cloacina, 'goddess of the tide/ Whose sable streams beneath the city glide'.⁵⁷ But a socially committed dramatist like Harrison would not object to being placed in company with the author of *The Beggar's Opera*. Harrison's coprology shares with Swift and Gay not only humanity but humour; it certainly provides him, as the examples from *Trackers* and 'Reading the Rolls' demonstrate, with some of his most scintillatingly witty puns and rhyme sequences.

Perhaps the greatest advantage of the cloacal trope in Harrison's innovative hands is that it allows him to address his reader as a corporeal subject of neither specific age nor specific gender. Small babies and old people defecate: so do both women and men. In his earlier work, for example in the poem 'Durham', Harrison sometimes used the image of the human body as involved in (hetero)sexual acts of love to explore 'the sick,/ sick body politic'.[58] Harrison has come in for criticism, even from his admirers, for the way that his poetry talks about women and their bodies – whether that of his mother, his wives, or his lovers.[59] When his poetry explores sexual themes in relation to bodily experience, it is indeed from a male heterosexual perspective that needs to be mediated by any female reading subject. But when it comes to his nappy-clad divine baby and four-year-olds in the lavatory, he has discovered a way of appealing to a universal human corporeality that is neither sexed (in the biological sense) nor gendered (in the acculturated one). Nor does this distinctive corporeal subject – at least in nature – belong to any particular class: we all – both the homeless on the South Bank and the readership addressed in 'Reading the Rolls' – inevitably make our offerings to Cloacina.

'Stoic crap': *The Kaisers of Carnuntum*

This play, performed just twice in the Austrian amphitheatre which had hosted a performance of *Trackers* in 1990, is Harrison's most extended engagement with ancient Rome, and by far the funniest of all his works for theatre and cinema. It was commissioned by a local producer named Piero Bordin after the success of *Trackers* at Carnuntum. Bordin then needed to respond to Harrison's unusual requests for help from lion-tamers and 'the local fire brigade and army, hunting-horn bands, safari-park animals, and choirs drawn not only from Austria but from Hungary and Slovakia'.[60]

In response to the Carnuntum site, Harrison threw himself into research on its importance as the capital of the Roman north-eastern frontier province Pannonia Superior. It was a large city on the Danube, with a population of more than 50,000 inhabitants. Its remains include not only the amphitheatre, said to be the fourth largest in the Roman Empire, and a gladiator school, but a palace, houses, a forum, public baths and other amenities. He discovered that Marcus Aurelius, the famous Stoic Emperor, began writing his *Meditations* (also known as *Ta en Karnountōi* or *To Myself*) while campaigning against the rebellious Germanic tribes of the Roman Empire, the Macromanni and the Quadi. He lived there for three or four years, between 171 and 175 CE. These years also furnish the historical background to the opening sequence of Ridley Scott's *Gladiator* (2000). The audience at the performances are repeatedly addressed, in a pantomimic manner, as the direct descendants of these local barbarians.

Harrison discovered from inscriptions, coins, Herodian's *Roman History* Book I and the *Historia Augusta* that Marcus Aurelius often took his son Commodus on military campaigns when he was a child. The eleven-year-old Commodus was with him in Carnuntum in 172, and already connected in propaganda with Hercules. When Commodus became Emperor, statues portraying him as Hercules were set up everywhere.[61] *Kaisers* is nominally set in 192. It portrays a version of the events when Commodus was assassinated and declared a public enemy after declaring himself 'Roman Hercules' and 'Conqueror of the World', and even renaming Rome 'Colonia Commodiana'. This followed his own performances at the plebeian games in the autumn of 192, where Dio Cassius (LXXIII.17–22) reports his slaughtering of ostriches and his impersonation as gladiator of Hercules the Hunter. But memories of his trips to the amphitheatre during his boyhood residence in Carnuntum two decades earlier are also central to the play's depiction of his megalomaniacal psyche.

The ancient co-texts, besides the accounts of Commodus in the *Historia Augusta* and Dio Cassius, are Marcus Arelius' *Meditations* and the huge Greek dictionary called the *Onomasticon* by Julius Pollux, a Greek scholar from Egypt patronized by Commodus. The figure of Hercules unites the several thematic strands in the play. He is the symbol of Commodus and of the violence of Roman imperialism. He was also resuscitated in the propaganda of the Hapsburg emperors; the Pillars of Hercules were used as insignia by Karl V, and Joseph II was depicted when he was born in 1742 as the infant Hercules strangling serpents.⁶² Harrison connects the far-right nationalism and xenophobia of Jörg Haider's FPÖ, in 1995 supported by nearly a quarter of Austrians, with both the Third Reich and their Hapsburgian imperial ancestry. But the third strand is the adoption by Stoics such as Marcus Aurelius, and Seneca as the presumed author of *Hercules Oetaeus*, of Hercules as symbol of the Stoic Sapiens, or wise man, the epitome of manliness, resilience, self-control and virtue in the face of calamitous ordeals, suffering and death.⁶³

It is the Stoic Emperor who introduces the Hercules theme, in one of the many flamboyant triple rhymes:

> Rome had to be an Hercules
> to turn barbarians like these
> into cultivated Viennese.⁶⁴

Halfway through the play, we even hear Marcus Aurelius singing a section of his *Meditations* (Book XI.18) in Greek, English and German. But in the mouth of Commodus, Harrison, who is not temperamentally in tune with Stoicism, mercilessly mocks the ancient philosophical school: 'Daddy's a killjoy, a conqueror of Germans/ less into piss-ups than preaching Stoic sermons.' Commodus thinks that the agony suffered by amphitheatre victims would be a suitable test for Stoics' fortitude:

> I'd like to put my father in this cage
> to see if his Meditations could calm the lion's rage.
> I'd split my sides laughing that would be a hoot
> watching philosophy face up to the brute.
> I suppose he could always strike the beast a blow
> with a rolled up papyrus of Ta en Karnounto.
> It would be wonderful to see them eat his words
> and shit out that Stoic crap as steaming lion turds.

The first half of the play is dominated by Commodus, resurrected in 1995 to reintroduce gladiatorial games to Carnuntum after many centuries. The entire amphitheatre floor now represents the provinces of the whole Roman empire, each one represented by the type of animal which it has sent to be butchered for pleasure. Commodus boasts,

These are my conquests. You could feed the Roman army
if you processed all I've slaughtered into sliced salami.
The animals I've slaughtered in the Colosseum here
could keep the world's MacDonalds in burgers for a year.[65]

But Commodus subsequently decides to be transformed 'into the god Hercules' incarnation'. Here Barrie Rutter donned a lionskin and club, but also a bra, suspender belt, and silk knickers and stockings, resulting in many Austrian audience members walking out in disgust.[66] Commodus reminds the audience that Hercules had once been enslaved to a Lydian queen and forced to wear women's attire:

Go on laugh. I dare you. Anyway they're not mine;
I nicked them from Jörg Haider's washing line.
You Marcomanni and Quadi though, you're not too hot
on your mythology, you barbarian lot!
If you ever read beyond the pages of *Die Presse*
you'd know that Hercules was also a cross-dresser.
You'd know that Queen Omphale once made Hercules
dress in lacy knickers just like these.

The task of explaining the Stoic appropriation of Hercules is given to the character of Commodus' subordinate Julius Bollux (as Harrison decided to rename Julius Pollux). In one of Harrison's most breathtaking displays of erudition, Bollux addresses Marcus Aurelius, referring to the fragmentary treatise on Herakles by Herodorus of Pontic Heraklea, who sees

a spiritual symbol in the guise of Hercules.
And for Stoics like your Highness the lion-skin
which your son so sacrilegiously goes swaggering in
signifies the garb of reason.[67]

The juxtaposition of Stoic Hercules with the physical presence of Rutter, roaring and stamping his way across the amphitheatre in this flamboyant outfit, could not have been more ludicrous. The most hilarious and shocking moment was his explanation that he not only enjoys cross-dressing, but is exuberantly bisexual and zoophilic:

And I admit I'm double-doored. Had piles of pokes
with birds as poker and as poked by blokes.

> COMMODUS FUTUTOR, known to shaft
> both sexes, man and beast, both fore and aft.[68]

No wonder the older Austrians in the audience looked so uncomfortable, while their younger counterparts grinned conspiratorially.[69]

The play, however farcical, deals with other dark themes than imperialism and racism. There is a continuous contrast between the theatre of the Greeks, where atrocity was merely enacted, and Roman entertainments where humans as well as beasts suffered atrocious deaths in front of bloodthirsty audiences. Inspired by an ancient mosaic in the Carnuntum Museum, Harrison used the character of Orpheus to calm the caged beasts, and to educate the audience in the Roman practice of dressing criminals destined for execution in the garb of mythical victims such as Orpheus and Prometheus:

> The Greeks would have this fool torn apart off-stage
> and get some messenger to tell of the lions' roar and rage.
> Well I'm a Roman and he's really going in
> with these lions who'll divest him of his skin.
> He's stepped off that museum wall just up the road
> playing music to the animals and mosaically bravoed.[70]

But Orpheus is also the persona who leads the eventual assassination of Commodus, proving that art can fight oppression.

The most tragic episode is dominated by Commodus' mother Faustina, played by Harrison's long-term partner Sian Thomas. Her aria-like speech was written almost overnight. Faustina had been in Pannonia with her husband in the 170s. Her first theme is the way that the difference between the characters of Marcus Aurelius and Commodus led to rumours that she had been unfaithful, slept with gladiators and sailors and conceived Commodus by another man.

> There are followers of yours who just can't bear
> to think that such a saint had such an heir,
> and to preserve your role as Stoic saviour
> invented my lascivious behaviour.
> It would keep the Stoic icon undefiled
> if adultery had doomed me with this child.[71]

Her second theme is the psychological challenge faced by all woman, like the mothers of Hitler, Mussolini and Stalin, who give birth to babies who grow up to be criminal dictators. But she also implies that Marcus Aurelius, for all his Stoicism, is culpable for ignoring the brutalities that took place during his reign. When men were being torn to pieces by the beasts, she says,

> You were dictating with averted gaze what was to grow
> into the chapter titled Ta en Karnounto.[72]

Stoic moral hypocrisy and blind-eye-turning, in Harrison's universe, is no more forgivable than megalomaniacal depravity.

'Cementing over cemeteries': *The Labourers of Herakles* (1995)

In 1990, Alan Rusbridger, then Features editor of *The Guardian*, had been impressed by *Trackers*. In early 1991, he asked Harrison to write some poems on the Gulf War. Harrison responded with two of his most admired poems, 'Initial Illumination' and 'A Cold Coming', published in March 1991. Harrison's association with the newspaper continued, with gaps, for more than a decade.[73]

In September 1995, just three weeks after the performance at Delphi of *The Labourers of Herakles* on 23 August, he was sent to see the Bosnian War in person. He came under fire in an armoured vehicle, and the newspaper published 'The Cycles of Donji Vakuf'.[74] Because he took his role as 'news poet' so diligently, all the preceding months, when writing the *The Labourers of Herakles*, he was reading every scrap of news he could find about the situation in the Balkans.[75] He had long planned a play exploring the contribution to theatre made by Phrynichos, an Athenian tragedian of the generation before Aeschylus, who was said in antiquity to have been the first to introduce female characters to the stage (*Suda* Φ 762).[76] But this project turned into a manifesto on the sufferings of the Muslim population of Bosnia.

The play was commissioned to mark the site at Delphi where it was then intended to build a new theatre (this never transpired), and co-produced by the European Cultural Centre of Delphi and the UK National Theatre Studio. It was sponsored, to Harrison's delight, by the Herakles General Cement Corporation, which is headquartered in Athens. It was written for an audience largely consisting of Greeks with an education in ancient Greek theatre, and contains both phrases in modern Greek and the most dense quotations of untranslated ancient Greek – the surviving fragments of Phrynichos' plays – in any work ever published by Harrison. It would not be an easy drama to revive in performance.

Jocelyn Herbert's set consisted of a circular stage demarcated by nine cement mixers. Behind them loomed a thirty-five-foot cement silo bearing the Herakles General Cement Corporation's logo, the head of Herakles wearing the traditional lionskin. The ground was littered with other construction work paraphernalia and cement sacks. The cast consisted of modern construction workers who have ancient doublets, actors who cite the titles and perform surviving fragments of Phrynichos' tragedies, including his *Alcestis, Antaios, Danaids, Women of Pleuron, Tantalus, Phoenissae* and *Sack of Miletos* (*Miletou Halosis*) as well as unattributed fragments. The *Sack of Miletos* is significant in theatre history, because it was a history play, portraying the defeat of the Athenians' Milesian allies by the Persians in 494 BCE. The Athenians were angered because Phrynichos reminded them just two years later of their own problems, fined him and forbade him to put the play on again (Herodotus VI.21). Harrison uses this tradition to make points about both censorship and the use of the stage for exploring contemporary political issues. He appears in his own persona towards the end of the play, to explain it:

> Although I speak in English and not in ancient Greek
> it's the poet Phrynichos on whose behalf I speak.
> To honour Phrynichos who gave theatre a start
> in redeeming destruction through the power of art,
> and, witnessing male warfare, gave the task
> of mourning and redemption to the female mask,
> to honour such a poet all modern actors need
> to celebrate his genius, and get their spirits freed
> from Europe's impasse, where art cannot redeem
> the cry from Krajina or the Srebrenica scream . . .

At least 135 Croatians were killed in Krajina in the autumn of 1991 and buried in shallow mass graves; more than 8,000 had been massacred at Srebrenica the month before *The Labourers of Herakles*, July 1995.

The master trope of the play – the analogy between the perishable human body and structures made of stone or cement, which echoes the interest in 'stone bodies' in *The Loiners* – is declared in the early sequence where the 'ancient statue of Herakles' appears. The silo rumbles, the timbers supporting it collapse, and he emerges as if from the Underworld. But Labourer 1 demolishes the statue, hurling its dismembered pieces into the cement mixers, and then behaves like the filicidal Herakles himself. He slashes at cement sacks, which represent small children, and impales them. Two of the other labourers become transformed into ancient actors playing the roles of the bereaved women of Miletos in Phrynichos' *Miletou Halosis*, and put the sacks, representing their dead children, into the cement mixers.

The play concludes with songs of the labourers, one of whom has taken the role of Herakles who died in flames wrapped in a toxic robe. Their poetry develops the theme of the creation of material artefacts which devour human flesh–the weaving of 'caustic camouflage no cooling water quenches', producing 'Muslims that are mouldering in mass-execution trenches', making the children of Sarajevo 'amputees' by shells, and wrecking the life of the 'mother of the mortared mosque's dismembered muezzin'. All these events taking place, just north of Greece, are reiterations of the terrible story of siege and destruction told in Phrynichos' banned tragedy. Herakles' own 'ethnic cleanser's conscience crawls with caustic worms', while the aggressors in Bosnia are 'cementing over cemeteries with centuries of dead'.

These human bodies are burned, consumed, dismembered and desecrated by similar technology to the bulldozers that should instead be building theatres. Yet the play ends on a faintly optimistic note. Harrison returns with Herakles' club. It is set alight and turned into a torch. Labourer 1/Herakles reminds the audience that after the Persian wars the Greeks rekindled their fires with the Delphic flame at the very place where the performance has taken place.

> The fire that burned Miletos and the flame
> that makes me writhe with anguish are the very same
> element that we hold up here tonight
> as a beacon for the future with its ambiguous light.
> This fire for the future that still comes flickering through
> [ALL] HALOSIS MILETOU

In the next chapter, we shall see how Harrison's fascination with the ambivalent power of fire both to illuminate and to destroy underlies *Prometheus*, his extraordinary feature film of 1998.

7

'End to end in technicolour': *Prometheus* (1998) and Other Films

'Prosodic motion'

After the cement-mixers of *The Labourers of Herakles* (1995), Harrison returned to the Greek construction industry at the climax of *Prometheus* (1998), 'the only major release feature-length film-poem ever made'.[1] The sequence of statues melting down, partly inspired by an epigram of Palladas Harrison had translated long ago (see p. 32), was filmed in a quarry belonging to Titan Cement in Elefsina. *Prometheus* is only the most ambitious and substantial of Harrison's four film-poems on classical themes, all recorded partly in Greece between 1992 and 2000, and all featuring his favourite statue motif and the idea of a long journey across central or eastern Europe: the others were *The Gaze of the Gorgon* (1992), *A Maybe Day in Kazakhstan* (1994) and *Metamorpheus* (2000). These and Harrison's seven other experiments with combining film and poetry are his least familiar works, although his achievement in this medium, especially in *The Shadow of Hiroshima* (broadcast on Channel Four Television on 6 August 1995, the anniversary of the nuclear attack), is regarded as setting the definitive standard in British cinema. The films are unique in that all the poetry evolved simultaneously with the filming process.[2]

The scripts have been published, constituting what Nick Lowe has called 'instalments of a life at work in an evolving form: a personal narrative whose central self-discovery is the power of poetry-in-film to provide voices for the voiceless in a way startlingly distinct from any other use of the medium'.[3] Harrison's two prose essays discussing film, 'Flicks and This Fleeting Life' and '*Prometheus*: Fire and Poetry', are also published.[4] But most of the films, for complex copyright reasons, have not been made easily available to the public.[5]

This situation could change, but currently they have not been properly understood and valued. This problem has encouraged me to incorporate more description of the contents of these works than I have included in chapters devoted to theatre and freestanding poems.

Harrison's appreciation of cinema stems from his childhood, when his father took him to see gangster movies, and someone – he believes one of his grandfathers, a retired signalman – accompanied him, when he was only eight, to the News Theatre in Leeds City Square to watch newsreel about the liberation of Belsen. He saw every classic of world cinema shown when he was studying at Leeds University. His first personal experience of editing came with the montage of martial clips from documentaries and newsreel with which his Nigerian *Lysistrata*, *Aikin Mata*, had opened in 1964 – once again proving his prescience. Although it is now ubiquitous, the incorporation of video within live theatre, although not altogether unprecedented in eastern European performances, was unheard of in Britain in 1964. In that production, Harrison's Lysistrata put a sudden stop to the filmed combatants by throwing a water-pot at the screen on the back wall, exploiting the power of the 'hard cut'.[6]

Harrison has explained that his desire to make his own film-poem was fed by several experiences. He was motivated by the poor editing of the images with which a television arts programme had accompanied his reading of some poems from *The Loiners* in 1972. Key influences on his technique have included Sergei Eisenstein, whose shooting of *Alexander Nevsky* was informed by the director's passion for Milton's *Paradise Lost*.[7] Harrison has studied Pier Paolo Pasolini, who used his own verse as a template for sequence editing.[8] Harrison wrote lyrics for the songs in George Cukor's ill-fated musical movie *The Blue-Bird* (1976). During its filming in Leningrad, he saw Andrei Tarkovsky's *Mirror*. It includes a poem recited by Tarkovsky's father which affected him deeply.

In 1981, Harrison wrote a verse commentary in the metres of Robert Service, 'the Scots-born Yukon Balladeer',[9] for an edition of the BBC documentary series 'The World About Us'.[10] This was his first time in a cutting room, and the moment when he discovered that if verse is to accompany film, longer camera holds are needed at the beginning and end of shots. The documentary's director, Andrée Molyneux, then invited him to work on a Christmas TV special, *The Big H* (1984), which was not a film-poem. It was a film of verse about King Herod being performed by Leeds schoolchildren. It briefly meditates on classical languages.[11]

It was in making films with BBC director Peter Symes, which began with *Loving Memory* in 1987, that Harrison experimented with mutually reinforcing words and images through careful editing of clip against metre, producing what he calls 'the scansions of edited sequences';[12] 'the scansions of the screen and the prosodies of poetry coexist to create a third kind of mutually illuminating momentum that is the film/poem whose potential range and depth has not been fully explored'.[13] Symes and he explored the connection between metrical poetry and film, which uses twenty-four or twenty-five frames per second and can be seen as 'a prosodic motion'. There is a parallel between the succession of images in a film and how the beats in a verse line 'succeed one another and build into gratifications or disappointments of expectation'.[14] Harrison uses most standard cinematic techniques in his film-poems – dissolve-and-fade, close-up, tracking shots and especially panning. The camera's movement as it scans groups of people, or a street, or the course of a river, is often timed to fit the rhythm of his verse.

Film had further advantages. It enabled Harrison to reach a wider audience by being broadcast on television. He made special efforts in his films 'to make things accessible enough to be shown anywhere'.[15] Harrison wanted to 'move poetry out of the ghetto of late-night programmes for the initiated, and put it in front of a mainstream audience'.[16] The other advantage was that film, if strictly controlled by poetic voice-over and structured visual sequences, can make 'footage of terror' bearable: 'the word, if it was seductive enough and powerful enough, could make the ear, as it were, go into close-up and take the imagination *further* than it would have gone had it simply been presented with the raw archive.[17]

'Grunting to the barbed-wire lyre': *The Gaze of the Gorgon* (1992)

Harrison's forty-nine-minute film about the wars that scarred the twentieth century veers from sounds and sights of exquisite beauty to the most harrowing footage in his *oeuvre*. It includes a soprano performance of a Lied by Schumann and lingering close-ups of delightful sculpted Muses, but these are intercut with clips and still photographs from both world wars and the Gulf War of

1990–1, code-named Operation Desert Shield. The director was Peter Symes, with whom Harrison had established a deep creative understanding. The central image is the face of the Gorgon on the pediment of the temple of Artemis in Corfu Archaeological Museum. In Harrison's only extended engagement with Homer, the most important co-text is the *Iliad*. In another unusual move, although he is the voice speaking the poetry, it is put in the mouth of the German poet Heinrich Heine. This is Harrison's most intense encounter with German culture, in which he had become absorbed during his relationship with his first wife, Rosemarie Crossfield Dietzsch. Her parents were German refugees.[18] The filming process also fed his interest in Austria, where he produced *The Kaisers of Carnuntum* three years later.

The motifs of war, the *Iliad*, Heine and Germany are connected by the moment in 1911 when men digging for Kaiser Wilhelm II, who had a summer palace in Corfu, exhumed the terrifying Gorgon sculpture with which Wilhelm became obsessed. The man who likened Jews to a poisonous fungus on the German oak even made drawings, which appear in the film, 'proving' that the Gorgon's strange posture was modelled on the swastika.[19] The palace had been built in 1890 for Empress Elizabeth of Austria, affectionately known as Sissy. It was called the Achilleion because it was a monument to the Iliadic hero. Harrison discovered that the statue there of Heine, whom the culture-loving Sissy had invited to live as her guest when he was ill with venereal disease, was taken down by Wilhelm because Heine was not only a political radical but Jewish:

> *Get rid*
> *of Sissy's syphilitic Yid!*
> *Dammit! The man's a democrat,*
> *I've got no time for shits like that.*[20]

The Gorgon represents all agents who cause human suffering through the brutality and machinery of war. The central idea is that the Gorgon's gaze, which turns living being into stone, returns cyclically to petrify entire races and continents. While the film was in development, Harrison was also working on his play about the invention of chemical weapons, *Square Rounds* (1992), echoes of which can be heard in the Gorgon's snakes 'hissing like chlorine gas at Ypres'.[21] In 1991 he also wrote 'A Cold Coming' in response to a shocking photograph from the Gulf War. The film includes a distressing sequence showing the faces of disfigured or dead soldiers, 'the Kaiser's Gorgon choir', who are turning into stone and 'grunting to the barbed-wire lyre'. This contrasts with the 'tragic mask of ancient days' held by a dainty statue of Melpomene, the tragic muse, who used to help humans contemplate their predicament.[22]

The film meditates on the dialectical connection between masks and death: in ancient Greek thought, the gaze of the Gorgon, the archetypal mask-head, was literally lethal because it turned the viewer into stone.[23] This dialectic is expressed in the opening frame which introduces the *Iliad*, just as the film ends visually with a bust of Homer in the Achilleion and a man singing a Greek folk-song. The opening frame consists of a quotation from Simone Weil's *The Iliad, or the Poem of Force*, presciently written in 1939 during the Nazi occupation of France and the aftermath of the Spanish Civil War. It reads: 'To the same degree, those who use force and those who endure it are turned to stone.'[24] As Henry Stead points out, Weil also identifies the death of Hector as an example of the extreme force that turns humans into material objects by killing them:

> Exercised to the limit, it turns man into a thing in the most literal sense: it makes a corpse out of him…The hero becomes a *thing* dragged behind a chariot in the dust…The bitterness of such a spectacle is offered to us absolutely undiluted.[25]

In Harrison's film, the abuse of Hector's corpse is key. It is portrayed in a large painted fresco in the Achilleion, Franz Match's 'Triumph of Achilles', commissioned by Sissy in 1892. While the camera first surveys it, Heine comments:

> Along with me the Empress/versifier
> revered blind Homer and his lyre,
> the ancient poet whose *Iliad*
> was the steadiest gaze we've had
> at war and suffering…[26]

The next visual image is the statue of Achilles which Wilhelm commissioned. Where Sissy's Achilles statue, 'Dying Achilles' by Ernst Herter (1884), showed the superhero suffering and prostrate, Wilhelm's 'Triumph of Achilles' by Johannes Götz (1909) is a terrifying, upright hoplite, with a gorgon carved on his shield and the inscription 'The greatest German to the greatest Greek' on its plinth. The camera then returns to the painting, to linger not on Achilles on his chariot but on the women of Troy, especially Andromache, fainting at the sight of her husband's cadaver.

> The soon-to-be-defeated rows
> of Trojans watch exultant foes
> who bring the city to the ground
> then leave it just a sandblown mound.

These verses correspond with specific passages in the *Iliad* – Andromache's crazed dash to the walls when Achilles has killed Hector (XXII.437–72) and the simile of the boy kicking down a sandcastle (XV.362–4). The poet concludes the commentary on this painting with a return to the parallels between the Holocaust and the destruction of Troy, remembered only because of Homer:

> A whole culture vanished in the fire
> until redeemed by Homer's lyre.
> A lyre like Homer's could redeem
> Hector's skull's still-echoing scream.[27]

Yet, as Weil insisted, the victorious Greeks were also 'in the Gorgon's gaze'. Both 'victims and the victimisers' are dehumanized by acts of atrocious violence; people with rigid religious or political views have been looked upon by the Gorgon, too.

The bulk of *Gaze of the Gorgon* is filmed in the Achilleion, but it has a vast historical and geographical sweep. It opens in Frankfurt, where a modest memorial to Heine is compared with imposing statues of Goethe and Schiller, and young drug addicts, contemporary victims of the Gorgon, shoot heroin into their veins. Towards the end, the scene shifts to the Bronx in New York, where African and Hispanic Americans dance joyfully beside the Heinrich Heine Memorial. This white marble fountain was designed for his home city of Düsseldorf to mark the centenary of his birth in 1897, but antisemitism put a stop to this plan. Its sculptor, Ernst Herter, took it to the USA. The America reference leads into the final sequence of horrific images of charred Iraqi corpses and a burnt-out tank, with the Gorgon's face superimposed,[28] as caused by Operation Desert Shield and also inspiring 'A Cold Coming'.

These are not the first nor even the most shocking images in the film. The newsreels from the mass graves of the First World War, and the concentration camps of the Second World War, are breathtakingly dreadful. Perhaps the most shocking clip follows close-ups on the Achilleion's graceful Terpsichore, muse of dance: it shows a shattered human foot being amputated.[29] This immediately follows some of the most memorable verse in the film, recited over a beautiful carved image of a particular type of ancient lyre:

> The *barbitos*, the ancient lyre,
> since the Kaiser's day,
> is restrung with barbed wire.
> Bards' hands bleed when they play
> the score that fits an era's scream,
> the blood, the suffering, the loss.
> The twentieth-century scream
> is played on barbed-wire *barbitos*.[30]

'Doomed Argonauts': *A Maybe Day in Kazakhstan* (1994)

Perhaps the least analysed of all Harrison's works, except in a study by Robert Speranza (2002), *A Maybe Day in Kazakhstan* reflects on the fragility of the uneasy new democracy in Kazakhstan – for Kazakhstanis, the old annual May Day celebrations now mean that 'maybe' things can change for the better.[31] The film was funded and produced by Channel Four Television in association with the Foundation of Hellenic Culture. The stars are a group of Greeks whose forefathers had moved to the Black Sea, perhaps at the time of Catherine the Great's Hellenization initiative, but whom Stalin brutally deported, especially from Georgia, to central Asian collectives between 1937 and 1949. The camera lingers on their faces, especially of the older men and women, while Harrison intones couplets such as 'Cold dark deportation trains/ still jolt and judder through their brains'.[32]

Many have now subsequently moved to their ancestral homeland in Greece; the journeys made by them and their forebears are equated with those of the argonauts for whom Harrison had written arias in his *Medea: A Sex-War Opera*. The film meditates on a group of Kazakhstani Greeks who now survive by selling obsolete Soviet memorabilia at an Athenian flea-market, and latterly ascend to the Acropolis, where the classical Athenian democracy was born. The film is dedicated to Melina Mercouri, intended to be its voice-over. But this veteran campaigner for democracy and social justice in Greece, and advocate for the return of the Parthenon sculptures held in the British Museum, was mortally ill. Harrison had to step in.

Co-directed by Harrison and Mark Kidel, and edited by Julian Sabbath, this film contains some of the most bravura cutting of image against word in Harrison's entire filmic *oeuvre*. The introductory sequence consists of precision cutting of images of the people in the outdoor market for Soviet souvenirs to the rhythmic music played by an old man, with an intriguing twinkle in his eye, on his Black Sea lyre or *kemence*, played with a bow. Paradoxically, however, *A Maybe Day in Kazakhstan* feels more like a documentary than most of Harrison's film-poems. The viewer is informed not only about the Kazakhstan Greek community, but about Soviet propaganda and ancient democracy and 'Kleisthenes,/ democracy's first dreamer'.[33] Harrison was influenced by the British documentary tradition founded by John Grierson, who developed film as a way of investigating and recording everyday social and working life. One of the first films Grierson produced was the GPO Film Unit documentary *Coal Face* (1935), which influenced Harrison's *Prometheus* (see below).

The theme of the market where the impoverished migrants try to earn their livelihood selling Red Army uniforms and other Soviet knick-knacks is developed in a typical Harrisonian critique of free-market capitalism in the film's long central stanza. This is where the comparison with the Argonauts is first introduced:

> Pavement peddlers trading trash
> from Communism's fatal crash,
> salvaging the washed-up cargo
> from their ill-fated, shattered *Argo*.[34]

As the camera zooms in on a statuette of Lenin, Harrison's voice-over develops the image:

> Doomed Argonauts condemned to peddle
> the bric-à-brac of badge and medal
> from that doomed voyage that maroons
> Lenin here with fork and spoons.[35]

The next frames focus on a plastic puppet of Leon Trotsky, and the poet reiterates the comparison a third time. 'The foundered Argo's former crew' are stranded 'in free flea-market forces'; and now the reason for the Greek mythical references becomes apparent. The film has tricked us into thinking we are in central Asia, but no. As a reflection, at first unfocused, of the Parthenon comes into view, Harrison's voice-over informs us, 'This market wasn't Kazakhstan/ but where democracy began.'[36] The remainder of the film explores the streets of Athens and the Acropolis; these people are disoriented, triply exiled, on a quest from Greece to the Black Sea, from the Black Sea to Kazakhstan, and now back to Greece again. While the film moves into its last sequence, with the Kazakhstan Greeks forming a musical band and ascending to the Parthenon, a woman's voice sings a haunting lament, to the tune of 'The Red Flag', recalling how her people had been sent east, and, as they approached the cotton-farming collective, glimpsed 'the cotton glow, a golden fleece/ cold in moonlight far from Greece'.[37]

The 'band of Greeks who get called Russian' are led by a small girl, dressed in red, who seems to symbolize hope. At the Parthenon, noisy pulleys cut through the soundtrack; a large stone is lifted by a crane.[38] Harrison alludes to Shakespeare's *Sonnet* 55, which begins 'Not marble nor the gilded monuments/ Of princes shall outlive this powerful rhyme'; his lines run 'Not marble, but millennia weigh/ on cables that'll maybe fray'. The stone's movement offers a visual parallel to the poet's discussion of democracy's original foundation by Cleisthenes, and democracy's need for permanent re-creation.

At the end, the girl climbs down the south-western side of the Acropolis to the ancient theatre of Dionysus. The film ends on a note (unusual for Harrison) of cautious optimism, which would be obvious to any viewer/listener regardless of their knowledge of ancient Greece. But there is a profound visual undertext which requires knowledge of Aeschylus' *Oresteia*. The girl walks slowly across the orchestra of the theatre towards the stage on a 'carpet' made of red flags,[39] just as Agamemnon in the first tragedy of the *Oresteia* treads the crimson carpet as he enters the palace. This may have been meant partly as a tribute to Mercouri, whose performance of the role of Clytemnestra in this scene in Karolos Koun's 1980 *Oresteia* had entered theatrical legend. But the motif also has political implications. Agamemnon meets his own death, and the constitution of Argos descends into a cruel tyranny. What kind of political future can either Kazakhstan or this child expect? There is a cryptic answer in the return of the mysterious elderly lyre-player of the opening sequence, whose music seems to encourage the girl to dance; the face of the carved satyr on the stage front (an image of which Harrison had made use in *Trackers*) is compared with his.[40] So the political question the film asks is finally articulated, solely by visual imagery, as the distinction between ancient Greek dramatic genres. Is the future like a tragedy or will it bring the joyous release of the culminating satyr play?

'History and lack of hope': *Prometheus* (1998)

> Fire and poetry, two great powers
> that mek this so-called gods' world OURS!

So speaks an old man, who has turned into Prometheus, to an audience of miners in Harrison's first feature film. The poet had been fascinated by the fire glowing in his family fireplace as a child. He feels that his poetic gift was nurtured by gazing into its flames; later, he compares fires in dark grates and the light emitted by the screen in darkened cinemas.[41] *Prometheus* was screened at some esoteric venues, broadcast by UK Channel Four television, and subsequently disappeared almost completely from public view. Outside the UK, it made little impression. Yet Harrison's *Prometheus* is a significant artistic reaction to the fall of the British working class as the twentieth century staggered to its close, a fall symptomatic of the international collapse of the socialist dream. The film also offers a path-breaking adaptation of classical myth for a radical political purpose.

Harrison believes that the ancient Greek tragedy entitled *Prometheus Bound*, the authorship of which is contested, is indeed by Aeschylus, the poet of the Athenian democratic revolution. Aeschylus' Prometheus is stubborn, audacious, gloomy, inspirational, intellectual, poetic, and has a diachronic view of history. He can see far away across the world, into the past and the future. Harrison's film is also stubborn, audacious, gloomy, inspirational, intellectual and poetic, with an international perspective and diachronic historical viewpoint. It escorts its audience on a procession of arresting images from northern England to eastern Europe and Greece, via the bombing of Dresden, the collapse of socialism and the Holocaust. This procession advances – its sequential logic dictated by poetic values rather than strict chronology – with a measured pace enhanced by Alastair Cameron's meticulous camera work and by precision editing.

The opening sequence reveals Kratos and Bia, masked nuclear power workers, looming through the steam of cooling towers. Another episode involves the wild-eyed Io finding comfort by embracing the monumental gold statue of Prometheus, which dominates the later stages of the film. A haunting image is the Oceanids (women workers at a fish-canning factory), their pale fishnet veils fluttering across sad, beautiful masks designed by Jocelyn Herbert. They float on a raft down the River Humber, in an industrial heartland, to Richard Blackford's atmospheric music, emitted by the Humber Bridge's suspension cables. Hermes (whose connection with the lyre Harrison had explored in *Trackers*), has struck the sound from this steel construction, a potent symbol of humankind's ability to overcome natural obstacles through a combination of Promethean intelligence, which transforms the world at the level of mind, and Promethean industrial fire, which transforms it at the level of matter.

The role of Hermes, played with menace by Michael Feast, is upgraded from the Aeschylean archetype. Hermes' dialogues with Prometheus constitute the intellectual kernel of the film. Feast's upper-middle class English accent, hard as cut glass, contrasts with Walter Sparrow's Promethean Old Man, who puts his warm, northern, working-class voice to superb use. The oratorical highlight is his nostalgic monologue on smoking,[42] which ruminates on the pleasure and sexual allure cigarettes, as represented on screen, used to offer: 'Who smokes now? Them were the days / when women smoked in negligées.' The Old Man's smoking habit constitutes, in Marxist terms, an example of the Dialectical Unity of Opposites. To smoke is a sign of working-class identity and even solidarity (smoking remains a class issue in the UK), and the ultimate sign of the personal liberty which the Old Man refuses to yield to his capitalist masters. Yet it is forced upon him by multinational tobacco corporations and is killing him. Some unintelligent anti-smoking campaigners in the UK complained that Harrison's film was an apology for cigarettes.[43] It is not. Harrison dislikes smoking. The Old Man is dying of his addiction; the actor playing him, Walter Sparrow, died of lung cancer after the film was made.

The film is neither a translation nor an adaptation but it is inspired by the tragedy and is informed by its confrontations. The cast includes familiar figures – Prometheus, Oceanids, Hermes, Io – plus miners, a miner's small son, his mother and grandmother. The screenplay even quotes the ancient tragedy in ancient Greek: Hermes' first apostrophe to Prometheus (*PV* 976–78) is addressed with contemptuous malice to miners descending a mineshaft.[44] Elsewhere Harrison uses English translation of the Greek, notably in the early scene in which the boy's homework consists of reading a trenchant version of Prometheus' 'philanthropy' monologue (*PV* 447–53), 'Men had eyes but didn't see', concluding,

> With Prometheus life began
> to flourish for benighted Man.
> My gift of fire made Mankind free
> but I stay in captivity.[45]

The rich research into previous receptions of myths which we have noted in the cases of *Phaedra Britannica* and *Medea: A Sex-War Opera* is just as in evidence here. The film is partly about what the Aeschylean Prometheus has meant to later generations of humankind, especially to romantics, radicals and revolutionaries. It is a late twentieth-century antiphonal response to Shelley's *Prometheus Unbound*, with its choric plurality of voices, frustrated revolutionary power and sense of the torment implicit in the march of human history. Harrison himself invites us to draw such connections between his film and Shelley's poem in 'Fire and Poetry', much of which he wrote in the Baths of Caracalla, where Shelley penned *Prometheus Unbound*.

Harrison also explores the relationship between the Prometheus myth and the history of Marxist politics. Some of the film feels like a symphony on ideas developed in the classics of Marxist theory. It explores the material and economic processes that have underpinned capitalism and twentieth-century communism: there has certainly never been an artwork more aware of its own contextual mode and underlying means of production. Coal is extracted from the earth, cast into fire, and miners' bodies are transformed visually into bullion – a horrific metamorphosis from concrete to abstract labour and thence to Symbolic Capital. Yet Harrison's scholarship never stands between him and the people he portrays. His classical heroes never overshadow his local heroes. One reason he likes film is that 'the cinema screen can give heroic stature to the most humble of faces ... an essential requirement in a film where the most unlikely wheezing ex-miner is slowly made to represent Prometheus himself'.[46] The reason why Harrison's film has been little watched is that it draws epic inferences from a controversial political event, the landmark conflict in British post-war socio-economic history.

Twice in the early 1970s, under Edward Heath's Conservative government, the National Union of Mineworkers had brought Britain to a near-standstill by striking against pit closures. In both 1972 and 1974, the country was forced to work a three-day week to reduce energy consumption. The strikes improved miners' pay, conditions and status. The Conservatives never forgave them. The Right Wing's new warrior, Margaret Thatcher, returned to power in 1983, after defeating Argentina, 'the enemy without', in the Falklands War. Her priority was now the defeat of the 'the enemy within'. In early 1984, the National Coal Board announced the closure of twenty pits (as it turns out, far more than twenty pits were eventually closed). The closures would make more than 20,000 men redundant, removing the income from many more Britons in allied industries, and destroying numerous communities across the poorest regions of Wales, Scotland and north-east England.

Although Harrison's *Prometheus* is set in its own 'present' of the 1990s, the strike is signalled as the point at which Kirkby, the northern English community it portrays, had been thrown into crisis; the Old Man carves a coal figure in Promethean pose captioned 'Striking Miner, 1984'; a newspaper article traces the pit closures back to the strike.[47] In defending the mining communities, Harrison has accepted into art heroes even less acceptable than the homeless of *Trackers*. It is one thing for a poet to support oppressed causes that have been legitimized by mainstream liberal ideology, such as women and ethnic minorities, in whose name countless productions of Greek tragedy have emerged. It is quite another to make heroes out of the white male working class, especially the NUM.

At the time of the strike the union was a conflicted organization, including principled family men, intransigent ideologues, moral heroes, moderates desperate for a quiet life, hot-headed youths spoiling for a fight, grey-headed sages, scabs and secessionists. Its leadership was split between those striking to keep the mines open and those striking for the right to dignity, work and remuneration, not necessarily the right to dangerous work in the unhealthy conditions of the mining industry. Yet these ordinary, hard-working, proud, community-minded, argumentative and increasingly desperate men were almost universally presented as violent thugs; the right-wing press insinuated that they were corrupt and in league with Libya and the Soviet Union (a ludicrous claim in the UK, where Communism failed to take root in the working class). Mainstream media set about discrediting Arthur Scargill, the union's president, by implying that he was an avaricious bully and even a traitor. One reason for the opprobrium heaped on Harrison's poem 'v.', first published just after the end of the strike in 1985, was that it is prefaced with a quotation from Scargill (see above p. 80).

Harrison's constant theme – the inaudibility in 'high' artistic culture of working-class voices – resounds in *Prometheus*. The boy thoughtlessly lights a fire with his father's archive of cuttings on the pit closures, destroying even the last memorials of the miners' subjective experiences. The Promethean fire bestows on the miners of Kirkby not only audible voices but the capacity to speak in verse. Hermes is suspicious of poetry because 'Poets have taught mankind to breach/ the boundaries Zeus put round speech', and the miners, imprisoned in a cattle truck, lose their customary dialectal habits and become extempore poets themselves.[48]

This engaging scene is an antidote to the silencing and misrepresentation of the miners. At the time, the footage on news programmes showed few miners' faces. Neither the miners nor their leaders ever had the remotest chance of fair representation. They displayed emotional strain, swore publicly, had strong accents, unfashionable haircuts, unglamorous clothes, few media contacts and no experience in the manipulation of public opinion. They inevitably lost the PR wars before the strike had begun. The victims in this epochal conflict remained silenced in the public imagination until the mid-1990s, when the Berlin Wall had safely fallen and the mining industry in Britain had been annihilated. Tens of thousands of people still live in the former mining communities – they are poor, suffer high levels of petty crime and addiction, attend failing schools and possess nearly worthless real estate. It is in this context of erasure by non-representation that Harrison's treatment of the miners' strike needs to be appreciated.

Illumination can be gained from comparison of *Prometheus* with three films that share its subject-matter, although not its classicism, and are approximately contemporary. Mike Figgis' one-hour documentary *The Battle of Orgreave*

(2001) finally allowed the mining families involved in that confrontation to relate it from their own perspective. A realist (but ultimately escapist) attempt to tell the miners' tale, which has enjoyed relatively wide circulation, on account of the presence of Ewan MacGregor as the love interest, is Mark Herman's 1996 *Brassed Off*, the story of the fictional Grimley Colliery Band, based on the famous miners' brass band at Grimethorpe. This film is curiously optimistic in its message, implying that working-class people are so resilient that they can wisecrack their way through removal of their livelihood.

Prometheus shares subject matter with one film which has received international exposure, and has subsequently been turned into a phenomenally successful musical, Lee Hall and Stephen Daldry's moving *Billy Elliot* (2000). This portrays an eleven-year-old boy's desire to study ballet. Its context is Easington, a tough colliery town in County Durham. Billy's father and brother are miners, daily attending the picket line. The film is sympathetic to the miners (although critical of their narrow construction of masculinity). But its message is about transcending class origins and tribal culture; *Prometheus*, on the other hand, addresses humanity's collective need to transcend its own tragic history. The shift from the individual to the collective, from the specific to the general (in the terms of Aristotle's *Poetics*, chapter 9, from the historical to the philosophical), is made by grafting the struggle of the British miners onto the ancient Greek myth. Harrison has forged a new cinematic language, based on myth, which accommodates the figuring of the real and the contemporary. This is mythic language which can be spoken by gods and miners alike. It is unique. Through the special diction of poetry, everyday people speak and their environment is illuminated.

Harrison believes that 'poetry can 'enter the inner world of people in documentary situations'.[49] His labours included the collection of materials in order to offer a true memorial to the British miners and their past. Harrison had originally planned to create a theatrical performance of *Prometheus Bound* on a slag-heap in Yorkshire. But when it became clear that all the pits would close, he visited them, collecting signage and equipment which physically appear in the film. He also collected newspaper and magazine cuttings (especially accounts of accidents with high death tolls), photographs and postcards. The terrible legacy of pollution left by heavy industry is as prominent a topic in his notebooks as in the film, whose landscapes make bleak visual poetry out of derelict cooling towers.

This is the Classical Tradition at its most potent. If nothing else, it provides overwhelming proof that Capitalism and Classicism need not go hand in hand. The film which *Prometheus* superficially most resembles is probably Theo Angelopoulos' meditative *Ulysses' Gaze* (1995), with which it shares the idea of a journey through disintegrating regions of east European communist industrialization, monumental civic statuary, a subordination of narrative to an exploration of themes, and movement backwards and forwards in time. The two films also share a commitment to examining the cinematic gaze and film as the medium of memory, but Angelopoulos' epistemological concerns are replaced in *Prometheus* by a vibrant and class-conscious view of the role of cinema: the Old Man spends much of the film in the derelict building of the Palace Cinema in Knottingley, a real relic of twentieth-century working-class culture. More importantly, *Ulysses' Gaze* is not a verse film-poem, a genre of which Harrison is one of the earliest and most important exponents, if not quite its actual inventor.

On 10 March 2002, Independent Television (ITV) broadcast Harrison's new film *Crossings*, which revisits Auden's *Night Mail* but with a different political vision. *Night Mail*, despite its date, avoided the realities of unemployment and poverty in 1930s Britain. But seventeen years after the 1984–5 strike, the miners are still on Harrison's mind; as the train in *Crossings* reaches northern England, the narrator views the ruins of the once-proud industrial landscape (its farmland also recently devastated by the slaughter of cattle during the foot-and-mouth epidemic of 2001):

> The modern Nightmail threads through the map
> of mining communities thrown on the scrap,
> collieries culled like Shilbottle, Shotton,
> winding gear felled, and workforce forgotten.
> Along with culled cattle, culled kingdoms of coal
> one dumped on the bonfire, one on the dole.

Harrison was here more influenced by Auden's involvement with the GPO Film Unit documentary *Coal Face*, the verse of which was intended for a female chorus, especially this stanza:

> O lurcher loving collier black as night,
> Follow your love across the smokeless hill.
> Your lamp is out and all your cages still.[50]

The song appears near the end of *Coal Face*, made a year before the more famous mail train documentary.[51]

The notebooks relating to *Prometheus* include images of Prometheus on ancient vases, of the high temple of capitalism constituted by the Rockefeller Center and careful transcriptions from LSJ of whole entries under items of Greek vocabulary. Poetry figures large: passages of Hesiod are pasted in *Prometheus* Notebook 1. Other words are written out for contemplative purposes: 'Sprengbombe-high explosive bombs', 'Vernichtungsfeuer-annihilating fire' and Vernichtungslager-extermination camp'.[52]

The film uses Classics to address the most challenging of artistic topics, especially for a non-Jew – the Holocaust.[53] Others have used Greek tragedy to explore the Second World War, for example the viewpoint of German soldiers as presented through the myth of Oedipus in Rainer Simon's film *The Case for Decision Ö* (1991), or through the *Oresteia* and other House of Atreus tragedies in Jonathan Littell's docu-novel *The Kindly Ones* (2006).[54] But the representation of the Holocaust has been the most notorious controversy in critical theory and postmodern thought. It has been argued that any kind of fictive construct is disrespectful, that it inevitably transforms memory (which in the case of the Holocaust is a dangerous process), and that non-survivors, let alone non-Jews, should not write it.[55] Others have simply viewed the topic as too horrific to be imagined, let alone expressed, and that the sole rational reaction to such 'ineffability' is a reverential silence.

Critics have discussed different aesthetic modes for negotiating the moral and cognitive minefield laid by the murder of millions – truthful memoir, documentary, docufiction, realist fiction, parable, fable, consciously distortionist cartoon, comic grotesque or allegorical fantasy. But in *Prometheus* Harrison evaded selecting any single mode. He combined a realist 'documentary' strand (for example, in the picture of pilgrims' candles at Auschwitz) with a symbolic and surrealist mode created by audio-visual effects, such as the screaming miners being melted down in a German foundry, or the cattle trucks and industrialization of death in the abattoir, where Io's suffering is movingly portrayed by the athletic Fern Smith.

In *Prometheus Bound* Io is viciously persecuted, half turned into a cow and sent on a lonely journey eastward by a vindictive divinity. Her leaping entrance, tortured by the gadfly, followed by her account of eviction from her ancestral home, is one of the most extraordinary treatments of a persecution victim's subjectivity anywhere in ancient literature. It makes the matter of being transformed into an animal, and treated like one, emotionally plausible. Harrison wanted his viewers to see, with brutal literalness, what it means to be turned into a cow (or into a human treated like a cow) destined for a death chamber. His Io is pursued across Europe by 'Poor KRATOS and his sidekick Bia', who 'miss the swastikas of yesteryear':

> They've come to Dresden and they've sighed
> for the good old days of genocide.
> How they've yearned to reinstate
> the furnace as a people's fate.

They arrest Io and hurl her into a cattle truck. They use cattle-prods to force her into the abattoir, where the camera studies her slaughter, the disgusting industrialization of death and the processing of her carcass, which is finally cremated.[56]

Prometheus is slightly reminiscent of the allusive use of myth in Primo Levi's 'The canto of Ulysses', which also revolves around hell fires, added in 1958 to *Survival in Auschwitz*.[57] Froma Zeitlin suggests that Harrison had unconsciously absorbed images from the dreadful Nazi propaganda film, *Der ewige Jude* (1940), which he has seen. This includes a horrifying episode showing the kosher slaughter of animals, in concealed slow motion, to imply that Jews are barbaric and deserve similar treatment. But Io is also female. This acts as a reminder that fewer women survived the selection for the gas chambers because they were deemed less valuable as labourers. This may explain why there have been many more male writers of Holocaust memoirs.[58] The shocking force of Io's death certainly exempts Harrison from the charges of disrespect often levelled at artists representing the Holocaust.[59]

The countries of the former eastern bloc are presented charitably. Harrison spent eighteen months in Prague in the mid-1960s, and experienced at first hand the effects of communism gone bad in the period leading up to the Soviet invasion of Czechoslovakia in 1968. But his first wife's father had been a communist under Hitler, living in East Germany. Harrison does not engage with the propaganda images on which the West was fed an undiluted diet during the Cold War. His Eastern Bloc countries are always viewed with a humane and rational gaze. Bulgaria provides the film's most searing image of simple humanity, when a poor baker woman gives the desperate Io a loaf of bread. Yet the Eastern Bloc of his film also provides, with uncompromising truth, the most horrific images of industrialization and pollution – one of the terrible prices that twentieth-century socialism had to pay in the name of the proletariat. When the statue of Prometheus reaches Nowa Huta, Hermes wantonly muses on the chemical poisoning of man's environment. Seeing it as the punishment that the industrial working class must pay for their insouciance, he concludes:

> So such Promethean shrines,
> chemical and steel works, mines,
> still anger Zeus because they stand
> for the Promethean contraband,
> nonetheless make him content
> by blighting man's environment.[60]

The budget for the film was pitifully small – only £1.5 million. Sometimes it shows. The most cataclysmic sequences, when the whole world is in conflagration, would have profited from sleeker production values. But the tiny budget may have had a beneficial impact: Harrison believes that great art requires almost preternatural effort. The fact that the film was physically extremely arduous to make enhances the sense of exertion and struggle. Yet at times this epic on the horror and hope of humankind is extremely funny, especially when contemplating its own aesthetics; in one hilarious episode the Old Man humorously develops the conceit that it is the political machinations of the Conservatives which have driven him into perpetual rhyming couplets.[61]

Prometheus is on a grand conceptual scale and deserves a wider audience. Since it is unlikely ever to be screened in commercial multiplexes, its audience will inevitably consist of members of the liberal intelligentsia, many of whom will not be able to abide Harrison's 'unreconstructed' politics. But others will recognize that Prometheus is less a protest piece or left-wing agit-prop than a tearful threnody for a lost dream, a lost utopia.[62] In 1937, an English socialist poet, John Lehmann, fell in love with Soviet Georgia. He published a fascinating book entitled *Prometheus and the Bolsheviks*, read by few outside the British Left, which Harrison discusses in 'Fire and Poetry'. Lehmann recounts the Hesiodic dream he experienced while sleeping in a deckchair on a Soviet steamer crossing the Black Sea. He is visited by Prometheus, the longest-term resident of the Caucasus. The Titan has been liberated by Bolshevism, and is about to take out party membership. Even our historical awareness of the squalid future and fate of Soviet communism cannot obscure the buoyancy of this dream. Lehmann's narrative closes optimistically: the people of Georgia are on their way to equality, freedom and a fair society.

Psychologists say that hope is essential to human well-being. The weekly purchase of a lottery ticket allows us to dream that personal wealth is imminent. From the early nineteenth century until the 1980s, everyone who could not tolerate the many intolerable aspects of capitalism had been able to participate in dreams of ideal socialism. Communism, socialism, the labour movement and trade unionism offered forms of group consciousness which helped humans all over the world imagine that progress to a better society was not only possible but was beginning to be delivered in reality. However, during the last thirty years, socialism has become discredited. Our society has no collective lottery ticket. Harrison's film was a howling lament for the death of aspiration, an indictment through word and image of the dangerous hopelessness of the cynical millennial Zeitgeist.

At a climactic moment the film's composer, Richard Blackford, sings a lament in the persona of a Jewish cantor, and is disrupted by the arrival of the contemptuous Aeschylean lackey Hermes. The god violently snuffs out the candles left by Jewish pilgrims and snarls a speech to camera explaining why: 'Fuhrer Zeus' hates

> These candles that can help them cope
> with history and lack of hope.[63]

Harrison is here responding to Seamus Heaney's famous lines in the *Cure at Troy* (1990), his version of Sophocles' *Philoctetes*:

> When History says, don't hope,
> On this side of the grave.
> But then, once in a lifetime
> The longed-for tidal wave
> Of justice can rise up,
> And hope and history rhyme.[64]

But in *Prometheus* Hermes even snuffs the hope-candles out. For Harrison, hope and history can never be made to rhyme.

He is unconvinced of the possibility, in the light of human history, of maintaining an affirmative perspective. His charred Iraqi in 'A Cold Coming' warns the poet against assuming that a collective and progressive global sensibility is possible, that he has 'the imagination to see the world beyond one nation'.[65] Harrison expressed his fear that humanity is doomed to the horror of global war in a speech he wrote for Hermes. It is so prescient that it now seems strange that it was excluded from the final cut of *Prometheus*:

> We're immortals. We can wait
> for mortals to disintegrate.
> Waiting's the policy at present
> waiting, say for Cross or Crescent
> to clash in Crusade and jihad.
> Now that would make Zeus really glad.

These lines were written just a few years before 9/11.

Harrison's ideological edginess was revealed in the tone of many reviews, which tended to mask political disagreement under aesthetic complaint. It is instructive to compare the enthusiasm of the critical response to a successful version of another Aeschylean tragedy, *Suppliants*, which has shown how 'politically correct' opinions can be so diluted as to take the visceral punch out of Greek tragedy altogether. Charles Mee's *Big Love* is an amusing sex comedy,[66] which 'turns Aeschylus into a chocolate for the knowing bourgeoisie...happy to consume culture that is wacky, well-pedigreed, and watered down'.[67] But Harrison is uncompromising in his awareness of the problem in using elite Western art to represent Western non-elites as well as non-Westerners (as in *Aikin Mata* and *Phaedra Britannica*). The father in *Prometheus* has a healthy hatred for the classical books that dominate the education and culture of his masters. As the cynical Iraqi says to the Harrison in 'A Cold Coming',

> That's your job, poet, to pretend
> I want my foe to be my friend.

'The scream of Orpheus': *Metamorpheus* (2000)

Harrison's last Classics-themed film developed his longstanding interest in Orpheus. Long before, in 'Guava Libre' (1975), he had identified himself with the mythical bard in a poem about Jane Fonda, then leading other feminists in a campaign against the Vietnam War. Orpheus was a symbol of all poets in *The Kaisers of Carnuntum* and would be again in 'Queuing for Charon' (2001). Like *The Gaze of the Gorgon* and *Prometheus*, *Metamorpheus* includes several statues, here carved Bulgarian representations of Orpheus. It was screened on BBC 2 on 17 December 2000.

Metamorpheus is his work in the filmic medium most concentrated on the details of a single version of a myth, in a self-conscious manner which Antony Rowland has described as similar to Ezra Pound's, especially in the visual and aural deployment of Harrison's 'Orpheus' notebook as the film's source.[68] It shows his skills at 'prosodic motion' at their most developed, for example in the juxtaposition of the phrase 'twists and turns of my obsession' with footage of a child speeding down a winding flume in a waterpark.[69] But it is also the most metapoetic of Harrison's films. Its focus is the theme of poetry and the divergent ways it is treated by poets and the public on the one hand and within academe on the other. Poets are represented by Orpheus and Tony Harrison, who appears in person and on whose head Orpheus' decapitated head is modelled; academics are represented by 'The Professor', Harrison's friend Oliver Taplin, and Otto Kern, the editor of the canonical edition of Orphic texts, *Orphicorum Fragmenta* (1922).

Orpheus becomes the founding father of all poetry while his dismembered head and lyre are followed on a forty-four-minute journey from the Thracian mountains to Lesbos, called 'the most songful of all islands' by an elegiac poet, Phanocles, of the late fourth century BCE. Phanocles' poem, to which Taplin had drawn Harrison's attention, is the movie's ancient co-text. It does not explore the familiar story of Orpheus' love and loss of Eurydice. The tale narrated in both poem and film is Orpheus' love for a handsome youth named Kalais, his murder by the women of Thrace because 'he was the first to reveal gay male love to the Thracians and did not recommend desire for women',[70] and the journey taken by his dismembered head and lyre down river and across the sea.

Several features distinguish this film from the other three discussed here. First, it is Harrison's longest engagement with the theme of homosexuality since the problematic misogynist Hercules of *Medea: A Sex-War Opera*. Harrison's depiction of the gay Orpheus is unremittingly sympathetic:

homophobia is presented in an important sequence, on the three-sided border of Bulgaria, Turkey and Greece, as equivalent to crass nationalism. The first sequence riffs playfully on meanings of the term 'bugger', and a few minutes later the camera caresses the profile of a beautiful young Bulgarian man, which is then 'supered over' by the face of a youth on an ancient vase; later, attention is drawn to the 'adoring male admirers' of Orpheus, dressed in Thracian costume, on a dazzling red-figured krater.[71] The camera lingers on female couples sunbathing, the most famous of all poets from Lesbos being 'Sappho, the tenth Muse, whose love poetry to her girlfriends gave the name of Lesbos to love between women'; this sentence is in prose because it is delivered by the Professor.[72]

Second, Orpheus' supernatural power to entrance animals gives Harrison an opportunity to use landscape and footage of wildlife, neither of which is often a preoccupation of his dominantly urban-centred poetry. Enhanced by Blackford's exquisite score, the lyre, hurled into the river by the Thracian women, drifts through the air in slow motion, before landing in the water, through which it swirls to rippling harp music. Wonderful shots of wildlife are intercut with Orpheus' drifting lyre and head: butterflies, eagles, wildcats, blackbirds, boars, magpies, pelicans, woodpeckers, seagulls, snakes and grasshoppers. Farm animals also feature, whether donkeys working by the river, a herd of goats in an industrial landscape, or the cows who wade and drink in a luxuriant sequence while Orpheus' lyre, itself made from a tortoise shell, floats past them. This allows Harrison to make a resounding intertextual visual reference to the lyre invented by Hermes in *Trackers*.

But the theme which dominates the film's emotional and intellectual registers is the friction between poetry and scholarship. This is reproduced formally in the alternation between the poet's verse (Harrison speaks in the second half of the film from Orpheus' dismembered head) and the Professor's academic sequences in prose. Taplin rose to the challenge, and his eloquent yet accessible explanations of the Orpheus myth, and how it related to his physical surroundings, make fascinating documentary television in themselves.[73] Yet they also seem designed by Harrison to make the film's viewer/listener eagerly anticipate their closure so that we can hear the magic of verse and music again. The film begins with Harrison explaining that he has invited the Professor to retrace the Orphic journey, because scholarship 'could open those locked

Orphic doors'.[74] By the end of the film, however, Harrison's voice figures scholarship as the enemy of poetry, or at least deaf to the suffering of humanity expressed in poetry and symbolized by the cruel death of Orpheus:

> I think it needs that ancient scream
> to pierce the skulls of academe.

Harrison and Taplin had been friends since the *Oresteia* nearly two decades earlier.[75] Something happened to estrange them during the filming of *Metamorpheus* (they have since become reconciled), but neither has spoken publicly about the rift.

The tone is at times surprisingly hostile and personalized. The poet recalls his invitation to Taplin, when he said, 'You've got the leisure and the long vacs', and that the food and wine would be good: 'you can have a trip/ half-scoffing and half scholarship'.[76] Taplin is shown eating in two sequences, with close-ups on his mouth; Harrison comments after the Professor is shown leaving a restaurant, 'Typical scholar! Scoffs his fill/ and leaves the poet to pay the bill.'[77] The film also alternates sequences of Bulgarians at hard physical work, farming, waiting tables and grave-digging, with sequences in which Taplin is seated. In one, he lies asleep on a boat, an academic book placed across his eyes to shade them from the sun.

The Professor, it seems, has become a target for the poet's class anger about the security, sense of entitlement and comforts guaranteed by a bourgeois professional salary and lifestyle. How far had Harrison always intended the film to make a statement about the rival claims to poetry staked by artists and academics? Does *Metamorpheus*, alternatively, reflect developments during its filming, and thus offer a unique insight into how Harrison's emotions interact with his art directly as it is being created? He never showed the script to Taplin before finalizing the edit of the film, so we shall probably never know.

8

'Witnessed horror': *Fram* (2008) and Harrison's Euripides

> A messenger who's thought about the things he's seen and not an unmediated image thrown on to a screen show's a human mind and heart's had time to brood on the witnessed horror...
>
> (Gilbert Murray, in *Fram*)

Euripides in Sevastopol

In 2008 I had lunch with Harrison in his favourite London restaurant, the Café Koha in St. Martin's Court off the Charing Cross Road, and showed him two photographs. One was a recent snap of the northernmost Greek theatre ever excavated. It lies outside Sevastopol in Crimea, founded as a Russian city on the site of an ancient Greek city-state known as Tauric Chersonesos.[1] The other was a copy of a photograph from the National Army Museum, taken in 1855, during the Crimean War, also near Sevastopol. The work of Roger Fenton, the first war photographer, it depicted Lieutenant-Colonel William Munro and other members of the 39th (Dorsetshire) Regiment of Foot outside their barracks.[2] I was researching a book on Euripides' tragedy *Iphigenia among the Taurians*, better known by its Latin title *Iphigenia in Tauris*, which is set in the ancient Tauric Chersonites' sanctuary of their maiden goddess, equivalent to Artemis. I had discovered that Colonel Munro had overseen the collection of ancient Greek objects discovered by British soldiers around their camps.[3]

The British soldiers, including many Irish, came across chunks of masonry and ancient artefacts – fragments of sculpture and vases – an engraving of which was published in the *Illustrated London News*.[4] They took them to

Colonel Munro. He had arrived on the screw steamer *Golden Fleece* (suitably named for a Black Sea voyage!) at the port of Balaclava, as the siege-lines around Sevastopol were tightening. The bulk of the time was spent in the trenches. It was attrition warfare, but the Colonel found compensations. He was something of an intellectual, an antiquarian and botanist who corresponded with Queen Victoria.

The educated officer class became aware that their camp was situated near the setting of *Iphigenia in Tauris*. The cliffs on the Crimean coast, still known as the 'Parthenit' or 'Parthenizza' promontory, from the maiden goddess, the *Parthenos*, was the site where some English marines created their encampment in the winter of 1854–5.[5] It was thought to be the location of the temple in Euripides' play. Rumours spread that one of the churches in the area 'was remarkable as being evidently a beautiful Greek temple, metamorphosed into a Christian church, into whose walls the bases and capitals of Ionic columns and other parts of Greek architecture had been built'. These words were written by the artist William Simpson in association with this scene which he drew in 1855 for his book *The Seat of War in the East*.[6]

My plan was to persuade Harrison to translate *Iphigenia in Tauris* and stage it in the ancient Tauric theatre itself. Sadly, this site-specific project was never realized, despite our memorable reconnaissance visit to (then Ukrainian) Crimea and the ancient theatre in September 2011. V. I. Putin made that impossible when Russia re-annexed the peninsula soon afterwards. What did transpire, after Harrison became Leverhulme Artist in Residence at Royal Holloway University of London, where I was then employed, was a new play set at Sevastopol during the Crimean War. But it featured a 'play-within-the-play', a version of the Euripidean tragedy, enacted in the camp by soldiers in costumes, including women's gowns, looted from local aristocratic houses. Harrison had uncovered evidence that such cross-dressed theatricals had taken place in both the British and the French camps during the siege of Sevastopol.

Iphigenia in Crimea stars a philhellene Lieutenant who is the best friend of Colonel Monroe (as the British press usually spelt the name). In the play-within-the-play he takes the roles of both Iphigenia and the *ex machina* goddess Athena. Harrison had remembered the real Lieutenant-Colonel standing second from the left in Fenton's photograph: his name was Robert Tinley. Perhaps the working-class Sergeant in Harrison's play, who takes the role of

Thoas, the uncouth Taurian king, is a response to the tall figure of Sergeant Major Joseph Jobberns in the photograph, on the far right of his senior officers.

The play premiered on BBC Radio 3 on Sunday 23 April 2017, directed by Emma Harding, with Blake Ritson as the Lieutenant and John Dougall as the Sergeant.[7] Here is the speech in which the Lieutenant explains to the Sergeant how the passion for ancient Greece which he shares with Monroe inspires him to produce *Iphigenia in Tauris* in Tauris – Tauric Chersonesos – itself:

> Colonel Monroe and I, both classicists when young,
> spoke to each other in the ancient tongue,
> and in the temple of Athena, with champagne,
> toasted the glory to be gained in this campaign.
> We didn't want to leave but bore the loss
> by remembering Greeks built Chersonesos,
> the very place, this place, lest we forget,
> where Euripides' *Iphigenia*'s set.
> The ancient Greeks helped both of us withdraw
> from the dire demands of 1854,
> me into poetry, the Colonel into pots.
> In old Chersonesos he's dug up lots.
> Whenever the action starts abating
> the Colonel sends his men out excavating.
> The Colonel has what's excavated crated
> to be shipped back home to be appreciated.
> In every break in fighting, each small lull
> his men race to get the Colonel's crates packed full,
> fragments of antiquity piled high,
> lamps, bronze coins, terracotta, amphorae . . .
> For me when there are brief lulls in the fray
> I'll read a line or two out of my play,
> the one by Euripides that takes place here
> in this particular bit of old Crimea.
> I study the text I started at eighteen
> and carried with me everywhere I've been.
> In my cabin on long voyages, in my tent
> the play went with me everywhere I went.
> Already I know all of it by heart
> and could, if called upon, play every part.

> If you don't believe me, Sergeant, I'll recite
> the whole damn thing in Greek one peaceful night.
> SERGEANT
> What an honour, sir! LIEUTENANT. Sergeant, you're too kind!
> SERGEANT [*aside*] You must be out of your posh little mind.[8]

In a manner similar to *Trackers*, the elite associations of classical literature for the British gentleman educated in the imperial nineteenth century are examined in a distant location, where fragments of antiquity are surfacing, and are undercut by a low-status interlocutor. This chapter closes with a brief return to the Iphigenia and Black Sea themes in Harrison's work.

His response to the photograph of the Crimea officers is hardly the first time that photographs have proved seminal in Harrison's creative processes. We saw earlier that the disorientation of the poet in 'Newcastle is Peru' is encapsulated in the final visual image, a photograph he sees in a newspaper.[9] 'A Cold Coming', one of his most celebrated poems, was inspired by Ken Jarecke's unforgettable photograph (1991) of an Iraqi soldier burned alive struggling to escape his truck on the road to Basra during the Gulf War. The picture is so shocking that the American media originally refused to publish it, although *The Observer* and *Libération* in France were less pusillanimous.[10] This poem, which records the voice of the dead Iraqi, the features of his hideously burned face bizarrely reminiscent of the Greek tragic mask, expresses Harrison's understanding of the relationship between this mask and the public witnessing of agony: the Iraqi asks the authorial voice, 'Isn't it your sort of poet's task to find words for this frightening mask?'[11] This trope and the allusions to dead babies and bereaved mothers suggest that the ancient text dominant in Harrison's mind was here Euripides' *Trojan Women*, on which, as we shall see, he had recently been working.

Greek tragedy is a masked art; wearing a mask can, paradoxically, permit the viewing of the unviewable. As Nietzsche put it in *The Birth of Tragedy*, Dionysiac art compels us to gaze into the horror of existence, yet without being turned into stone by what we see.[12] In the programme note to his *Oresteia*, Harrison developed this Nietzschean idea by suggesting that the Greek tragic mask allows its wearers to keep their eyes open in situations of extremity, just a visor allows a welder to look into the flame. This powerful simile is suggestive for the function of the genre as a whole. To watch a thoughtfully directed

Greek tragedy is to assume an aesthetic mask through which we can bear to contemplate extremity.

This idea is similar to one of the most brilliant arguments Aristotle proposed in defence of all mimetic art: artistic representations of reality are educative precisely because they allow us to contemplate horrific things 'which cause us pain to witness in reality' (*Poetics* 4.1448b 10–12). Aristotle cites the examples of disgusting creatures and human corpses. We can't bear to look upon the corpses of the Iraqis our own soldiers and pilots have killed, nor on our own angry poor we have created by class war and unemployment, and have difficulty even imagining an art form adequate to the representation of the subjectivity of the millions of dead victims of the Holocaust. But through the familiar, formal lineaments of Greek tragedy, by peering, at first cautiously, through its mask, even the countless forgotten people whose suffering we have permitted can be briefly remembered, rendered faintly visible and audible. Theodor Adorno may have said that writing poetry after Auschwitz was barbaric, but he qualified this by also saying that 'suffering has as much right to expression as a tortured man to scream'; at the height of the Vietnam War, Walter Kaufmann argued that the value of tragedy lies in its 'refusal to let any comfort, faith, or joy deafen our ears to the tortured cries of our brethren'.[13]

Within Harrison's *oeuvre*, the themes of photography and Euripidean tragedy are intertwined, especially in *Fram*, where photography is discussed by Gilbert Murray, the most significant translator of Euripides for the British stage of all time. Euripides' exquisite messenger speeches, embedded reportage charged with horror and pathos, usually delivered by nameless lower-class onlookers, have been instrumental in shaping Harrison's core concept of poetry as witness. The language of Euripidean messengers lies behind his analogy between tragic poetry and a mask through which we can contemplate otherwise unbearable horror.

Crimea has contemplated barbaric wars over its long history. Blood has been spilt over groups struggling for control of Crimea by ancient and Byzantine Greeks, Cimmerians, Scythians, Venetians, Genovese, Romans, Goths, Huns, Bulgars, Kipchaks, Tatars, Eastern Slavs from Kiev, Mongols and Ottomans. Eight thousand Tatars died when Stalin ordered their deportation from Crimea; the atrocities committed by the Nazis in the Second World War at Sevastopol, Simferopol and Kerch were almost indescribable. But the Crimean War (1853–6), as the first war to be recorded in photographs, has a particular status in the history of trauma. It was to play a major role in the inauguration of the witnessing of human misery via visual media.

Harrison had translated Aeschylus' *Oresteia* for the National Theatre, and adapted the Aeschylean *Prometheus Bound* into a feature-length film poem. He had embedded Sophocles' *Trackers* into a new play entitled *Trackers of Oxyrhynchus*. But his contact with the third great Athenian tragedian, Euripides, at least over the last twenty years, has been more extensive than with either of the others. It is the difficulties some of his Euripidean endeavours have encountered which have obscured the instrumentality of Euripides in his total project.

Harrison's Hecubas

Harrison's earliest meeting with any Greek tragedian may have been when a teacher at Leeds Grammar School made him play the Cyclops in Shelley's translation of Euripides' satyr drama *Cyclops*, on the insensitive ground that his working-class Leeds accent befitted the uncouth man-eating giant.[14] If so, his first lines will have been these iambic pentameters:

> What is this tumult? Bacchus is not here,
> Nor tympanies nor brazen castanets.
> How are my young lambs in the cavern? Milking
> Their dams or playing by their sides? And is
> The new cheese pressed into the bull-rush baskets?
> Speak! I'll beat some of you till you rain tears –
> Look up, not downwards when I speak to you.[15]

When the Cyclops has been blinded, however, the drama ends not without pathos as the lonely giant staggers around, doleful and in pain. This early encounter with satyr drama bore fruit when Harrison was drawn to the fragments of Sophocles' sayiric *Trackers* in later life.

The other recollection concerns Harrison's work in a local brewery. In a 2013 interview with the award-winning sports writer Anthony Clavane, who is also now an Associate Lecturer at the London College of Communication, Harrison said that self-deprecation was in the very bloodstream of Yorkshire working-class writers:

We have gone back, though. You just think 'what's the point of doing it?' I tried to reclaim great poetry in northern English. It was written in an alliterative style, for being outside in the street, in places like Leeds market, where I worked. And the music hall inspired a lot of my theatre. I saw Laurel and Hardy live. I went to Leeds music hall and I'd take my homework.

But what homework did the grammar school boy deemed clever enough for the top Classics stream take with him to the music hall?

I'd have Aristophanes in my pocket, or Euripides. I used to work as a barrel roller in Tetley's. I found an old note where I was trying to devise a Greek chorus out of people working in Tetley's. It was an amazing place. I drew on the rhythmical energy of the workmen for my poems and plays.[16]

It is *Euripides* whom Harrison here names in connection with his ambition to create theatrical choruses vocalizing their thoughts in working-class accents, turning the rhythmical energy of the demotic outdoor speech of northern factories into great poetry.

Four qualities of Euripides have made his dramas offer the perfect model for Harrison's distinctive approach to drama. First, he was famous in antiquity for giving his tragic characters speech that sounded natural, contemporary and everyday: Aristotle claimed that Euripides had been the first dramatist ever to do this (*Rhetoric* III.2.5). Second, he was perceived as giving lower-class characters and women more important roles than the other tragedians: in Aristophanes' *Frogs* he claims to have made tragedy more 'democratic' by allowing women and slaves talk as much and as well as male masters of households (949–52). Third, Euripides was renowned for the beauty of his songs, which were popular hits, the music-hall classics of his era. They were supposedly learned off by heart even by the ordinary Athenian soldiers imprisoned in the quarries of Syracuse in Sicily in 413 BCE (Plutarch, *Life of Nicias* 29). But fourth, Euripides was regarded as the most tragic of the poets, as Aristotle deems him (*Poet.* 1453a29–30), because his plays were the most effective at eliciting the tragic emotions of pity and of terror. Amongst other things, he pioneered the use of dying or bereaved children in the evocation of the extremities of human pain.[17]

The Greek tragedy which in antiquity was held to possess almost miraculous power to make its spectators feel pity was by Euripides.[18] Harrison knew that, according to Plutarch, it could reduce even the cruellest tyrant to tears (*Life of*

Pelopidas, 29).¹⁹ It was his *Trojan Women*, mentioned above in relation to 'A Cold Coming'. *Trojan Women* depicted the sufferings of Hecuba and Andromache, the grandmother and mother of the murdered Astyanax, whose corpse is prepared for burial on stage, and mother and wife of the warrior Hector, whose corpse was brutally mutilated. This play and *Herakles* have been two of the handful of works of world literature which I believe have most fruitfully informed Harrison's creativity, even though, paradoxically, no translation by him of either of them has ever been performed.

Harrison already engaged with Euripides during his creation of *Phaedra Britannica*, in which his fascinating hybrid poetic form formed a slow, intense crescendo towards the affecting rhetoric of the 'messenger speech' where Burleigh, Thomas' tutor, reports the young man's death. A monstrous apparition, perhaps sent by the god Siva, has terrified the cavalcade of horses in which he was riding:

> The horses panic. A regular stampede!
> He calls out to his own. They take no heed.
> The one he's riding bolts and all in vain
> he shouts *whoa, whoa*, and tugs upon the rein.
> He wastes his strength. From each champed bit
> flies froth and slaver and blood-red spit.²⁰

But the first staging of a Harrison translation, rather than adaptation, of a Euripidean tragedy did not come until March 2005 and his ill-starred *Hecuba*, starring Vanessa Redgrave, which premiered at Albery Theatre in London (now renamed the Noël Coward Theatre). Behind this text, once again, there lies a photograph which had impressed Harrison: it shows refugees from Anatolia crammed into the Opera House in Athens in 1922, after the mass 'exchange of populations' between Greece and Turkey, an event which the Greeks call, simply, '*the* catastrophe'. Women are seen hanging blankets over the theatre boxes to try to achieve a degree of privacy for their desperate, homeless families.²¹ But Harrison's notebooks reveal that it was the plight of the tortured, raped and consequently often pregnant Iraqi women prisoners in the prison at Abu Ghraib which fed the anger palpable in this translation.²²

I was official RSC classical consultant on this production, early in the process, when Laurence Boswell was directing it. The women of the chorus were miserable, and found Boswell's directorial style macho and intimidating, even humiliating (their words) which felt painful given the position of the women they were representing – captive slave women subject to violence and rape at the hands of their new masters. I was invited to write an essay for the theatre programme, and Boswell demanded that I change it since it did not entirely fit with his own un-nuanced interpretation of the play; I have written dozens of such essays and never received a request to rewrite one from any other director. The relationships between Boswell and Redgrave and Boswell and Harrison were inflammable. These psychological conditions were obviously not right to make great theatre, and the critics pounced.[23]

Once Harrison took over the direction and led the production to Washington, DC and Delphi, it became much more dramatically effective and successful.[24] What was lost in the kerfuffle surrounding the show was the excellence of Harrison's translation.[25] Euripides has found few translators capable of combining his grace and pungency in contemporary language. But Harrison's sprung blank verse rhythm, interspersed with occasional rhyming couplets and shorter lines to reflect the Greek lyric sections, and his sensitivity to Euripides' rhetorical fireworks, especially his imagery and alliteration, produced a remarkable modern playscript.

Harrison's *Hecuba* also did justice to Euripides' exploration of the notion of the witnessing of atrocity. The chorus emphasize the visual impact of the fall of Troy: 'I had to watch my husband hacked/ to bloody pieces.../ I see Troy recede and know its streets are blackened rubble, craters, weeds.'[26] The death of Polyxena is described twice, once predictively by Polyxena herself. When told she is to be sacrificed to appease the ghost of Achilles, she is concerned that her mother will have to *see* her die:

> Now you'll have to watch men grab
> your uncoralled and cragbred cub.
> You'll have to watch it happen,
> being torn from your loving hug.
> Sacrificed, spread-eagled, struck,
> my girl's gullet slashed open.
> despatched down to the world below
> where dead Polyxena will lie.[27]

The second narration of her death is longer, and is delivered by the Greek herald Talthybius. Hecuba wants to know how her daughter's life ended, saying to him, 'Speak, though your words, I know, will break my heart.'²⁸ Talthybius is reluctant, saying that it will reduce him again to the tears he wept as he watched the atrocity, but then delivers one of the most affecting 'messenger speeches' in Greek tragedy, emphasizing the piteous sight of the solitary young woman facing so many ranks of armed men.²⁹

The tension between seeing somebody suffer and listening to an account of their suffering becomes almost unbearable after Hecuba inveigles Polymestor into the tent. Harrison extracts the maximum possible effect from the remarkable feature of this play, that the same assault on the Thracian father and his children is represented three times in speedy succession. First, we hear his screams from backstage and his laments for his butchered sons, even though we may not witness the violence itself. Then Polymestor emerges, blinded and on all fours, to sing a wild song which functions as a sort of messenger speech-aria explaining his reactions to the violence. Finally, with the arrival of Agamemnon, Polymestor delivers his own formal, rhetorical messenger speech. The victim becomes both the chief witness and the prosecutor, evoking the most powerful pictures in the audience's minds, a process reinforced by the pitiful sight of his own now sightless eyes.³⁰

The other Euripidean tragedy dominated by the ageing queen of Troy, *Trojan Women*, has been central to Harrison's conception of Greek theatre. He revealed this almost in passing during his Presidential Address 'Facing up to the Muses' to the Classical Association on Tuesday 12 April 1988, at the University of Bristol. He said that he saw the very first words of Hecuba to herself in *Trojan Women*, *ana, dysdaimon*, 'Lift your head up, unlucky one' (98), as a 'motto for the tragic mask, an injunction to present itself suffering and all to the audience'. The mask enables us 'to gaze on the terror and not turn to stone'.³¹ More than twenty years before his *Hecuba*, he written a play entitled *The Common Chorus* to support the women protesting at the Greenham Common US missile base. He imagined these Peace Camp women performing two ancient Greek dramas 'for the benefit of the guards behind the wire who were defending the silos where the weapons of our ultimate extinction were stored'.³² Part 1 (which was once performed at the University of Leeds) was based on Aristophanes' *Lysistrata*, while Part 2 was based on Euripides' *Trojan Women*.

In this *Trojan Women*, Harrison used the clairvoyant Cassandra to conjure before the audience's eyes vivid scenes of militarism, violence and bereavement.

The herald Talthybius also describes Andromache's parting with the corpse of her baby son. Yet again, a spectacular photograph had stimulated Harrison's poetic and theatrical creativity: taken in 1983 by Raissa Page, it recorded women dancing hand-in-hand in a circle on top of a Greenham Common missile silo.[33] He has said that he likes to imagine both Lysistrata and Hecuba in their midst, that the presence of nuclear weapons at this deadlocked stage of the Cold War 'made us stare into the face of oblivion', and that it is our responsibility, therefore, to listen as the 'later mortals' to whom she 'commits the suffering of her women at the end of *The Trojan Women*'.[34] As his Lysistrata says, a nuclear holocaust would destroy the entire record of human culture, including the very texts that by recording past agonies might have persuaded us to avoid conflict in our own time:

> In the Third World War we'll destroy
> not only modern cities but the memory of Troy,
> stories that shaped the spirit of our race
> are held in the balance in this missile base.
> Remember, if you can, that with man goes the mind
> that might have made sense of the Hist'ry of Mankind.
> It's a simple thing to grasp: when we're all dead
> there'll be no further pages to be read,
> not even leaflets, and no peace plays like these,
> no post-holocaust Aristophanes.[35]

'And no post-holocaust Euripides either! No Hecuba entrusting her story to the future,' Harrison adds to his quotation of this passage in the Introduction to *The Common Chorus*.[36]

Fram: 'always-open-eyes'

Harrison's other Euripidean early venture was *Medea: A Sex-War Opera* (1985), discussed above in Chapter 5. It included a version of the child-slaying sequence from Euripides' *Herakles* as well. But in *Fram*, the role of Euripides' *Herakles* in distilling Harrison's views on the Greek tragic messenger speech – the role of poetry in witnessing and recording horror – is given its most mature form. *Fram* is opened by Gilbert Murray, the Greek scholar who died in 1957.

The frame story is set fifty years later, when he emerges from his Memorial in Westminster Abbey. Murray has himself written a play about the Norwegian explorer Fridtjof Nansen and asks the spirit of Aeschylus to assist him. But Murray was more closely identified with the tragedian Euripides. He published the most influential book on Euripides of all time, *Euripides and his Age*, in 1913.[37]

Fram is a complex play. Two of its dimensions are related to Harrison's engagement with Euripides' *Herakles*. First, the relationship between the depressive and ultimately suicidal Hjalmar Johansen and the Herculean figure of Nansen, thrown together in a horrifying ordeal during Nansen's attempted expedition to the North Pole in 1893–6. This echoes the last part of Euripides' play, which consists of an extended dialogue between Herakles, who has in a psychotic fit killed his wife and children and is now suicidal, and Theseus, his old friend whom he had rescued from Hades in the last, terrifying labour, the Underworld expedition.

But the most Euripidean aspect of *Fram* is its discussion of the power of language, and especially of poetry performed by skilled actors, to evoke agony. This theme is materially signified on stage by the tragic mask picked up by different characters. Harrison makes Murray argue doggedly that poetry is the most powerful medium for conveying the experience of others. While his actress Sybil Thorndike gets changed, Murray lifts a tragic mask to his face and gives a short lecture to the audience on one line from Euripides' *Herakles*:

> And while you are doing that I'm going to cover mine
> to initiate our effort with one ancient tragic line.
> *Gilbert Murray enters with the mask of Greek Tragedy. He holds
>   it before his face.*
> οὐκ ἄν τις εἴποι μᾶλλον ἢ πεπόνθαμεν.   (Eur. *Herc.*, 916)
> *Revealing himself, and placing mask downstage centre.*
>
> No to cast aspersions on your state of education,
> But is anyone out there in need of a translation?
> Let me see a show of hands. O, I see, quite a lot.
> No fellow classicists? Obviously not!
> οὐκ ἄν τις εἴποι μᾶλλον ἢ πεπόνθαμεν (*Herakles*),
> one of the greatest tragedies of the great Euripides.
> The messenger enters. His first words in Greek are these:

οὐκ ἄν τις εἴποι μᾶλλον ἢ πεπόνθαμεν.
What he's saying's that the horror that's occurred's
too terrible for anyone to put into mere words.
And then from line nine-two-two to ten-fifteen
he lets us know in detail the horrors that he's seen.
Ninety-three lines in graphic, passionate succession
giving the unspeakable poetical expression.
Forgive the ancient Greek. I'm only showing off.
   He bows.
Gilbert Murray, classicist, translator, prof.[38]

Murray then explains that has written a play about Nansen because he had been a great humanitarian. They had helped found the League of Nations together; Nansen had worked tirelessly to further the safe repatriation of refugees and the provision of passports for the stateless. But of the two friends, only Murray survived to witness the carnage of the Second World War, and the notion of witnessing brings him back to the theme of Greek tragedy:

> To speak of the war's atrocities is an almost hopeless task
> even for this open-mouthed and eloquent Greek mask.
> I happen to believe that the ancient tragic speech
> is the highest form of eloquence a man can hope to reach.[39]

The play asks whether tragic poetry is the most effective form of eloquence by comparing the power of different media to record suffering and arouse emotions that will make audiences take action in response. The question dominates the climactic scene of Part I, at a meeting in London in 1922 of several parties raising money to alleviate an urgent humanitarian catastrophe.

The test case is the 1921–2 Povolzhye famine in the Volga region of Russia, when an estimated five million people starved to death. We hear a cruel, sardonic account of how an inappropriately fat Isadora Duncan had performed a dance called *The Russian Famine* in Moscow in order to call attention to the unfolding disaster. The philanthropist Eglantyne Jebb watches a film publicizing the famine made by the *Save the Children Fund*; she compares the effectiveness of colour and monochrome movies and of drawings and photographs; she also muses on the possibility of images being projected into people's sitting rooms, by devices which Harrison's National Theatre audiences, with the benefit of hindsight, recognized laughingly as television sets. Yet she criticizes the more sensational techniques used in the films made by the Herbert Hoover's American Relief Administration, represented at the meeting by the cynical emissary Sheldon. Nansen is giving public lectures on the disaster, and makes full use of shocking, even obscene still photographs to reinforce his message. But Murray is convinced that new media must not be allowed to eclipse the unique power of messages delivered by the crafted spoken word, and he speaks to Nansen:

> The tragic mask for me has come to symbolise
> the art of facing horror with always-open eyes.
> No eyelids on a tragic mask. It has no choice but see
> and its mouth is always open to utter poetry.[40]

Murray gradually builds his arguments, and in due course delivers a speech which I believe is the nearest thing Harrison has ever written to a personal artistic manifesto, beginning with the lines quoted as the epigraph at the beginning of this essay. Murray becomes forthright. Poetry was invented for this purpose:

> to give focus to our suffering and to our pain
> and the more it's done through language the more we'll stay humane.
> Reliance on devices like the photograph and slide
> will lead, I rather fear, to linguistic suicide.[41]

His theory is put into practice by Sybil Thorndike's searing monologue in the persona of a starving woman of the Volga, one of the most virtuoso speeches Harrison has ever composed, and which was performed at the National Theatre with unforgettable power by his long-term partner, Sian Thomas. And Thorndike precedes it by quoting one of Harrison's favourite poets, Shelley: '"The greatest instrument of moral good",/that's the imagination.'[42]

Gilbert Murray's example

Earlier in *Fram*, Thorndike had reminded Gilbert Murray that they collaborated on several productions of Greek tragedies, as the two did in reality:

> You're the last person needs reminding that in my long career
> I have given my Clytemnestra, Hecuba, Medea.[43]

It was as a still young man in his twenties, when he retired in 1889 on the grounds of ill-health from the Chair of Greek at Glasgow, that Murray embarked on five years in which he worked to make Euripides available to a range of different audiences: to scholars through his Oxford Classical Text Edition of the plays, and to readers without Greek through his published verse translations. These translations found realization in important stage productions. Harrison's interest in Murray is partly a reflection of Harrison's deep knowledge of the earlier history of Greek tragedy on the British stage.

Greek tragedy was first performed in English in professional theatres in the Edwardian era, when the pioneering director Harley Granville Barker directed Murray's verse translations of Euripides from 1904 onwards, at the Court Theatre, the Savoy and other, mainly London, venues. With the exception of *Hecuba*, all the Euripidean plays which have been reimagined in stage versions by Harrison – *Hippolytus* in *Phaedra Britannica*, *Medea* in *Medea: A Sex-War Opera*, *Trojan Women* in *The Common Chorus* and *Iphigenia in Tauris* in *Iphigenia in Crimea* – were those staged by Harley Granville Barker (although he did two more, *Electra* in 1906 and *Bacchae* in 1908, as well). This overlap can be no coincidence: Harrison chooses ancient plays because they have something to say to modernity, and so did Granville Barker; both of them were working at times when the unequal position of women was under a spotlight, and this is reflected in the choice of plays. Harrison knows his theatre history backwards, and recognizes in Gilbert Murray one of his principal forebears.

The Edwardian Euripides experiment began with *Hippolytus* in May 1904 at the Lyric Theatre. The tragedy had a powerful effect and was felt to be shockingly 'modern'.[44] The second Granville Barker/Murray collaboration on *Trojan Women* in 1905, however, foreshadowed Harrison's concept of a political theatre. This production marks the first time a staging of a translated Greek tragedy, rather than a rewriting as a neoclassical tragedy, had ever been used, at least in Britain, as a form of political protest. The suffering of the women of Troy intentionally evoked the shameful treatment of Boer women and children in specially designed concentration camps (this was the first time this sinister term was used) by Britain during the Anglo-Boer War of 1899–1902. Murray had already gained a reputation for being an outspoken critic of the war – a deeply unfashionable position. He had sponsored the South African Conciliation Committee, which recognized that European imperialism in Africa was the cause of the crisis. He had also donated the then significant sum of £100 to the Boer Women and Children's Hardship Fund.[45]

The performance was harrowing and liked less than *Hippolytus* by the critics. Max Beerbohm, no political radical, criticized it for being far too 'penitential'.[46] Murray's old friend Leonard Hobhouse, a committed liberal thinker, could not even bear to watch it, writing to Murray to explain why: the production was too chillingly reminiscent of the suffering of the Boers at British hands. This play 'revived troubles that lie too near'.[47] Of all Greek tragedies, only *Trojan Women* and *Hecuba* confront their audience with women and children deported to prisoner-of-war camps while their homes burn. Only *Trojan Women* presents the corpse of a child, small enough to be carried into the theatre on his father's shield. The Edwardians were correct in assuming that Murray's version of this intense play, and its 1905 production, exemplified his 'pro-Boer' political stance.[48]

Harrison had researched the performance history of Murray's translation, including the Old Vic production starring Sybil Thorndike at the end of the First World War, in 1919. It was a fundraiser for the newly founded League of Nations, in which Gilbert Murray played a significant role.[49] It is discussed in *Fram*, when Murray is arguing that theatre can be help raise public awareness of concerns.

> We've raised money and subscribers to the *League of Nations*
> by playing the most popular of my Euripides translations,
> *The Trojan Women*, with Sybil in the lead.[50]

A moving photograph of Thorndike in the role of Hecuba, with the corpse of Astyanax in her arms (played by one of her own children), was seen by Harrison when he was writing *Fram*.[51]

The Granville Barker/Murray *Medea* of late 1907, staged at the Savoy Theatre, proved even more controversial. It was selected as appropriate for a year which had seen an upsurge of public interest in the movement for women's suffrage. In 1907, Gilbert Murray was a Fellow of New College, Oxford, before his appointment to the Regius Chair of Greek in 1908. Although he was later to distance himself from the militant wing of the women's suffrage movement, he had supported its aim since 1889. He believed that the ancient Greeks were 'the first nation that realised and protested against the subjection of women',[52] and Thorndike recalled him saying that *Medea* might have been written for the women's movement.⁵³ He knew the play would be found shocking. Granville Barker had moved his company to the capacious Savoy and was anxious, as he explained in a letter to Murray in the summer of 1907, to find 'something sensational' with which to open there.⁵⁴ The political climate must have made *Medea* seem an attractively 'sensational' choice.

The first Women's Parliament met at Caxton Hall in February 1907, and the first mass arrests of suffragettes shocked the public. No fewer than sixty-five served sentences in Holloway Prison. Several photographs familiar to Harrison preserve the electrifying moment when the well-known suffrage campaigner and actress Edythe Olive, who had impressed as the crazed Cassandra in the 1905 *Trojan Women*, emerged as Medea from her house in Corinth and lectured the audience on the injustices suffered by women.⁵⁵ There were gasps in response to her famous lines on cruelty of the dowry system, men's right to demand sex, the loneliness of housebound wives and the dangers of childbirth.⁵⁶ In *Euripides and his Age*, Murray writes, 'To us he seems an aggressive champion of women... Songs and speeches from the *Medea* are recited today at suffragist meetings.'⁵⁷ The actresses in the Granville Barker/Murray productions, including Sybil Thorndike who after the First World War was to become the most prominent performer of Murray's translations of Euripides, were all committed to the cause, Edythe Olive passionately so. She won the role of Medea against opposition from Granville Barker's wife Lillah McCarthy. McCarthy later starred as Hecuba in revivals of *Trojan Women* and as Iphigenia in the first, 1912 production, at the Kingsway Theatre, of Murray's translation of *Iphigenia in Tauris*. He had published it in 1910, by which time he was Regius Professor of Greek at Oxford.

This translation is outstanding. With its dialogue in his trademark archaizing rhyming couplets, and its lyrics in contrasting, rhythmically pointed verse forms, it created an alluring, antique atmosphere. Murray revelled in the multitude of rituals and the ceremonial language of the priestess of Artemis, even if his excessive archaism in the use of 'thy' and 'thee' instead of 'your' and 'you' was unfortunate.

> One lock of hair to wreathe thy tomb,
>   One tear: so far, so far am I
> From what to me and thee was home,
>   And where in all men's fantasy,
>   Butchered, O God! I also lie.⁵⁸

Although they were derided by T. S. Eliot,[59] as Murray resentfully recalls in *Fram*,[60] the public loved Murray's translations and found them deeply pleasurable to hear and perform.

Harrison has heard in the Murray translations the qualities that made them in their day so popular among a public far beyond the poetry-reading elite for whom the politically more reactionary classical modernists were writing, Eliot and Ezra Pound. Murray's verses are lively, varied, sonorous and notably speakable. Actors enjoyed delivering them as much as their audiences enjoyed hearing them. They made playscripts out of Greek tragedy that worked in theatrical *practice* in English-speaking theatres. No wonder Harrison has adopted Murray as a forefather.

The stones of Crimea

When I first suggested doing an *Iphigenia in Tauris* in Tauris/Sevastopol, Harrison was cautious. The play is a sometimes light-hearted escape drama with a problematically Hellenocentric view of the supposedly unenlightened barbarians of the Tauric Chersonese. In the event, he sidestepped this problem by his decision to have the play performed 'within the play' by a nineteenth-century British imperialist Lieutenant with whose ideology we are not invited to identify. One factor which persuaded Harrison to consider *Iphigenia in Tauris* was that it was one of the plays chosen for production by his adoptive ancestors – Murray, Granville Barker, and those suffragette actresses – in the practice of putting radical English-language verse translations of Greek tragedy on stage.

There were other reasons why Harrison agreed to this project, besides the poetic opportunity presented by its vivid messenger speeches. He has been haunted by murdered Iphigenia since the 1981 *Oresteia*; the strange tale of her life in exile after Artemis rescued her, told in *Iphigenia in Tauris*, allowed him to revisit some the same traumatized family half his own lifetime later. Russia, the Eastern Bloc countries of the former Soviet Union and the Black Sea have often featured in his previous work, from the Prague and St Petersburg/Leningrad poems in *The Loiners* and the use of the Argonautic myth's relationship to Georgia and the Black Sea in *A Maybe Day in Kazakhstan*

(1994) to *Prometheus* (1998). The project necessitated a reconnaissance trip to Crimea and the ancient Greek archaeological sites there, above all the theatre at Sevastopol itself. So in the late summer of 2011, Harrison, his archaeologist daughter Jane Harrison, his partner Sian Thomas and David Braund (a friend of mine who was until recently Professor of Black Sea Archaeology at the University of Exeter) spent a week in the digs and museums of southern Crimea. I learned about the place occupied in Harrison's creative processes by tactile, sensory, physical interaction with material environments and human encounters.

Besides his new play *Iphigenia in Crimea*, which Harrison wrote after that memorable Crimean adventure, it also produced 'Black Sea Aphrodite', first published in the *London Review of Books* in 2013. This starts from the mosaic made of large, coarse pebbles which we saw being reassembled for the first time since antiquity in the museum of Tauric Chersonesos:

> Chersonesos, Crimea. Archaeologists reassemble
> miscellaneous pebbles to restore Aphrodite
> found on the Black Sea the year of my birth,
> 1937, by Kiev's Prof. Belov.[61]

The image of the pebbles morphs from creative to destructive. The poem opens out to include women stoned for adultery, and the crazed Orestes at whom the local cowherds lobbed rocks in the first messenger speech of Euripides' *Iphigenia in Tauris* (307–33), a passage translated by Harrison in *Iphigenia in Crimea* like this:

> The foreigner collapses as his madness receded,
> his chops were all slobbery, and when we see him fallen
> to a man we start chucking rocks at the strangers.
> But the other foreigner wipes his friend's face of slaver
> and shields his body with his thick woven cloak
> making sure our missiles went wide of their mark,
> protecting his friend with an unselfish kindness.
> When he came to his senses he leaped to his feet
> and saw the numbers attacking and groaned aloud
> and went on being pelted with pebbles and stones.../..../
> We surrounded them and knocked their swords from their grasp
> with a barrage of stones.[62]

But 'Black Sea Aphrodite' ends by turning the pebbles/missiles back into something once again full of affirmative, generative power: a group Harrison calls 'we' joyfully swim in the straits of Kerch, the ancient city of Pantikapaion, between Crimea and the Taman peninsula:

> We bathe in the Black Sea then hold hands and run,
> surfing so much foam-born pebble potential,
> devotees of the goddess defying the stoners.

All five of us charged into the beautiful waters at the mouth of the Sea of Azov and swam for joy after a memorable visit to the dusty excavations at the Athenian settlement at Nymphaion, a few miles south of Kerch/Pantikapaion, on 7 September 2011. The beach looks across from the Athenian city to Russia, at the precise point of the Cimmerian Bosporus where Io of *Prometheus Bound* leapt from Europe into Asia, also the precise scene of our revel.

9

'Surviving the slopes of Parnassus': 'Polygons' (2015) and Other Poems

Autobiography of a radical poet-classicist

Harrison's elegy 'Polygons', published in the *LRB* in 2015, when he was in his late seventies, is his last long autobiographical poem. It provides the culmination to a series of such poems, since his pivotal 1969 'Newcastle is Peru' (discussed in Chapter 1), in which Harrison seems to commit, in his early thirties, to spending his life writing poems which annexed literary culture in the name of the colonized and oppressed in both hemispheres. He also seems to commit to fusing political commentary with a private dimension, which is almost always present in his poems (contrary to the opinion of some who have criticized him for a supposed lack of inwardness[1]). This concluding chapter traces the development of his self-crafted authorial persona across the decades until 'Polygons', nearly fifty years later. It asks how his authorial presence has been informed by his evolving engagements with classical and other canonical authors, especially the classical images in John Keats' odes.

After *The Loiners*, Harrison always wrote poems in his own 'I' voice to fuse personal experience with acerbic, public political commentary, as the archaic Greek island poets, Archilochus, Sappho and Alcaeus had done. Harrison seems to have made the decision to relinquish writing poems in voices other than his own at about the time of 'Newcastle is Peru'. He had even briefly experimented with a different master voice in prose with the Cuban revolutionary homophobe in his essay, 'Shango the Shaky Fairy', published in 1970.[2] A few other speakers feature in 'The White Queen' poems of *The Loiners* (1970), which are set in or engage with the colonization of Africa or America. The first, fourth and fifth Juvenalian poems, 'Saturae', 'Manica' and '*from* the

Zeg-Zag postcards', are delivered from the mouth of a white expatriate academic and homosexual suffering from venereal disease, 'an ageing, priapic Prufrock lusting through the wasteland of empire's dying days'.[3] The third poem, 'Travesties', purports to be a translation from Hieronymus Frascatorius' Latin epic poem *Syphilis* (1530), complete with routine references to Apollo and the siege of Troy, which alleged that this venereal disease was imported from the New World. But the second poem, 'The Railroad Heroides', shows that Harrison's own consciousness lies somewhere beneath all these poems, even if in different disguises.

It takes its title from the poetic love letters Ovid wrote in the voices of mythical women to men, but inverts the relationship. The speaker's identity does not become clear until two-thirds of the way through. He is on a train to Leeds after returning from Africa via Tenerife and France and is Harrison himself. He has left behind a Tuareg women with whom he'd had a sexual encounter, and writes to her hoping that her tribe has survived bloodshed and she is still alive. Harrison's own persona, it transpires, has not been unimplicated in the sexualization of colonized continents in the previous poem.

'The Railroad Heroides' is the most successful of the series, but the poems read together constitute an experiment with different voices addressing a single theme. The exercise may have helped Harrison to decide on the form best suited to his life's project. Some critics have taken exception to the way his personality and consciousness dominate his poems. Terms such as 'self-regarding' and 'egotistical' are sometimes to be found in reviews: Alan Brownjohn found Harrison's insights in *From 'The School of Eloquence'* 'hammered into crude containers for heavy irony and his very own brand of chip-on-the-shoulder coarseness'.[4] But Harrison would respond that elite individuals have never felt any need to apologize for writing in their own personas. Moreover, writing all his subsequent poems in his own voice does not mean that he relinquished his interest in recording the speech of others.

The bulk of his poems contain fragments of speech by a wide range of people, living and dead, which break through the first-person narrative and meditation, bringing a conversation, performance or reading-matter Harrison had experienced to life with vivid heteroglossia.[5] He told Richard Hoggart that the Greek dramatists were essential to the development of this polyphonic public voice;[6] many of his poems, where he has an interchange with an interlocutor, seem like staged miniature scenes from intense dramas, especially when imagery suggestive of the ancient theatre is included. In 'The Morning After', the public street bonfire celebrating victory at the end of the war on VE day leaves a 'scorched circle on the road', like the orchestra of the ancient theatre, which links it directly with the impact of the atomic bomb in the Japanese theatre of war.[7]

One part of Harrison's project, as we have seen throughout this book, has been to declare his entitlement to high culture, especially the classical world, in his own inimitable working-class voice. 'Study', published in 1978, recalls the death of his uncle Joe, who had been afflicted by a stammer, in his parents' 'best' room, which Harrison was allowed to use as a study, and the wordless grief that enshrouded the scene. But 'Study' concludes with the line, 'My mind moves upon silence and *Aeneid* VI.'[8] Since in that book Aeneas visits the Underworld and speaks to dead people including his father, perhaps Harrison is wondering whether he will ever talk to Joe again. But the point is more complex: *Aeneid* VI also contains Anchises' prophecy of Aeneas' achievements and the future rise of Rome. Harrison, alienated by his education, is silently thinking about Classics, poetry and his own ambitions for the future even at a time when his family is desolated. 'Cypress and Cedar' (1983) was written when Harrison was attempting to build a home in the USA, 'beneath the Swanee river and the Styx'. He was becoming depressed, and his ruminations on carpentry are interrupted by memories of Racine's *Phèdre* and the days when he had been an avid reader of Homer instead of 'an even avider verandah drinker'; he wonders whether an Englishman who had died there was really the victim of a type of snake mentioned in Virgil's *Georgics* III.[9]

Voices themselves – silenced and liberated, singing or speaking high poetry or obscenities, in regional or patrician accents, ancient and modern languages – are a continuous preoccupation in all his *oeuvre*. In 'Them & [uz]' (1978), which even includes an ancient Greek sound of lament in the Greek alphabet, Harrison recalls how he was brutally interrupted when asked by his schoolteacher to recite Keats' 'Ode to a Nightingale':

> 4 words only of *mi 'art aches* and . . . 'Mine's broken,
> you barbarian, T. W.!' *He* was nicely spoken.[10]

The following year, now ten years after 'Newcastle is Peru', his regard for Keats became the springboard for the remarkable 'A Kumquat for John Keats'.

At the age of forty-two, he tells us, after a year 'full of bile and self-defeat', he finds himself in the countryside in Florida and discovers the kumquat fruit. Eating one whole, skin and pulp together, produces a taste that is both sour and sweet at the same time. For Harrison, now at midlife, it seems to symbolize the combination of bad and good, horror and ecstasy he has experienced. This puts him in mind of the most well-known poem about the dialectical unity of life's polar emotional extremes, Keats' 'Ode on Melancholy':

> Ay, in the very temple of Delight
>   Veil'd Melancholy has her sovran shrine,
> Though seen of none save him whose strenuous tongue
>   Can burst Joy's grape against his palate fine...[11]

Keats had seen joy as a grape to be savoured, but only by people who can truly know what it is to be miserable as well. Harrison fantasizes about offering Keats a kumquat as a perfect image of this duality. But there are impermeable barriers between them. Keats died at the age of twenty-five, whereas Harrison has lived until early middle age. More importantly, their lives were separated by a century of grim history,

> years like an open crater, gory, grim,
> with bloody bubbles leering at the rim;
> a thing no bigger than an urn explodes
> and ravishes all silence and all odes.
> Flora asphyxiated by foul air,
> unknown to either Keats or Lemprière,
> dehydrated Naiads, Dryad amputees,
> dragging themselves through slagscapes with no trees,
> a shirt of Nessus fire that gnaws and eats
> children half the age of dying Keats ...

Here Harrison turns to Keats' 'Ode on a Grecian Urn', to ask whether there can be any kind of pastoral poetry after the invention of the nuclear bomb. Keats' Grecian urn, a 'Silvan historian' and 'a still unravished bride', preserves its silence about life in 'slow time' during an idyllic pastoral past. But nuclear bombs detonate, and Harrison effectively makes Keats' ode explode into fragmented pieces, destroying 'pastoral assumptions about time'.[12]

The 'Flora' of Keats' 'Sleep and Poetry' had represented Keats' early poems and their 'amorous pastoralism';[13] for Harrison, she is 'asphyxiated by foul air/ unknown to Keats or Lemprière' (the author of a classical reference work used by the Romantic poets). The 'white naiad in a rippling stream', who represents what a poet can perceive in his mind's eye in Keats' 'To George Felton Mathew', is now dehydrated; the Dryads lulled to sleep 'by zephyrs, streams, and birds, and bees' in Keats' 'Ode to Psyche' become amputees;[14] the radiation figured as the shirt of Nessus – the robe anointed with the hydra's poison with which Deianeira accidentally kills her husband Herakles in Sophocles' *Women of Trachis* – is Harrison's own grim addition to these rural classical personnel. He returns to the 'Ode on Melancholy' when regretting that he can't, of course, offer Keats a kumquat, because 'dead men don't eat kumquats, or drink wine,/ they shiver in the arms of Prosperine'. Harrison's puts a twist on Keats' admonition to his reader not to 'suffer thy pale forehead to be kiss'd/ By nightshade, ruby grape of Proserpine', with a dark allusion to a fruit of deadly toxicity.[15]

'Whene'er I venture on the stream of rhyme', said Keats in his 'Oft have you seen a swan superbly frowning', he identifies with a proud swan.[16] The singer-poet/swan identification reappears at the opening of one the most informative of all Harrison's autobiographical poems, his scathing 'Laureate's Block'; the image goes all the way back to Aeschylus' Cassandra in *Agamemnon* (line 1444). This polemical poem was published in *The Guardian* on 9 February 1999. Beneath the title were printed the words, 'for Queen Elizabeth'. The poet Ted Hughes had died on 28 October 1998, leaving the post of Poet Laureate vacant. Harrison must have known that his caustic recusatio would ensure that he was not offered the post, for which he had been tipped by some observers. But it made him even more unpopular at a time when his star was waning. He had begun to fall out of favour even among the radical intelligentsia when he derided Richard Eyre for accepting a knighthood (see below), and Melvyn Bragg for becoming a peer. His unapologetic class politics did not fit the new agenda of Blairite Britain. In 'Laureate's Block', this proud swan identifies the radical politics of other non-laureates, Gray and Milton, as his inspiration. He imagines the monarchy ceasing with the death of Elizabeth II, to spare the country 'some toad's ode' at Charles's coronation, for Harrison would 'like all suchlike odes there've ever been,/ binned by a truly democratic nation'.

Harrison's muses

Another part of Harrison's project has been to inscribe important moments in his private life into his poetic record. He often says that he doesn't want anybody to write his biography, because everything he regards as significant 'is there in the poetry'. Read this way, his poems create contradictions. In 'v.', for example, he anticipates being buried alongside his parents in Leeds, but in 'Polygons' he asks his survivors to scatter his ashes in Delphi; perhaps he is deliberately expressing his sense of a divided self, the son of a northern English baker who has become a cosmopolitan cultural figure. His view also seems a little disingenuous; others might see significance where he has controlled the narrative of his life to erase phenomena. He has a sister named Anne, for example, who shared his childhood. Yet she appears in none of his poems until 'Shrapnel' (2005), which links his memory of bombs falling on Leeds during the blitz with the London terrorist suicide attacks on 7 July. He draws an almost complete veil over the figure of his first wife, who is also the mother of his two children, Jane and Max, although they are both lovingly portrayed. 'Gaps' especially includes gentle memories of Max, who suffered a psychiatric breakdown as a young adult.[17] It is perhaps to protect them that he does not much discuss their mother. But he is close to neither his first wife nor his sister, and may feel that this is a sufficient explanation for their near-absence from his evolving poetic autobiography.

Many other women have made impressions on Harrison's poetry. They are often linked with classical imagery, as we have seen. 'The Viewless Wings' in *The Loiners* (1970), set in Grimley, recalls a lover he has had to leave behind in the Soviet Union. Harrison has taken the title from Keats' 'Ode to a Nightingale', where the poet says he will fly 'Not charioted by Bacchus and his pards,/ But on the viewless wings of Poesy'.[18] He invited this Russian woman, the night before he had to leave her, to watch the dawn break over the museum ship *Aurora* in Leningrad docks; the crew of this ship had mutinied in 1917, joined the Bolsheviks, and fired the blank from the forecastle gun to order the assault on the Winter Palace. Harrison's sense of the epic importance of this event in world history is adroitly conveyed by the Homeric epithet in the last two lines, describing 'AURORA, rosy-fingered kind, and battleship/ whose sudden salvo turned the east half red'.

The two women with whom he has had long-term relationships since his first marriage also feature memorably in his work. Teresa Stratas, his second wife, is herself of Cretan Greek descent. He speaks of her in his poems and in conversation with great tenderness and respect; it seems their marriage simply could not survive being separated for long periods by the Atlantic. He is poleaxed by his longing for her in his 1981 'Loving Memory'; this poem was triggered when he looked for the grave of another renowned soprano, Jenny Lind, in the Malvern Hills, amongst the 'fosses where Caractacus fought Rome'. The reference to the ancient British chieftain anticipates the poem's meditation on the antiquity of the Malverns – some of the oldest rock formations in the world – revealing that Harrison's interest in paleogeology, central to 'Polygons', as we shall see, is longstanding.[19] But it is in the long, anguished 'The Mother of the Muses', which takes its name from a line in the Aeschylean *Prometheus Bound*, that Stratas' weeping presence and Harrison's love for her are palpable.

Written when her father Emmanuel (Manolis) Stratas died in a Canadian home for people suffering from senile dementia, it carefully recalls the last day the couple had spent with him, in deepest winter. Harrison's evocations of the effects of dementia on his father-in-law and several other patients are searing. The central theme is their loss of memory, which Harrison introduces by himself attempting to recall the passage in *Prometheus Bound* (later to feature in his movie *Prometheus*) where the Titan lists his gifts to mankind; these included writing, 'craftswoman, mother of the Muses, remembrance of everything' (461).[20]

But the great love of Harrison's life is the actress Sian Thomas, whom he started seeing in 1988 and with whom he has lived for nearly as long. In 1999, at the age of sixty-two, he wrote his fascinating love poem 'A Fig on the Tyne' to mark her forty-sixth birthday. Ruminating on scientists' reports that global warming will result in an expansion of the English wine industry, even in the poverty-stricken north, he ironically celebrates 'Dionysus redeeming dereliction'. The poem, which is sexually explicit, was partly inspired by D. H. Lawrence's 'Innocent England', in which this other working-class classically educated Englishman, who also liked Mediterranean climates, protested at the banning of his paintings showing pubic hair. Harrison quotes the first line of Lawrence's couplet, 'Fig trees don't grow in my native land;/ there's never a fig-leaf near at hand.'[21] The themes of an adored woman and fruit reappear in another poem of the same year, 'Fruitility', where Harrison explores his longstanding preoccupation with fruit in his poetry. He concludes with a memory of his mother, 'of all my muses' the first to teach him to love fruit, thus referencing once again the 'Mother of the Muses' in *Prometheus Bound*.[22]

Other poems of the late 1990s explore his relationships with friends and close collaborators. He was appalled in 1997 when Richard Eyre, who had directed the televised film of '*v.*' and the staunchly republican *The Prince's Play*, accepted a knighthood. He said so in a trenchant poem.[23] But 'Toasting Jocelyn' is one of his most joyful poems. Written to celebrate his beloved designer's eightieth birthday, it includes vivid memories of working with her on the *Oresteia*, *Trackers*, *The Kaisers of Carnuntum* and *Prometheus*, travelling on the rough roads around Delphi, and drinking pure water from the Castalian spring with her to pledge 'the tragic Muse/ and comic Muse, Melpomene and Castalia'. Jocelyn, he decides, has been a more inspiring Muse to him than either of them.[24]

'Polygons'

This long and wistful poem embeds a memorialization of Harrison's friend Seamus Heaney:

> A hanging newspaper clothes pegs keep open
> on the kiosk across from the shut, smashed hotel
> has a whole half-page picture of a poet I know well.

News of Heaney's death came to Harrison when he was himself convalescing on the rocky precipices around Delphi, making his 'coeval heart' judder 'with lurches of scree fall'. Heaney had once visited him in Delphi, where they had swapped drafts of their translations of Greek tragedy (and, Harrison tells me, he encouraged Heaney to translate *Aeneid* book VI). Now he sits in Newcastle with Sian, raising a toast of ouzo, clouded by a splash of water from the Castalian spring, to 'that great Irish spirit'. Above the stove is a forty-year-old poster from

> the Festival Hall,
> a reading with Ted Hughes, Seamus Heaney, and me,
> Tony Harrison, sadly the only one still alive.
> Both those I've read with have been in this kitchen.

Harrison's mind moves to his own death, and he takes comfort from Heaney's own last words, *noli timere*, do not be afraid.

The poem's titular polygons unify its strands, which meditate on his cancer treatment, the stones of the ruined architecture of Delphi, the shifting of the tectonic plates which created the craggy limestone of the Parnassian landscape and the way he associates metrical and geological formations:

> The tectonic soul-shift that tragedy comes from
> can shatter most lyrics but leaves Aeschylean
> anapaests uncollapsed, coping though quake-wracked.

He returns to the craggy, alliterative, normally unrhymed four-beat Anglo-Saxon line of his *Oresteia*, creating rhythmic syncopations which evoke continental drift and subterranean forces in motion. It uses its setting, Delphi, and the background of Mount Parnassus with its spring of Castalia, to unite a profoundly personal meditation, brimming with classical allusions and memories of his work on classical themes, on significant strands in his life. These include, besides his dialogues with other poets, his theatrical collaborations, especially with Herbert, and his long and happy love affair with Thomas.[25]

Harrison sets this poem in the longest historical context by associating the polygonal blocks of the Cyclopean wall beneath the temple of Apollo with the shape of the super-continents, Gondwana and Pangaea, that existed until 180 million years ago:

> blocks shaped like continents pre-early Jurassic
> where capers cascade down landlocked Pangaea,
> polygonal Gondwanaland, in tasselly swathes.

Through thinking about Delphi, he recalls some of his life's highlights: his 'clog-dancing satyrs/ with phalluses upright' at the première of *The Trackers of Oxyrhynchus*; he references his film work by descrbing the statue of Prometheus at Delphi, surrounded by flagpoles; his '*Oresteia*/ with its Egil-like kennings I thought Aeschylean', in a style 'like polygons though hewn out of English'.

The themes of death and Delphi connect his appreciative verses about other poets than the Greek tragedians, Egil and his friends Heaney and Hughes. He speaks of flowers named in Virgil and Ovid and Ovid's interest in Empedoclean cosmogony; the mention of Empedocles prompts reflection on another southern European place much visited by Harrison, and the setting of 'The Grilling', Mount Vesuvio. Ovid's narrative of 'Deucalion surviving the great inundation,/ finding dry land on the slopes of Parnassus' in *Metamorphoses* I is a major under-text. Compliments are paid to the Scottish *makar* (bard) William Dunbar, the Greek writers George Seferis and Nikos Kazantzakis, and especially to Byron, who with John Hobhouse inscribed his name on a Delphi column in 1809. It is with Byron's poetry about Delphi and the Muses that Harrison insinuates the idea of the darkness impending as he ages:

> His *Childe Harold's Pilgrimage* line on Parnassus,
> the mountain seen snow-capped walking down here:
> 'And thou, the Muses' seat, art now their grave.'
> And from *Darkness* the whole earth gone with the Muses:
> 'seasonless, herbless, treeless, manless, lifeless.'
> a landscape to wait for Melpomene in.[26]

Nature seems in agreement with Harrison's state of mind as he ruminates from Newcastle that winter is coming to Parnassus, and the Muses will be shivering:

> Melpomene's the only one doesn't need thermals
> but goes round Parnassus like a Newcastle lass
> on a pub-crawl at Christmas with bare legs and arms
> as though out for the night on the Costa del Sol.

And this Melpomene, whether she is a drunken Geordie or an ancient Greek divinity, provides Harrison with the memorable image of continuing survival on Parnassus, against the odds, with which 'Polygons' seems to summarize his life. He drinks water he has brought from Castalia,

> and use it to take my anticoagulant,
> to keep on surviving the slopes of Parnassus
> though Melpomene's the last Muse up on the summit.

The golden harp

'Polygons' read, when it was published, like a valedictory gesture. There will be no more long autobiographical poems. In late 2018, Harrison was diagnosed with the early stages of Alzheimer's disease and retired completely from public life. This seems especially cruel for a man whose entire life has been devoted to language, memorializing the inarticulate and restoring the consciousness of those erased from communal memory. His candour about his father-in-law's dementia in 'The Mother of the Muses' (1987) and intimate, gentle work with elderly sufferers in his film *Black Daisies for the Bride* (1993) now seem painfully prescient. But he would not want this book to end on a downbeat note. He is still perfectly aware of who he is, and of his close relationships; he is still quaffing retsina and laughing at Sian's immaculate impersonations and funny stories. He is still watching movies and reading avidly.

Harrison's passion for the products of human artistic creativity is inexhaustible. To say 'passion for the Arts' would be a ludicrous distortion, since 'the Arts' are not normally taken to include all the countless forms taken by words and images, across the social and cultural spectrum, which he has enjoyed and which have enriched his imagination. His prose essays reveal rich insights into his classicism by detailing the sheer diversity of his cultural experiences and how they have informed his own creative output. The most canonical high operas by Monteverdi, Verdi, Smetana and Orff jostle here with working-class entertainers George Formby and Vesta Tilley. Films only seen in arthouse cinemas, by Eisenstein, Torre Nilsson and Tarkovsky, appear alongside James Cagney in *White Heat* and Disney's *Bambi*. Almost forgotten translators like Edward Powys Mathers and minor novelists like Nancy Bogen rub shoulders with Dryden and Dostoyevsky.[27] The work in which he offered his most eloquent exploration of the way the Arts have been used to create and maintain social divisions was *The Trackers of Oxyrhynchus*, where the human-animal hybridity of the satyr, and what Adrian Poole has aptly called 'ribald generic indeterminacy' of satyr drama,[28] allowed him to meditate on the chasm in his own previous theatre between the supposedly 'high' culture of the *Oresteia* and the folk culture of *Bow Down* (1977) and *The Mysteries*.

Long before research into previous post-antique manifestations of Greek and Roman material had become a central interest in academic Classics, Harrison's appetite for it was inexhaustible. He needs to be acknowledged as one of the founders of Classical Reception. *Phaedra Britannica* was Classics at its most anticolonial; *Medea: A Sex-War Opera* meditated on the patriarchal needs that had been served by Medea's incarnations after Euripides. Some of Harrison's earlier poems introduced me and Henry Stead, when we were researching *A People's History of Classics*, to working-class classicists in the annals of British history, such as the Bradford quarry boy, Joseph Wright, who became Professor of Classical Philology at Oxford.[29]

Harrison has found in classical antiquity and its later applications his most fruitful medium for discussing the class politics of art. The boys at Leeds Grammar School studied Latin and Greek to make them feel superior to other children, but it did not work on the Loiner Poet. Yet, in the final analysis, it is the exuberance of his classicism for which he may be best remembered. An important sequence in his film-poem *Metamorpheus* takes place in a Bulgarian underground bar. Women dancers in flamboyant dresses and colourful high heels perform high kicks to the can-can music from Jacques Offenbach's uproarious *Orpheus in the Underworld* (1858). Offenbach's Olympian gods hold a party in Hades, itself partly inspired by the visit to the Underworld made by Dionysus and his able slave Xanthias in Aristophanes' *Frogs*. Harrison's classicism seems to me to bear close resemblances to with Offenbach's. Bored by Zeus's old-fashioned taste in sedate dances, Offenbach's Olympians invent the riotous 'infernal gallop', better known as the can-can.

Critics were appalled by the irreverence Offenbach had shown towards ancient Greek culture, his desecration of an Ovidian narrative and 'profanation of holy and glorious antiquity'.[30] But another way of looking at it was that Offenbach was using the Greeks to take society and entertainment into the future, or, as Harrison put it in his 1987 presidential address to the British Classical Association, 'Facing up to the Muses', to take the human race '*forward with the Greeks*'. To use his own inimitable phrase in another essay, 'The misanthrope: Jane Eyre's Sister', his whole life's work has truly been 'a Jack and the Beanstalk act'. He has braved 'the somnolent ogre of a British classical education to grab the golden harp'.[31]

Notes

Chapter 1

1. Statement at the Friends House, Euston Road, 16 September 2011.
2. See Hall and Stead (2020) Chapter 13.
3. Adams (1822) entry for 16 June.
4. Eggebrecht (1995) 8.
5. Ziolkowski (2015) 9.
6. Ziolkowski (2015) 5–7; Fleischmann (1965). In 1755, J. J. Winckelmann coined the phrase that inspired generations of Germans to imitate ancient Greek artists, 'eine edle Einfalt und eine stille Grösse' ('a noble simplicity and quiet grandeur'); see Pfotenhauer (1995) 30.
7. Anon. (1826) 457.
8. Vines (1930) 156.
9. Ziolkowski (2015) 4.
10. Hall and Stead (2020) 273; see H. Marshall (2010) 140–1.
11. Rihm (1997) 315–18.
12. See p. 119.
13. Deane (1999) 501.
14. Harrison (2016) 317.
15. Awtrey (2014) 98–100.
16. Settis (2006).
17. Hall (2008) 25–6.
18. Rowland (2019) 186–92.
19. Quote in Jameson (2015) 3.
20. Harrison (2016) 176.
21. Harrison (2016) 22, 127.
22. Harrison (2016) 298–9; Sappho fr. 168B Campbell.
23. Taylor (2015) 214–52.
24. Harrison (2016) 425.
25. Amours (1908) 162 line 632.
26. See especially Taplin (1997) 170.
27. Jaggi (2007).

28 Collected in Harrison (2017).
29 Haffenden (1991) 236.
30 Harrison (2016) 214.
31 University of Leeds, Brotherton Library Special Collections. Letter to Jon Silkin, 10 May 1964.
32 Jaggi (2007).
33 Secretan (1973) 67.
34 See the analysis in Robinson (1998) 44–5. On Harrison's elegiac sonnets, see above all Morrison (2019).
35 Young (1991) 158.
36 S. Regan (2019) 353.
37 This was how Harrison introduced himself when interviewed by Melvyn Bragg on the South Bank Show in 1980.
38 Harrison (1991) 280; Stravinsky (1947) 51.
39 Blakesey (2018) 55.
40 Moul (2010) 2–3 and n. 4.
41 See p. 108.
42 Harrison (1967) and (1969).
43 See Harrison (2018) 283–310.
44 Young (1984) 160.
45 Harrison (2016) 388 (Amphis fr. 8 Kassel-Austin). See Balmer (2019) 36; C. Marshall (2019) 162; Greco (2019) 163.
46 Secretan (1973) 68.
47 Hardwick (1999) 8.
48 Deane (1994) 30.
49 Hall and Stead (2020).
50 Harrison (2016) 126.
51 Harrison (2016) 151.
52 Harrison (2016) 130.
53 Gilroy-Ware (2013) 112.
54 See the title of Watkin (2006).
55 Young (1759) 21.
56 Orthwein (2017).
57 Tessa Roynon used the term 'radical classicism' in the abstract to her PhD thesis on Toni Morrison (2006), but explained it no further. See also Richardson (2015) 85, discussing Robert Brough, on whom see p. 83.
58 Barnard (2018) 9.
59 Harrison (2016) 122.
60 Davis (1997) 20–61; Hall (2008) 96–7.

61 Späth (2002) 48.
62 Harrison (2016) 69.
63 Clay (1992).
64 Harrison (2016) 65–6.
65 Harrison (2018) 83.
66 Harrison (2008) 3–4.
67 *The Yorkshire Post*, 21 September 1931, 6. I am grateful to Anna Reeve, a graduate student in the Classics Department at Leeds University, for helping me research these windows
68 A letter by Tom Phillips to *The Independent*, quoted in Butler (1977) 114.

Chapter 2

1 Harrison (2017) 469.
2 Lyon (1996–7) 13. He may be misinterpreting Carol Rutter's intention, when she included several photographs in her selection of Harrison's poetry *Permanently Bard* (1995), as implicitly critical of the poet's interest in visual culture.
3 Kennedy (2009) 167.
4 Harrison (2017) 76, 325.
5 Harrison (2017) 470.
6 Harrison (2016) 321.
7 Hickling (2003).
8 Hall (2006) Chapter 4.
9 Haffenden (1991) 231. On the relationship between public and private in Harrison, see the insights of his translator into French, Cécile Marshall (2010).
10 Harrison (2016) 20.
11 Harrison (2016) 37.
12 Harrison (2016) 53–4.
13 *Laocoön* has been published repeatedly in English translation since Lessing (1836); for discussions of these concepts, see Park (1969).
14 Aeschylus, *Agamemnon* 238–43; Harrison (1981) 10.
15 On ekphrasis in classical epic, see Becker (1995) and Putnam (1998). On statues in ancient Greek literature, see Steiner (2002) and Hall (2006) Chapter 4.
16 Harrison (2016) 58.
17 Harrison (2016) 59.
18 Harrison (2016) 60.
19 See p. 126.

20 Nietzsche (1993 [1872]) 80; see p. 150.
21 Harrison (2016) 104n.
22 See p. 133.
23 Harrison (2016) 70-2.
24 Quoted in Bertram (2005) 23.
25 See Ford (2002) ch. 4.
26 *The Greek Anthology* 9.258=Harrison (2016) 95, no. 66.
27 Dougherty (2006) 129.
28 Harrison (2017) 240, 304; Tarkovsky (1986) 134.
29 *The Greek Anthology* 9.773=Harrison (2016) 94 no. 64.
30 *The Greek Anthology* 9.441=Harrison (2016) 95 no. 65.

Chapter 3

1 Harrison (1976) 11.
2 Harrison (2017) 157.
3 See Bower (2015) and Suhr-Sytsma (2017) 38, with further references in his n.33.
4 On Heaney's use of the parallels between Roman and British colonialism, which struck him in his teens when he was reading Virgil's *Aeneid*, see Hall (2019).
5 See Regan (2015), (2016) and (2018).
6 See further Hall (2017a).
7 Dexter (1993) 39.
8 See Bower (2018); Suhr-Sytsma (2017) 152-5. Harrison celebrated his friendship with Simmons in 'The Act' (1987), published in Harrison (2016) 281-4.
9 Hall, Macintosh and Wrigley (2004).
10 Cited from Dexter (1993) 34.
11 Dexter (1993) 39.
12 Dexter (1993) 134.
13 See Young (1984) 157-8; Nunn (2013).
14 Barnes (1975). Harrison updated his translation of *The Misanthrope* for a successful revival by Shakespeare at the Tobacco Factory in Bristol in 2010 (https://stf-theatre.org.uk/themisanthrope).
15 Letter to Harrison, 4 December 1974, in *Phaedra* Notebook 1.130-1.
16 The detailed attention that Racine paid to Euripides' play is carefully documented in Phillippo (2003). Nero became Emperor in 54 CE. Seneca committed suicide, on Nero's orders, in 65 CE. Despite the scholarly commonplace that Seneca may not have written the tragedies attributed to him, there is no valid reason to doubt that

Phaedra was his own work. The text's overwhelming influence since the Renaissance in any case renders the authorship controversy irrelevant to my argument.

17 *Phaedra* Notebook 1.1.
18 Turnell (1947) ix; Mauriac (1940) 203.
19 Cited from Dexter (1993) 34.
20 See Bishop (1983).
21 Dexter (1993) 45.
22 Hall (2010b).
23 Quick (2009) 140–9.
24 Dexter (1993) 53.
25 Gosling (1974), pasted into *Phaedra* Notebook 3.720.
26 http://theeclectist.blogspot.com/2012/06/interview-with-alaknanda-samarth.html
27 Hall (2010a).
28 *New-York Daily Tribune*, August 14, 1857; see Hall (2010a) 33–4.
29 Act I, scene 1, lines 10–21; Racine (1985) 19.
30 Harrison (1976) 1.
31 See the large photograph in *Phaedra* Notebook 1.192–3 and other neoclassical buildings in Hyderabad 1.211.
32 *Phaedra* Notebook 1.197.
33 Harrison (2017) 153.
34 James (1997) 279.
35 Hall (2010a).
36 Belmekki (2008).
37 Cross (1970) 44.
38 For full details, see Heffer (1998) 449–67 and http://edithorial.blogspot.com/2013/04/how-enoch-powell-got-vergil-wrong.html.
39 Heffer (1998) 91–3, 115–16; Roth (1970) 42–6, 51.
40 See James (1997) fig. 18, captioned 'A Centurion of the Raj'; Abbott (2003) with the photograph of the unidentified officer on p. 48.
41 Act III, scene 3, line 850, Racine (1985) 55; Harrison (1976) 30.
42 Harrison (1976) 7, with the illustration stuck into *Phaedra* Notebook 1.218.
43 See the letter from Rawson to Harrison in *Phaedra* Notebook 1.112–13 and the images at 1.146–7. The neoclassical painting is a mural in the Palazzo del Te, Mantua, after a design by Giulio Romano.
44 On the potency and multivalence of the figure of 'Sikander' in Indian historiography, see Vasunia (2013) 91–115.
45 Fraser (1851).
46 Holman (1961).

47 See Henry Martens' painting 'An Officer of the 1st Bengal Irregular Cavalry (Skinner's Horse)' in the National Army Museum, at https://artuk.org/discover/artworks/an-officer-of-the-1st-bengal-irregular-cavalry-skinners-horse-182783.
48 Harrison (1976) 9.
49 Harrison (1976) 14–15.
50 Act II, scene 1, lines 423–4; Racine (1985) 37.
51 Harrison (1976) 16.
52 Long (1869) li.
53 Butalia (1998) 273.
54 See Allen (1857).
55 Harrison (1976) 19.
56 *Phaedra* Notebook 1.1.
57 *Phaedra* Notebook 1.1, 1.4.
58 *Phaedra* Notebook 1.4.
59 Morley (1975).
60 Morley (1975).
61 Dexter (1993) 45.
62 Harrison (1976) 54.
63 Pittas-Herschbach (1990) discusses effect of Racine's decision not to include a chorus in *Phèdre*.
64 See e.g. Forbes (1878 [1856]) 635–6.
65 Volk (2006).
66 Harrison (1976) 19; *PV* 4–6; *Antigone* 474–6.
67 *Phaedra* Notebook 3.684.
68 See *Phaedra* Notebooks 2, inside of front cover and 1, inside of front cover.
69 See e.g. *Phaedra* Notebooks 1.180–211, 3.481, 430–1; texts quoted in Harrison (2017) 127–57 with bibliography cited in the endnotes.
70 Harrison (1976) 16.
71 Harrison (1976) 1–2.
72 Harrison (1976) 15, 22.
73 *Phaedra* Notebook 1.169.
74 Harrison (1976) 31.
75 Harrison (2017) 136–7.
76 The two words, along with an image of a crocodile, appear together on the inside cover of *Phaedra* Notebook 2.
77 See especially BC MS 20c Harrison 03/PHA/03, pp. 551 and 652.
78 Harrison (2017) 301.
79 Harrison (2017) 134–5.

80 On the fragmentary tragedy see Hall (2020); for a comparison of the ethics and emotions in Euripides, Seneca and Racine's versions, see Budzowska (2012).
81 Act II scene 5, lines 655-62, Racine (1985) 47.
82 Translation by Morgan (1885) 19 (slightly adapted).
83 Harrison (1976) 23.
84 Harrison (1976) 24.
85 See e.g. Fitch (1987) 208 and Keulen (2001) 148.
86 Harrison (2017) 148. *Phaedra* Notebook 4.730. This landmark translation was reprinted in facsimile by the Spenser Society as Simms (1887); see further Spearing (1909).
87 Harrison (1976) 31.
88 Harrison (2017) 144; *Phaedra* Notebook 4.751.
89 The interconnections between Stoicism and Roman imperial ideology in Senecan tragedy are analysed in Henry and Henry (1985). See below, p. 116-19.
90 Woodruff (1953) 15. Philip Woodruff was the pseudonym of Philip Mason (1906-99). See Vasunia (2005) 35 n.2.
91 See especially Segal (1986) 58-9.
92 Harrison (2017) 132-8.
93 Harrison (1976) 6.
94 Harrison (1976) 18 and 19.
95 Harrison (1976) 6.
96 Harrison (1976) 11.
97 Harrison (1976) 2.
98 Harrison (1976) 10.
99 Act III, scene 2, line 814; Racine (1985) 54; Harrison (1976) 28-9.
100 *Phaedra* Notebook 2.420.
101 Harrison (1976) 4.
102 Harrison (1976) 2.
103 Hall and Stead (2020) 219.
104 See Butler (2003) 182, 184; Levine (2003) 95; Kobes Du Mez (2015) 65-6. Harrison once planned a play in celebration of Josephine Butler's work for women prostituted in the north of England.
105 Kobes Du Mez (2015) 68-70.
106 Kobes Du Mez (2015) 90.
107 Styan (1983) 102.
108 *Phaedra* Notebook 1.170-1.
109 *Phaedra* Notebooks 1.224-5, 3.536-7.
110 On *Phèdre*'s canonization as the supreme dramatic exemplar of French classicism, see the sophisticated study of Wygant (1999).

111 See the review in *The Observer Review*, Sunday 11 April 1976, pasted into *Phaedra* Notebook 4.959.
112 Gussow (1988).
113 Patel (1989).
114 As 'T.W. Harrison' (1967) and (1969).
115 See Hall and Macintosh (2007) vi–22.
116 McDonald (1991) 97–146.
117 Taplin (2002) and Taplin (2005).
118 See the website at http://www.apgrd.ox.ac.uk. Works by Harrison are discussed in several of the APGRD's books, including Hall, Macintosh and Taplin (2000), Hall, Macintosh and Wrigley (2004), Macintosh, Michelakis, Hall and Taplin (2005), Hall (2013); they have been addressed in the doctoral theses I have supervised by Helen Eastman (2015), Caroline Latham (2016) and Charlotte Parkyn (2018).
119 Macintosh (2019).
120 See Hall and Stead (2020) 8 with bibliography n.23.
121 Hall and Stead (2020) with bibliography n.24.
122 Hall (2010a).
123 'Preface' in Harrison (1976) v–xxv; revised version in Harrison (2017) 127–57.
124 Nilsson (1968).
125 Hall (2010b) 16.
126 Revised version in Jones (1788).
127 Vasunia (2007), revised version in Vasunia (2013) 279–99.
128 Vasunia (2005) 36.
129 Vasunia (2005) 13 and 14. See e.g. the *East-India Register and Directory* for 1843, xix.
130 Vasunia (2005) 40 with n.22.

Chapter 4

1 Lee Hall (2019) 24.
2 See e.g. Elliott (1989); Davidson (1991).
3 O'Brien (2014) 233.
4 See Lewis (1990) 159.
5 Peter Hall (1983) 237.
6 Personal correspondence with Unsworth; see also Hall (2009).
7 Rutter (2007) 143–4.

8 Harrison (1981) 6.
9 *Oresteia* Notebook 10.2, 10.340.
10 Taplin (1997) 172. He also argues that the two flocks of sheep in the libretto of the opera *Yan Tan Tethera* (1986, music again by Birtwhistle) correspond to a double theatre chorus.
11 Harrison (1991) 279.
12 See Parker (1986) 338–40. There are acute insights into the masks of this *Oresteia* in H. Marshall (2010) 52–9.
13 Quoted in Fay and Oakes (1991) 289–90 from *Sunday Times*, 29 November 1981.
14 Harrison (2002) 8.
15 Harrison (2017) 333–74.
16 Taplin (2005) 242.
17 Taplin (2005) 242.
18 Harrison (1981) 58.
19 *Oresteia* Notebook 1.19.
20 *Oresteia* Notebook 9.1987.
21 *Oresteia* Notebook 4.958–60.
22 Harrison (1981) 10.
23 Harrison (1981) 21.
24 Smalley (1991) 75–6.
25 Harrison (2016) 9, 13.
26 Harrison (2016) 113–14.
27 See below pp. 156–7.
28 Latham (2016) 119.
29 Harrison (1981) 28.
30 *Oresteia* Notebook 6.1453; Goldhill (2007) 99.
31 During an actors' workshop, at which I was present, at the National Theatre Studios in September 2012 when Harrison was developing *Iphigenia in Crimea*.
32 Hall (2012).
33 Harrison (1981) 15, 55, 78, 83.
34 In *The New Statesman*, 4 December 1981.
35 *Oresteia* Notebook 10, 2340.
36 Case (1985).
37 See e.g. Whitaker (2013) 177–217; Byrne (2006).
38 Harrison (2016) 167.
39 Wroe (2000).
40 Spencer (1994) 66.
41 Warner (1982) 25.
42 Harrison, quoted in the programme for *The Oresteia* (National Theatre, 1981).

43 *Oresteia* Notebook 4.800.
44 McDonald (2003) 32.
45 Aeschylus, *Agamemnon* 437–47; Harrison (1981) 15. Harrison's version of the first half of this choral passage has been included in his *Collected Poems* as 'The Ballad of the Geldshark. From Aeschylus': Harrison (2016) 114.
46 See Hall (1998), (2005) and (2010c) 210–20.
47 Aeschylus, *Agamemnon* 10–11; Harrison (1981) 3.
48 Latham (2016) 75–6.
49 Aeschylus, *Agamemnon* 1457–1504; Harrison (1981) 43–4.
50 Harrison (1981) 59.
51 *Oresteia* Notebook 4.849, 4.891.
52 Harrison (1981) 98.
53 *Oresteia* Notebook 1.157.
54 Stead (1980).
55 *Oresteia* Notebooks 5.968–91, 5.1007, 9.2157, 5.1102, 9.2169, 10.2268, 5.1146–7.
56 *Oresteia* Notebook 1.216–17; Dolan (1988) 91.
57 *Oresteia* Notebook 10.2183 and 10.2236–7.
58 Zeitlin (1978).
59 See e.g. Padley (2008) 6–14.
60 See further below, p. 70.
61 See also 'Essentials', 'Dark Times' and 'Red Lights of Plenty' (Harrison (2016) 210, 152, 231–3, 341) and C. Regan (2019b).
62 C.W. Marshall (2013).
63 Gill (2012).
64 Hairsine (1997) 209–10.
65 Haffenden (1991) 246.
66 Harrison (2016) 176, 137.
67 Harrison (2016) 157.
68 *Oresteia* Notebook 3.482 and inside front and back covers.
69 *Oresteia* Notebook 1.3.
70 Harrison (1981) 18, 53, 59, 74.
71 Harrison (1981) 77.
72 *Oresteia* Notebook 5.1007.
73 *Oresteia* Notebook 4.917–947) See Latham (2016) 146 n.28.
74 Levi (1991) 164.
75 Harrison (1981) 90, 26.
76 Lee Hall (2019) 25.
77 Harrison (1981) 42.
78 *Oresteia* Notebook 1.153 and Harrison (1981) 9–10.

79 Aesch. *Ag.* 36–7; Harrison (1981) 4.
80 Harrison (2016) 112–13; on the Brecht poem to which he is responding, see Hall and Stead (2020) 126.
81 Harrison (2016) 133–4.
82 Harrison (2016) 135.
83 Latham (2016) 260.
84 Harrison (1981) 13, 24, 44, 22, 16, 27, 30–1, 36, 38, 46–8, 29, 52, 79, 53, 59, 63–4, 79.
85 Lee Hall (2019) 25.
86 Harrison (1981) 90, 92–4, 111.
87 Review in *The New York Times*, 20 December 1981.

Chapter 5

1 Harrison (2016) 263–79.
2 Morrison (1987) 57.
3 Tusa (2001); see Butler and Klepuszewski (2012).
4 A special performance was broadcast on Radio 4 in 2013 to mark the twenty-fifth anniversary of the film version, directed by Richard Eyre, seen on Channel 4 in 1987.
5 Representative responses are reproduced in Harrison (1989); see O'Brien (1998) 60.
6 See Harrison (2017) 459–60.
7 Harrison (2016) 263.
8 Harrison (2017) 462.
9 Gray (1751) 8.
10 Harrison (2016) 264.
11 Harrison (2016) 269.
12 C. Regan (2019a) 139 and (2016).
13 Arthur Rimbaud, Letter to Georges Izambard (13 May 1871), in Rimbaud (2005) 370–1.
14 C. Regan (2019a) 140.
15 Harrison (2016) 271.
16 Harrison (2016) 264.
17 Byrne (2019); see Harrison (2016) 150.
18 Rowland (2019) 195 n.53.
19 *Exploring* 'v.', BBC Radio 4, broadcast 18 February 2013. See also Jaggi (2007).
20 Wilmer (1992).
21 Harrison (2016) 273.
22 Stratas' singing voice features in Harrison's film *The Blasphemers' Banquet* (1989).

23 Macintosh (2000).
24 Durdik (1878).
25 Macintosh (2019) 105.
26 Harrison (1986) 371.
27 Tommasini (1996).
28 Harrison (1986) 383–4.
29 Eur. *Med.* 573–5; Harrison (1986) 433.
30 Macintosh (2019) 105–6.
31 *Oresteia* Notebook 5.1102.
32 Harrison (2016) 414.
33 Hair (1996) 6.
34 Hair (1996) 89.
35 Lévi-Strauss (1963) 217; a paraphrase of Thompson (1981) 213 and 240.
36 Harrison (1986) 368.
37 Harrison (1986) 369.
38 See Hall (2014) 171–2.
39 Harrison (1986) 369.
40 Harrison (1986) 446.
41 Harrison (1986) 371; Macintosh (2019) 108.
42 Harrison (1986) 446.
43 Harrison used an anonymized 1837 reprint of Talboys (1820).
44 Macintosh (2019) 108 n.17.
45 Harrison (1986) 410–11.
46 Harrison (1986) 414.
47 Harrison (1986) 412, 413, 415.
48 Harrison (1986) 413.
49 Harrison (1986) 418.
50 Harrison (1986) 418–19.
51 Fitch (1987) 146–7.
52 Harrison (1986) 420, 427, 430.
53 Harrison (1986) 435.
54 Harrison (1986) 437.
55 Harrison (1986) 420.
56 Easterling (1977).
57 Harrison (1986) 414.
58 Harrison (1986) 431.
59 Harrison (1986) 440.
60 Harrison (1986) 374.
61 Harrison (1986) 375.

62 Harrison (1986) 378.
63 Harrison (2017) 55-80.
64 Harrison (1986) 392.
65 Harrison (1986) 369.
66 Harrison (1986) 372.

Chapter 6

1. In January 2017, after nearly thirty years since first opening in London, it returned to the Finborough Theatre, directed by Jimmy Walters.
2. The most detailed analysis of both productions is in H. Marshall (2010) 130-69, to which I owe a great deal.
3. Eastman (2014) ch. 4.
4. H. Marshall (2007).
5. Harrison's no. 43=*The Greek Anthology* 11.291.
6. Corcoran (1993) 158-62 and Covey (1995) 139-41.
7. Morrison (1987).
8. Harrison (2016) 162.
9. Kramer (1997) 11, 31-62.
10. See Henderson (1991) 187-203; Lee (1971) 7-22, with especially Martial VI.8.1.
11. Translated by Balmer (2004) 81. On scatology in English satire from Nashe to Pope, see Lee (1971) 23-53.
12. Introduction to Persels and Ganim (eds.) xiii; Jonson, *The Staple of News,* 3.2.207-11; Boehrer (1997) 1-2.
13. Harrison (2016) 135. On the way this poem 'dialogizes the social and cultural past (and present)', see Kirk (2003) 96.
14. Lee (1971) 16, 18. Dante's sorcerers have their mouths where their anuses should be.
15. Lee (1971) 23-53.
16. Vallot, d'Anquin and Fagon (1862) 209-10. 16. See Marin (1989 [1986]) 218-41.
17. Shrager (1982) 39-44.
18. Shrager (1982) 67-73.
19. Carlyle (1898) 159, 164.
20. Lewin (1999) 5.
21. Persels and Ganim (2004) xiii-xxi.
22. Lee (1971) 1.
23. Swift (1725-6) 922. See Lee (1971) 59-60.
24. See p. 50.

25 Hillman (2007) 61.
26 See Nietzsche (1967) 25 (8), with Blondel (1991) 220.
27 Letter to the *Independent*, 3 November 1987, in Butler (1997) at 114.
28 See Byrne (1997b) 15 and Crucefix (1997) 161.
29 Harrison (2004) 28.
30 Harrison (2004) 29.
31 Harrison (2004) 40.
32 Harrison (2004) 48–9.
33 Lines 59–63 as translated by Page (1941) 35.
34 Lines 68, 74, 76, 81.
35 Parkyn (2018) ch. 2 analyses the changes and supplements Harrison made to the text of the fragment.
36 Kelleher (1996) 20.
37 Harrison (2004) 66.
38 The reading of Kelleher (1996) 64.
39 Eyre (1997) 45.
40 Harrison (2004) 130.
41 Harrison (2004) 138; see Poole (1999); Pérez (2015) 14–17.
42 Harrison (2004) 139.
43 Harrison (2004) 147.
44 Harrison (2004) 148.
45 Harrison (2016) 428–36. It was also included in his collection *Under the Clock* (2005).
46 See Hall (2011).
47 Harrison (2016) 430.
48 Harrison (1970) 73.
49 See especially LaGuardia (2004).
50 Rabelais (1653) 64.
51 Harrison (2016) 431.
52 Stanhope (1901) 192.
53 Harrison (2016) 431.
54 Harrison (2016) 433.
55 Sider (1997).
56 Harrison (2016) 436.
57 'Of Walking the Streets by Day' (1716) lines 115–16, reproduced in Dearing (1974) 144.
58 Harrison (2016) 71; see Thompson (1997) 128.
59 Spencer (1994) 3 and ch. 2. See also above p. 139.
60 Kustow (1995–6) 237.

61 Rostovtseff and Mattingly (1923).
62 *Kaisers* Notebook 2.456–9.
63 Larson (1991).
64 Harrison (1996) 68.
65 Harrison (1996) 82.
66 McDonald (1995).
67 Harrison (1996) 96.
68 Harrison (1996) 89.
69 Kustow (1995–6) 236.
70 For the mosaic, see Smid (2019) 395 fig. 10.
71 Harrison (1996) 97–9.
72 Harrison (1996) 101.
73 See Rusbridger (1997).
74 Armitstead (2019) 44–5.
75 Copley (2018).
76 See Hall (2006) 119–20.

Chapter 7

1 Speranza (2002) 170.
2 Bertram (2002) 45–68; Speranza (2002) 3, 121–2; Simon Armitage quoted on the *Poetry Foundation* website at https://www.poetryfoundation.org/poets/tony-harrison.
3 Lowe (2007) 150.
4 In Harrison (2017).
5 They can be viewed by appointment at the BFI in London or the Archive of Performances of Greek and Roman Drama at Oxford. I am very grateful to Peter Symes for providing me with personal copies.
6 Harrison (2017) 434.
7 Harrison (2017) 275–6.
8 Harrison (2017) 275–6.
9 Harrison (2017) 452.
10 Broadcast on 27 September 1981 at 1915 (*Radio Times* issue 3020).
11 Harrison (2007) 54–6; see Byrne (1998) 22–59.
12 Harrison (2017) 278.
13 Harrison (2007) 456–7.
14 Harrison (2017) 278–9.
15 In a 1997 feature on Channel 4's *Film Night*.
16 Molyneux (1991) 371.

17 Channel 4, *Film Night*, 3 June 1997.
18 See the darkly humorous portrait of her mother in 'Schwiegermutterlieder', Harrison (2016) 51–2.
19 33:45 minutes; Harrison (2007) 172.
20 Harrison (2007) 167.
21 Harrison (2007) 168.
22 Harrison (2007) 171.
23 See Vernant (1991) 111–50.
24 00:39 minutes; Weil (2005) 26. On Weil and the Classics, see Gold (2016).
25 Weil (2005) 3–4; Stead (2019) 216–19.
26 Harrison (2007) 166.
27 Harrison (2007) 168.
28 45:44 minutes.
29 31:25 minutes.
30 Harrison (2007) 170–1.
31 Lowe (2007) 153.
32 Harrison (2007) 225.
33 Harrison (2007) 230.
34 Harrison (2007) 228.
35 Harrison (2007) 228–9.
36 From 14:32 minutes in, Harrison (2007) 229–30, we see the reflection of the Parthenon in a mirror on the lid of a compass and discover we are in Athens.
37 Harrison (2007) 230.
38 21:35 minutes.
39 22:28 minutes.
40 23:35 minutes.
41 Harrison (2017) 249.
42 Harrison (1998) 27–9.
43 E.g. John Harlow in *Sunday Times*, 9 November, 1998, discussed in Speranza (2002) 233.
44 Harrison (1998) 18.
45 Harrison (1998) 7.
46 Harrison (1998) xxii.
47 Harrison (1998) 5.
48 Harrison (1998) 36–7.
49 Harrison (1998) xxiii.
50 Auden (1991) 137.
51 Speranza (2002) 225–6.
52 *Prometheus* Notebook 3.563.

53 On this topic, see the excellent study by Rowland (2001).
54 See Michelakis (2004) 199–200; Hall (2016).
55 For succinct overviews, see Friedlander (1992) 1–21 and Schwarz (1999) 1–42. For a different perspective, see Clendinnen (1999). On issues facing film directors dealing with the Holocaust, see Insdorf (1983) and Avisar (1988).
56 On Io in Harrison's film, see Stead (forthcoming).
57 On Levi and Harrison, see Rowland (2005) 101–8.
58 Schwarz (1999) 5.
59 See Langer (1995). Aeschylus has also been used by Jewish writers when addressing the issue of the Holocaust. The 2003 production in Tel Aviv of Rina Yerushalmi's *Mythos*, a Hebrew *Oresteia*, made references to the Holocaust in the depiction of mass graves at Troy.
60 Harrison (1998) 63.
61 Harrison (1998) 22.
62 Scribner (2003) Chapter 3.
63 Harrison (1998) 61.
64 Heaney (1990) 77.
65 Harrison (2016) 43.
66 Foley (2004) 107–8.
67 Rehm (2002) 111.
68 See Rowland (2019) 196–7; this notebook contains notes on Pound's discovery of the Sappho fragments that inspired Pound's 1916 poem 'Papyrus'.
69 15:20 minutes.
70 Powell (1925) 106–7, lines 9–10. An English translation is available at https://livingpoets.dur.ac.uk/w/Phanocles,_fragment_1_Powell?oldid=2551.
71 Antikensammlung Berlin, V.I.3172.
72 Harrison (2007) 396.
73 Lowe (2007) 155–6.
74 Harrison (2007) 381.
75 See Harrison (2017) 27, 130, 159–62.
76 Harrison (2007) 383.
77 Harrison (2007) 385.

Chapter 8

1 For a photograph of the theatre which I subsequently took myself, in September 2011, see Hall (2013) 64 fig. III.4.

2. Fenton's Crimea images have proved of great interest to historians of photography: see Grant (2005).
3. Hall (2013) 13–14 with fig. I.4.
4. *Illustrated London News*, 19 January (1856) 80.
5. See Hall (2013) 5 fig. I.1.
6. Simpson (1902 [1855]) with fig. 72. Harrison gave me a copy of this beautiful book, which been given to him by film director Tony Richardson. Richardson had used it when making his controversial movie *The Charge of the Light Brigade* in 1968. I have since donated the volume to the Archive of Performances of Greek & Roman Drama at Oxford University.
7. For the full cast and production team, see http://www.bbc.co.uk/programmes/b08n1ylb.
8. Harrison (2019) 175–6.
9. Harrison (2016) 69.
10. See Deghett (2014), where the photograph is reproduced, and also above p. 128.
11. Harrison (2016) 313.
12. 'Wir werden gezwungen, in die Schrecken der Individualexistenz hineinzublicken – und sollen doch nicht erstarren', from *Die Geburt der Tragodie*, section 17, English translation adapted from Nietzsche (1993 (1872)) 80.
13. Adorno (1966) 362; Kaufmann (1968), 182.
14. Harrison (2017) 246, 496.
15. Shelley (1824) 338.
16. Clavane (2013).
17. Hall (2010c) 141–4.
18. See Hall (2007).
19. Harrison (2017) 409–10.
20. Harrison (1976) 50.
21. A similar photograph can be viewed in Pappas (2016).
22. Marshall (2008) 222–3.
23. On the critical response, see especially Hardwick (2013).
24. Stein (2005).
25. See also Brodie (2014).
26. Harrison (2005) 35.
27. Harrison (2005) 9.
28. Harrison (2005) 19.
29. Harrison (2005) 20–1.
30. Harrison (2005) 39–45.
31. Harrison (2017) 190.
32. Harrison (2017) 232.

33 It was reproduced in Page's *Guardian* obituary by Hopkinson (2011).
34 Harrison (2017) 232.
35 Harrison (1992) 49.
36 Harrison (2017) 232.
37 See Hall (2018) 46–50.
38 The Greek line is pronounced *ouk an tis eipoi mallon ē peponthamen*; it means 'nobody could tell of suffering greater than what we have suffered'.
39 Harrison (2008) 11.
40 Harrison (2008) 45.
41 Harrison (2008) 55.
42 Harrison (2008) 58; see Shelley (1840) 17.
43 Harrison (2008) 15.
44 Hall and Macintosh (2005) 495–6.
45 Hall and Macintosh (2005) 508–9.
46 *The Saturday Review*, 22 April 1905, 520–1.
47 Letter cited in Wilson (1987) 106 with n. 15.
48 Salter (1911) 9.
49 Harrison (2017) 411, 414.
50 Harrison (2008) 46.
51 The picture is reproduced in Hall and Macintosh (2005) xii, fig. 0.1.
52 See Wilson (1987) 9.
53 Thorndike (1936) 74.
54 Salmon (1986) 239.
55 See e.g. Hall and Macintosh (2005) 515, fig. 17.2, reproduced from *Illustrated London News* 131, 2 November 1907.
56 Murray (1906) 15–16.
57 Murray (1913) 32.
58 Murray (1910) 11.
59 See Ackerman (1986).
60 Harrison (2008) 4 and especially 47: 'But a certain someone's been unkind enough to say/ that poetry's not Professor Murray's principal forte/ And many agree with a certain someone's views/ on the outdated melodies of Gilbert Murray's muse.'
61 Harrison (2013).
62 Harrison (2019) 188.

Chapter 9

1 Murray (1989).

2 Harrison (2017) 67–74.
3 Nicholson (2007) 67.
4 Quoted in Byrne (2016) 117.
5 Geyer-Ryan (1991).
6 Hoggart (1991).
7 Harrison (2017) 203–4; Smalley (1991) 69–71.
8 Harrison (2016) 125; see H. Marshall (2017) 69–70.
9 Harrison (2016) 259–60.
10 Harrison (2016) 132; Keats (1841) 198.
11 Keats (1841) 208.
12 Smalley (1991) 59–60. See also the bleak reference to 'Hippocrene', recalling once again Keats' 'Ode to a Nightingale', in 'Cremation Elegy': Harrison (2016) 411.
13 Ulmer (2017) 54.
14 Keats (1841) 203.
15 Keats (1841) 208. On Harrison and Keats, see also Whale (2006).
16 Keats (1841) 237.
17 Harrison (2016) 215.
18 Harrison (2016) 57; Keats (1841) 199.
19 Harrison (2016) 207.
20 See p. 173.
21 Lawrence (1994) 487; Harrison (2016) 390, well discussed by Osterwalder (2005).
22 Harrison (2016) 363; see p. 173.
23 Harrison (2016) 334. Eyre (2019) later responded with a long and affectionate poem for Harrison's eightieth birthday.
24 Harrison (2016) 366.
25 The poem is analysed beautifully by Taplin (2019).
26 Byron (1837) 92, 329.
27 See Harrison (2017) *passim*.
28 Poole (1999) 57.
29 'Wordlists', Harrison (2016) 127; Hall and Stead (2020) 303–5.
30 Jules Janin in the *Journal des Débats* for 6 December 1858.
31 Harrison (2017) 179, 89. Harrison's exuberance as well as his darkness is well brought out in Cartledge (2019).

Bibliography

Abbott, P. E. (2003) 'The dress regulation of the Bengal artillery, 1845', *Journal of the Society for Army Historical Research*, 81, 47–57.

Ackerman, Robert (1986) 'Euripides and Professor Murray', *CJ* 81, 32–6.

Adams, J. Q. (1822) Entry for 16 June in *John Quincy Adams Digital Diary*, https://www.masshist.org/publications/jqadiaries/index.php/document/jqadiaries-v32-1822-06-16-p308.

Adorno, Theodor (1966) *Negative Dialektik*. Frankfurt: Suhrkamp.

Allen, W. H. (1957) *Allen's Indian Mail and Register of Intelligence*, vol. 15. London: W. H. Allen & Co.

Amours, F. J. (1908, ed.) *Scottish Alliterative Verse*. Edinburgh/London: Blackwood.

Anon. (1827) 'Commedie di Alberto Nota', *Monthly Review* vol. IV, no. 20, appendix, 449–50.

Armitstead, Claire (2019) 'Tony Harrison and *The Guardian*', in Hall (ed.) 41–52.

Astley, N. (1991, ed.) *Bloodaxe Critical Anthologies I: Tony Harrison*. Newcastle: Bloodaxe.

Attridge, Derek (1979) 'Dryden's dilemma, or, Racine refashioned: the problem of the English dramatic couplet', *Yearbook of English Studies* 9, 55–77.

Auden, W. H. (1991) *Collected Poems*, revised ed. London: Faber.

Avisar, Ilan (1988) *Screening the Holocaust*. Bloomington, IN: Indiana UP.

Balmer, Josephine (2004) *Catullus*. Newcastle: Bloodaxe.

Balmer, Josephine (2019) 'Lost in the original: Tony Harrison as a classicist poet', in Hall (ed.) 29–37.

Barnard, John Levi (2018) *Empire of Ruin: Black Classicism and American Imperial Culture*. New York: OUP.

Barnes, Clive (1975) 'A 'Misanthrope' for Modern Times', *New York Times*, 13 March, 44.

Becker, Andrew Sprague (1995) *The Shield of Achilles and the Poetics of Ekphrasis*. Lanham, MD: Rowman & Littlefield.

Belmekki, Belkacem (2008) 'A wind of change: the new British colonial policy in post-revolt India', *Atlantis* 30, 111–124.

Bertram, V. (2002) *Poetry and Contemporary Culture*. Edinburgh: Edinburgh UP.

Bertram, V. (2005) *Gendering Poetry*. London: Pandora.

Bishop, Norma (1983) 'A Nigerian version of a Greek classic', *Research in African Literatures*, 14, 68–80.

Blakesey, Jacob (2018) 'Tony Harrison the translator', *English Studies*, 99, 51–66.
Blondel, Eric (1991) *Nietzsche: The Body and Culture*, tr. Seán Hand. Stanford, CA: Stanford UP.
Boehrer, Bruce (1977) *The Fury of Men's Gullets: Ben Jonson and the Digestive Canal*. Philadelphia: UPenn Press.
Bower, Rachel (2015) 'Wole Soyinka in Leeds', online article at https://arts.leeds.ac.uk/nettw/wole-soyinka-in-leeds.
Bower, Rachel (2019) 'Tony Harrison: Nigeria, masque and masks', in Hall (ed.) 81–90.
Brodie, G. (2014) 'Translation in performance: theatrical shift and the transmission of meaning in Tony Harrison's translation of Euripides' *Hecuba*', *Contemporary Theatre Review*, 24, 53–65.
Butalia, Romesh C. (1998) *The Evolution of the Artillery in India*. Mumbai etc: Allied Publishers.
Butler, Christopher (1997) 'Culture and debate', in Byrne (ed.) 93–114.
Butler, Josephine E. (2003) 'The present aspect of the Abolitionist cause in relation to British India', in Ingrid Sharp (ed.) *The Queen's Daughters in India*, no. 22. London: Taylor & Francis.
Butler, Stephen and Wojciech Klepuszewski (2012) *All the Vs of Life: Conflicts and Controversies in Tony Harrison's Poetry*. Koszalin: WUPK.
Byrne, Sandie (1997a, ed.) *Tony Harrison: Loiner*. Oxford: Clarendon.
Byrne, Sandie (1997b) 'Introduction: Tony Harrison's public poetry' in Byrne (ed.) 1–28.
Byrne, Sandie (1998) *H, V., & O: The Poetry of Tony Harrison*: Manchester: Manchester UP.
Byrne, Sandie (2006) 'Sex in the "sick, sick body politic": Tony Harrison's fruit', in C. C. Barfoot (ed.) *And Never Know the Joy: Sex and the Erotic in English Poetry*, 373–88. Leiden/Boston: Brill.
Byrne, Sandie (2016) 'Poetry and class' in Edward Larrissy (ed.) *The Cambridge Companion to British Poetry, 1945–2010*, 116–29. Cambridge: CUP.
Byrne, Sandie (2019) 'Metre and memory (and Μνημοσύνη)', in Hall (ed.) 53–70.
Byron, George (1837) *The Complete Works*. London: Baudry's European Library.
Campbell, D. A. (1982, trans.) *Greek Lyric*, Vol. I. Cambridge, MA: Harvard UP.
Carlyle, Thomas (1898) *Latterday Pamphlets*. London: Chapman Hall.
Cartledge, Paul (2019) 'Will the real Tony Harrison please stand up?', *Argo*, 10, 41–2.
Case, Sue-Ellen (1985) 'Classic drag: the Greek creation of female parts', *Theatre Journal*, 37, 317–27.
Clavane, A. (2013) 'Tony Harrison: Leeds, poetry and *Granta Magazine*'s snobbery against the north', https://sabotagetimes.com/life/tony-harrisonleeds-football-poetry-and-granata-magazines-snobbery-against-the-north.
Clay, Diskin (1992) 'Columbus' Senecan prophecy', *AJP* 113, 617–20.

Clendinnen, Inga (1999) *Reading the Holocaust*. Melbourne: Text Publishing Company.

Copley, Hannah (2018) 'From Baghdad to Sarajevo to Beeston: the war poetry of Tony Harrison', *English Studies*, 99, 19–33.

Corcoran, Neil (1993) *English Poetry since 1940*. London: Longman.

Covey, Neil (1995) 'Notes toward an investigation of the marginality of poetry and the sympathetic imagination', *South Atlantic Review* 60, 137–51.

Cross, Colin (1970) *The Fall of the British Empire*. London: Paladin.

Crucefix, Martyn (1997) 'The drunken porter does poetry: metre and voice in the poems of Tony Harrison', in Byrne (ed.) 161–79.

Davidson, C. (1991) 'Positional symbolism and English medieval drama', *Comparative Drama*, 25, 66–76.

Davis, Gregson (1997) *Aimé Césaire*. Cambridge: CUP.

Deane, Patrick (1994) *At Home in Time: Forms of Neo-Augustanism in Modern English Poetry*. Montreal: McGill-Queens UP.

Deane, Patrick (1999) 'British poetry since 1950', *Contemporary Literature* 40, 491–506.

Dearing, Vinton A. (1974, ed.) *John Gay*, Vol. I. Oxford: Clarendon.

Deghett, T. R. (2014) 'The war photo no-one would publish', *The Atlantic*, 8 August, https://www.theatlantic.com/international/archive/2014/08/the-warphoto-no-one-would-publish/375762.

Dexter, John (1993) *The Honourable Beast*. London: Nick Herne Books.

Dolan, Jill (1988) *The Feminist Spectator as Critic*. Ann Arbor, MN: Michigan UP.

Dougherty, Carol (2006) *Prometheus*. London: Routledge.

Durdik, Petre (1878) *Euripidova Medeia*. Prague: Biblioteka Klassikuv.

Easterling, P. E. (1977) 'The infanticide in Euripides' *Medea*', *YCS* 25, 177–91.

Eastman, Helen (2014) *Greek Up North: A Study of Northern Broadsides' Productions of Ancient Drama*. PhD Diss. KCL.

Eggebrecht, H. H. (1995) *Terminologie der Musik im 20. Jahrhundert*. Stuttgart: Franz Steiner.

Elliott, J. R. (1989) *Playing God*. Toronto: Toronto UP.

Eyre, Richard (1997) 'Tony Harrison the playwright', in Byrne (ed.) 43–8.

Eyre, Richard (2019) 'Afterword: 'For Tony at 80': A Poem by Sir Richard Eyre', in Hall (ed.) 221–4.

Fay, Stephen and Philip Oakes (1991) 'Mystery behind the mask'', in Astley (ed.) 287–90.

Fitch, John G. (1987, ed.) *Seneca's Hercules Furens*. Ithaca, NY: Cornell UP.

Fleischmann, W. B. (1965) 'Classicism', in Alex Preminger (ed.) *Encyclopedia of Poetry and Poetics*, 136–41. Princeton: PUP.

Foley, Helene (2004) 'Bad women: gender politics in late twentieth-century performance and revision of Greek tragedy' in Hall, Macintosh and Wrigley (eds.) 77–112.

Ford, Andrew (2002) *The Origins of Criticism*. Princeton, NJ: PUP.

Fraser, James Baillie (1851) *Military Memoir of Lieut.-Colonel James Skinner*. London: Smith, Elder.

Friedlander, Saul (1992, ed.) *Probing the Limits of Representation*. Cambridge, MA: Harvard UP, 1992.

Geyer-Ryan, Helga (1991) 'Heteroglossia in the poetry of Bertolt Brecht and Tony Harrison', in Willie van Peter (ed.) *Explorations in language, literature, and culture*, 193–221. London: Routledge.

Gill, Jo (2012) '"Northern working-class spectator sports": Tony Harrison's *Continuous*', in Katharine Cockin (ed.) *The Literary North*, 157–74. Houndmills, Basigstoke/New York: Palgrave MacMillan.

Gilroy-Ware, Cora Hatshepsut (2013) *Marmorealities: Classical Nakedness in British Sculpture and Painting 1798–1840*. PhD Diss. York.

Gold, B. K. (2016) 'Simone Weil: receiving the *Iliad*', in R. Wyles and E. Hall (eds.) *Women Classical Scholars*, 360–76. Oxford: OUP.

Goldhill, Simon (2007) *How to Stage Greek Tragedy Today*. Chicago: Chicago UP.

Gosling, Kenneth (1974) 'More scope sought for black actors', *The Times*, 23 August.

Grant, S. (2005) 'A terrible beauty', *Tate, Etc.*, 5, http://www.tate.org.uk/context-comment/articles/terrible-beauty.

Gray, Thomas (1751) *An Elegy Written in a Country Church Yard*. 3rd edition. London: R. Dodsley.

Greco, Giovanni (2019) 'Wine and poetry: translating Tony Harrison in Italy', in Hall (ed.) 163–73.

Gussow, Mel (1988) 'A "Phaedra" From Britain's India', *New York Times*, 17 December, Section 1, 15.

Haffenden, John (1991) 'An interview with Tony Harrison' in Astley (ed.) 227–46.

Hair, Lindsey (1996) *The Right Words in the Proper Places: an Investigation of the Poetry of Tony Harrison, from Text to TV*, PhD Diss. Sheffield.

Hairsine, Neil (1997) *I is the Other: Conflicts and Continuities of Identity in Tony Harrison's* The Loiners *(1970),* Continuous *(1981) and* 'v'. *(1985)*. PhD Diss. Newcastle upon Tyne.

Hall, Edith (1998) 'Clytemnestra's manly heart in the *Agamemnon*', *Omnibus* 36, 27–30.

Hall, Edith (2005) 'Aeschylus' Clytemnestra versus her Senecan tradition', in Macintosh et al. (eds.) 53–75.

Hall, Edith (2007) 'Trojan suffering, tragic gods, and transhistorical metaphysics', in S. A. Brown and C. Silverstone (eds) *Tragedy in Transition, 16–33*. Oxford: Blackwell).

Hall, Edith (2008) *The Return of Ulysses*. London: IB Tauris.

Hall, Edith (2009) 'Greek tragedy and the politics of subjectivity in recent fiction', *CRJ* 1, 23–42, https://doi.org/10.1093/crj/clp006.

Hall, Edith (2010a) 'British refraction of the 1857 "mutiny" through the prism of Greece and Rome', in Hall and Vasunia, 33–48.

Hall, Edith (2010b) 'Mughal Princes or Greek philosopher-kings? Neoclassical and Indian architectural styles in British mansions built by East Indiamen', in Hall and Vasunia, 13–31.

Hall, Edith (2010c) *Greek Tragedy*. Oxford: OUP.

Hall, Edith (2006) *The Theatrical Cast of Athens*. Oxford: OUP.

Hall, Edith (2011) 'Karl Marx and the ruins of Trier', *ERH* 18, 783–97.

Hall, Edith (2012) 'The politics of metrical variety in classical Athenian drama', in D. Yatromanolakis (ed.) *Music & Politics in Ancient Greek Society*, 1–28. New York/London: Routledge.

Hall, Edith (2013) *Adventures with Iphigenia in Tauris*. New York: OUP.

Hall, Edith (2014) 'Why is Penelope still waiting? The missing feminist reappraisal of the Odyssey in cinema, 1963–2007', in K. P. Nikoloutsos (ed.) *Ancient Greek Women in Film*, 163–85. Oxford: OUP.

Hall, Edith (2015) 'Narcissus and the Furies: Myth and docufiction in Jonathan Littell's *The Kindly Ones*', in Justine McConnell and Edith Hall (eds.) *Ancient Greek Myth in World Fiction Since 1989*, 163–80. London: Bloomsbury.

Hall, Edith (2017) 'Tony Harrison: The bard of Beeston', *Prospect Magazine*, 15 May, viewable online at https://www.prospectmagazine.co.uk/magazine/tony-harrison-the-bard-of-beeston.

Hall, Edith (2018) 'Euripides, Sparta and the self-definition of Athens', in A. Powell and P. Cartledge (eds.) *The Greek Superpower*, 29–52. Swansea: Classical Press of Wales.

Hall, Edith (2019a, ed.) *New Light on Tony Harrison*. Oxford: OUP for British Academy.

Hall, Edith (2019b) 'Paving & pencilling: Heaney's Inscriptions in J. W. Mackail's Translation of the *Aeneid*', in S. J. Harrison et al. (ed.) Seamus Heaney & the Classics, 223–43. Oxford: OUP.

Hall, Edith and Fiona Macintosh (2005) *Greek Tragedy and the British Theatre*. Oxford: OUP.

Hall, Edith, Fiona Macintosh and A. Wrigley (2004, eds.) *Dionysus since 69*. Oxford: OUP.

Hall, Edith and Henry Stead (2020) *A People's History of Classics*. London: RTF.

Hall, Edith and Phiroze Vasunia (2010, eds.) *India, Greece and Rome, 1757–2007*, BICS suppl. 108. London: ICS.

Hall, Lee (2019) 'The man who came to read the metre', in Edith Hall (ed.) 21–8.

Hall, Peter (1983) *Hall's Diaries: The Story of a Dramatic Battle*, ed. John Goodwin. London: Hamish Hamilton.

Hardwick, Lorna (1999) 'Placing Prometheus', in Lorna Hardwick (ed.) *Tony Harrison's Poetry, Drama and Film*, 1–15. Milton Keynes: OU.

Hardwick, Lorna (2013) 'Translating Greek plays for the theatre today', *Target* 25, 321–42.

Harrison, Tony (1967) 'English Virgil: the Aeneid in the XVIII century", *Philologica Pragensia* X, 1–11, 80–91.

Harrison, Tony (1969) 'Dryden's *Aeneid*', in Bruce King (ed.) *Dryden's Mind and Art*, 143–67. Edinburgh: Oliver and Boyd.

Harrison, Tony (1976) *Phaedra Britannica. After Jean Racine*. 3rd edition with introductory essay & illustrations. London: Rex Collings.

Harrison, Tony (1978) *From The School of Eloquence and Other Poems*. London: Rex Collings.

Harrison, Tony (1981) *Continuous: 50 Sonnets from The School of Eloquence*. London: Rex Collings.

Harrison, Tony (1981) *The Oresteia*. London: Rex Collings.

Harrison, Tony (1986) *Theatre Works 1973–1985*. Harmondsworth: Penguin.

Harrison, Tony (1989) '*v*.' 2nd ed. Newcastle upon Tyne: Bloodaxe.

Harrison, Tony (1991) 'The Oresteia in the Making: Letters to Peter Hall' in Astley (ed.) 275–80.

Harrison, Tony (1996) *Plays Three*. London: Faber.

Harrison, Tony (1998) *Prometheus*. London: Faber.

Harrison, Tony (2002) *Plays Four*. London: Faber.

Harrison, Tony (2004) *Plays Five*. London: Faber.

Harrison, Tony (2005) *Hecuba*. London: Faber.

Harrison, Tony (2007) *Collected Film Poetry*. London: Faber.

Harrison, Tony (2008) *Fram*. London: Faber.

Harrison, Tony (2013) 'Black Sea Aphrodite', *LRB* vol. XXXV no. 22, 21 November. https://www.lrb.co.uk/the-paper/v35/n22/tony-harrison/black-sea-aphrodite.

Harrison, Tony (2015) 'Polygons', *LRB* vol. XXXVII no. 4, 19 February; https://www.lrb.co.uk/the-paper/v37/n04/tony-harrison/polygons.

Harrison, Tony (2016) *Collected Poems*. London: Faber.

Harrison, Tony (2017) *The Inky Digit of Defiance*, ed. Edith Hall. London: Faber & Faber.

Harrison, Tony (2019) *Plays Six*. London: Faber.

Heaney, Seamus (1990) *The Cure at Troy*. Derry: Field Day.

Henderson, Jeffrey (1991) *The Maculate Muse*. 2nd ed. New York/Oxford: OUP.

Hickling, Alfred (2003) 'Poetry or Bust', *The Guardian*, 8 September, https://www.theguardian.com/stage/2003/sep/08/theatre.

Hillman, David (2007) *Shakespeare's Entrails*. Basingstoke: Palgrave Macmillan.

Hoggart, Richard (1991) 'In conversation with Tony Harrison', in Astley (ed.) 36–45.

Holman, Dennis (1961) *Sikander Sahib.* London: Heinemann.
Hopkinson, A. (2011) 'Raissa Page obituary', *The Guardian* Photography Section, 21 September, https://www.theguardian.com/artanddesign/2011/sep/21/raissa-pageobituary.
Insdorf, Annette (1983) *Indelible Shadows: Film and the Holocaust.* New York: CUP.
Jaggi, Maya (2007) 'Beats of the Heart', *The Guardian*, 31 March. https://www.theguardian.com/books/2007/mar/31/poetry.tonyharrison.
James, L. (1997) *Raj.* London: Little, Brown and Company.
Jameson, F. (2015) *The Ancients and the Postmoderns.* London: Verso.
Jones, W. (1788) 'On the Gods of Greece, Italy, and India', *Asiatick Researches* 1, 221–275.
Kaufmann, W. (1968) *Tragedy and Philosophy,* New York: Viking Penguin.
Keats, John (1841) *The Poetical Works.* London: William Smith.
Kelleher, Joe (1996) *Tony Harrison.* Plymouth: Northcote House.
Kennedy, David (2009) '"Past never found" – class, dissent, and the contexts of Tony Harrison's *v*.', *English* 221, 162–81.
Keulen, Atze J. (2001, ed.) *L. Annaeus Seneca Troades.* Leiden, Boston and Cologne: Brill.
Kirk, Jon (2003) *Twentieth-Century Writing and the British Working Class.* Cardiff: University of Wales Press.
Kobes du Mez, Kristin (2015) *A New Gospel for Women.* Oxford: OUP.
Kramer, Reinhold (1997) *Scatology and Civility in the English-Canadian Novel.* Toronto, Buffalo, and London: University of Toronto Press.
Kustow, Michael (1995–6) 'A beast in the Coliseum', *Arion* 3, 236–40.
LaGuardia, David (2004) 'Doctor Rabelais and the medicine of scatology', in Persels and Ganim (eds.) 24–37.
Langer, L. (1995) *Admitting the Holocaust.* New York: OUP.
Larson, Victoria Tietze (1991) 'The "Hercules Oetaeus" and the picture of the "Sapiens" in Senecan prose', *Phoenix*, 45, 39–4.
Latham, Caroline (2016) *Reanimating Greek Tragedy: How Contemporary Poets Translate for the Stage.* PhD Diss. KCL.
Lawrence, D. H. (1994) *The Complete Poems.* London: Wordsworth Editions.
Lee, Jae Num (1971) *Swift and Scatological Satire.* Albuquerque: New Mexico UP.
Lessing, Gotthold Ephraim (1836) *Laocoon,* tr. W. Ross. London: J. Ridgeway.
Lévi-Strauss, C. (1963) *Structural Anthropology.* New York: Pelican.
Levine, Philippa (2003) *Prostitution, Race and Politics.* New York: Routledge.
Lewin, Ralph (1999) *Merde.* London: Aurum.
Long, James (1869) *Selections from Unpublished Records of Government for the Years 1748-1767,* Volume 1. Calcutta: Government Printing.

Lowe, Nick (2007) 'The screen of Orpheus', *Arion* 15, 149–56.

Lyon, John (1996–7) 'Doing it all: Tony Harrison', *Thumbscrew* 6, 11–18.

Macintosh, Fiona (2000) 'Introduction: the performer in performance' in E. Hall, F. Macintosh and O. Taplin (eds.) *Medea in Performance 1500–2000* (Oxford, Legenda), 1–31.

Macintosh, Fiona (2019) 'Harrison as scholar-poet of the theatre' in Hall (ed.) 101–10.

Macintosh, Fiona, Pantelis Michelakis, Edith Hall and Oliver Taplin (2005, eds.) *Agamemnon in Performance*. Oxford: OUP.

Marin, Louis (1989 [1986]) *Food for Thought*. Baltimore, MD/London: Johns Hopkins UP.

Marshall, Cécile (2010) '"Inwardness" and the "quest for a public poetry" in the works of Tony Harrison', in Merriman, Emily Taylor and Adrian Grafe (eds.) *Intimate Exposure: Essays on the Public-Private Divide in British Poetry since 1950*, 147–59. Jefferson, NC: McFarland & Co.

Marshall, Cécile (2019) 'The translation and reception of Harrison's poetry in France', in Hall (ed.) 155–62.

Marshall, C. W. (2013) 'The School of Eloquence: the development of Tony Harrison's sonnet sequence' file:///C:/Users/k1198403/Dropbox/BARD/The_School_of_ Eloquence_the_Development.pdf.

Marshall, Hallie (2007) 'Tony Harrison and Jocelyn Herbert: a theatrical love affair', *Arion* 15, 109–26.

Marshall, Hallie (2008) '"Remembrance is Not Enough": the political function of Tony Harrison's poetry', *Syllecta Classica* 19, 221–36.

Marshall, Hallie (2010) *Banging the Lyre: The Classical Plays of Tony Harrison*. PhD Diss UBC.

Marshall, Hallie (2017) 'Finding *Patria* and *Pietas* in Leeds: Tony Harrison and Virgil's *Aeneid*', *English Studies* 99, 67–76.

Marshall, Hallie (2019) 'The early years at the National Theatre: Harrison's Molière and Racine' in Hall (ed.) 91–100.

Mauriac, François (1940) *Journal [1932–39]*, vol. 3. Paris: Bernard Grasset.

McDonald, Marianne (1995) 'Marcus Aurelius: The Kaisers of Carnuntum', *Didaskalia* 2. https://www.didaskalia.net/issues/vol2no3/harrison.html.

Michelakis, P. (2004) 'Greek tragedy in cinema', in Hall, Macintosh and Wrigley (eds.) 199–218.

Molyneaux, Andrée (1991) 'Cutting his teeth: working with Tony Harrison on *Arctic Paradise* and *The Big H*', in Astley (ed.) 367–76.

Morley, Sheridan (1975) 'India, whose India?', *Punch*, 17 September, 468.

Morrison, Blake (1987) 'The filial art: a reading of contemporary British poetry', *Yearbook of English Studies* 17, 179–217.

Morrison, Blake (2019) 'Harrison as elegist', in Hall (ed.) 3–12.
Moul, Victoria (2010) *Jonson, Horace and the Classical Tradition*. Cambridge: CUP.
Murray, G. (1906, trans.) *The Medea of Euripides*. Oxford: OUP.
Murray, Gilbert (1910, trans.) *The Iphigenia in Tauris of Euripides*. New York: OUP.
Murray, G. (1913) *Euripides and his Age*. London, Williams and Norgate.
Murray, Oswyn (1989) 'Poetry and its public in ancient Greece', *TLS*, 16 June, 655.
Nicholson, Colin (2010) '"Reciprocal recognitions": race, class and subjectivity in Tony Harrison's *The Loiners*', *Race & Class* 51, 59–78.
Nietzsche, Friedrich (1967) *Werke*, ed. Giorgio Colli and Mazzino Montinari, vol. VII.2. Leipzig: C. G. Naumann.
Nietzsche, Friedrich (1993 [1872]) *The Birth of Tragedy out of the Spirit of Music*, tr. Shaun Whiteside. London: Penguin.
Nilsson, S. 1968. *European architecture in India, 1750–1850*. Trans. A. George and E. Zettersten. London: Faber.
Nunn, Trevor (2013) 'My theatre of dreams', *The Independent*, 1 November, https://www.independent.co.uk/arts-entertainment/theatre-dance/features/trevor-nunn-my-theatre-of-dreams-8915267.html.
O'Brien, Sean (1998) *The Deregulated Muse*. Newcastle-upon-Tyne: Bloodaxe.
O'Brien, Sean (2014) 'The poet in the theatre: verse drama' in S. Earnshaw (ed.) *The Handbook of Creative Writing Book*, 229–35. Edinburgh: Edinburgh UP.
Orthwein, Jake (2017) 'James Gray's radical classicism', https://filmschoolrejects.com/james-grays-radical-classicism.
Osterwalder, Hans (2005) '"Eros/Thanatos a pair": the dialectic of life and death in Tony Harrison's *Laureate's Block*', *Critical Survey* 17, 85–99.
Padley, Steve (2008) 'Hijacking culture: Tony Harrison and the Greeks', *Cycnos*, 18, 1–34.
Page, Denys (1941) *Literary Papyri*. London/Cambridge, MA: Harvard UP.
Pappas, G. (2016) 'When Greeks were refugees', http://www.pappaspost.com/photos-when-greeks-were-refugees.
Park, Roy (1969) '"Ut picture poesis": the nineteenth-century aftermath', *Journal of Aesthetics and Art Criticism* 28, 155–65.
Parker, R. B. (1986) 'The National Theatre's *Oresteia*, 1981–82', in M. Cropp, E. Fantham and S. Scully (eds.) *Greek Tragedy and its Legacy*, 337–57. Calgary: Calgary UP.
Parkyn, Charlotte (2018) *Inspiration from Tatters: Reconstructed Ancient Greek Plays on the Modern Stage*. PhD Diss. KCL.
Patel, Vibhuti (1989) 'Indianised adaptation of *Phaedra* in New York', *India Today, Magazine*, 28 February. https://www.indiatoday.in/magazine/international/story/19890228-indianised-adaptation-of-phaedra-in-new-york-815784-1989-02-28.

Pérez, Leticia González (2015) 'Nature and culture in Tony Harrison's *The Trackers of Oxyrhynchus*', *Tycho* 3, 5–24.

Persels, Jeff and Russell Ganim, eds. (2004) *Fecal Matters in Early Modern Literature and Art*. Aldershot, Hants and Burlington,

Pfotenhauer, Helmut (1995, ed.) *Frühklassizismus*. Frankfur-am-Main: Deutscher Klassiker Verlag.

Ploix, C. (2018) 'Harrison's *Phaedra Britannica* and *The Misanthrope*', *Perspectives* 26, 478–94.

Poole, Adrian (1999) 'Harrison and Marsyas', in Lorna Hardwick (ed.) *Tony Harrison's Poetry, Drama and Film: The Classical Dimension*, Milton Keynes: Open University, 56–68, http://www.open.ac.uk/arts/research/greekplays/publications/tony-harrisons-poetry-drama-and-film/harrison-and-marsyas.

Powell, J. U. (1925, ed.) *Collectanea Alexandrina*. Oxford: OUP.

Putnam, Michael (1998) *Virgil's Epic Designs*. New Haven: Yale UP.

Rabelais, François (1653) *The First [Second] Book of the Works of Mr. Francis Rabelais*, tr. Thomas Urquart. London: Richard Baddeley.

Regan, C. (2015) '"Ghosts" and the haunting of Harrison by Rimbaud', *Etudes britanniques contemporaines* 48, http://journals.openedition.org/ebc/2151.

Regan, C. (2016) *The Rimbaud of Leeds*. New York, Cambria Press.

Regan, C. (2019a), 12. "*v.*' Revisited: Harrison, Rimbaud and the French radical tradition' in Hall (ed.) 139–54.

Regan, C. (2019b) 'A Republican poet in the White Queen's Africa: reading Harrison's "The Railroad Heroides"' *English Studies*, 100, 63–74.

Regan, S. (2019) *The Sonnet*. Oxford: OUP.

Rehm, Rush (2002) (2002) '*Supplices*, the satyr play: Charles Mee's *Big Love*', *AJP* 123, 111–18.

Richardson, Edmund (2015) 'The harmless impudence of a revolutionary' in Stead and Hall (ed.) 79–98.

Rihm, Wolfgang (1997) 'Moderne also Klassizismus', in Hermann Danuser (ed.) *Die klassizistische Moderne in der Musik des 20. Jahrhunderts*, 315–18. Winterthur: Amadeus.

Rimbaud, A. (2005) *Complete Works, Selected Letters*. Chicago UP.

Robinson, Peter (1998) *Shared Intimacy: A Study of Tony Harrison's Public Poetry*, Ph.D. Diss. Hull.

Rostovtseff, Michael and Harold Mattingly (1923) 'Commodus-Hercules in Britain', *JRS* 13, 91–109.

Roth, Andrew (1970) *Enoch Powell*. London: Macdonald & Co.

Rowland, A. (2001) *Tony Harrison and the Holocaust*. Liverpool, Liverpool UP.

Rowland, A. (2005) *Holocaust Poetry*. Edinburgh: Edinburgh UP.

Rowland, A. (2019) 'Modernism and the "double consciousness" of myth in Tony Harrison's poems and *Metamorpheus*', in Hall (ed.) 185–204.

Roynon, Tessa (2006) *Transforming America: Toni Morrison and Classical Tradition.* PhD Diss. Warwick.

Rusbridger, Alan (1997) 'Tony Harrison and *The Guardian*' in Byrne (ed.) 133–6.

Rutter, Barrie 2007) 'Performing Tony Harrison', *Arion* 15, 143–8.

Rutter, Carol (1995, ed.) *Tony Harrison: Permanently Bard.* Newcastle: Bloodaxe.

Salmon, E. (ed.) (1986) *Granville Barker & his Correspondents.* Detroit MI: Wayne State UP.

Salter, W. H. (1911) *Essays on Two Moderns.* London, Sidgwick and Jackson.

Schwarz, Daniel (1999) *Imagining the Holocaust,* New York: St. Martin's Press.

Scribner, Charity (2003) *Requiem for Communism.* Cambridge, MA: MIT Press.

Secretan, Dominique (1973) *Classicism.* London: Methuen.

Settis, Salvatore (2006) *The Future of the 'Classical'*, tr. A. Cameron. Cambridge: Polity.

Shelley, P. B. (1824) *Posthumous Poems,* ed. M. Shelley. London: John and Henry L. Hunt.

Shelley, P. B. (1840) *Essays, Letters from Abroad, Translations and Fragments,* vol. I. Philadelphia, PA: Lea and Blanchard.

Shrager, Sidney (1982) *Scatology in Modern* Drama. New York: Irvington.

Sider, David (1997, ed.) *The Epigrams of Philodemos.* New York/Oxford: OUP.

Simms, C. E. (1997, ed.) *The tenne tragedies of Seneca.* The Spenser Society.

Simpson, W. (1902 [1855]), *The Seat of War in the East.* London: P. & D. Colnaghi & Co.

Smalley, Rebecca Emily (1991) *The Role of Memory in the Poetry of Douglas Dunn and Tony Harrison with Specific Reference to Elegy.* PhD Diss., Durham.

Smid, Katarina (2019) 'The Orpheus Monument in Ptuj', in Barbara Porod and Peter Scherrer (eds.) *Akten des 15. Internationalen Kolloquiums zum Provinzialrömischen Kunstschaffen.* 392–403. Graz: Phoibos.

Späth, Eberhard (2002) 'Tony Harrison: The Poet in a Post-Poetic Society', *European Journal of English Studies* 6, 43–59.

Spearing, E. M. (1909) 'The Elizabethan "Tenne Tragedies of Seneca"', *MLR* 4, 437–61.

Spencer, Luke (1994) *The Poetry of Tony Harrison.* New York: Harvester.

Speranza, Robert (2002) *Verses in the Celluloid: Poetry in Film from 1910-2002.* PhD Diss. Sheffield.

Stanhope, Philip Dormer (1901) *The Letters of the Earl of Chesterfield to his Son.* London: Methuen.

Stead, Henry (2019) 'The only tone for terror', in Hall (ed.) 205–19.

Stead, Henry (forthcoming) 'Fire, fennel and the future of socialism: Tony Harrison's Prometheus', in Sandie Byrne (ed.) *Tony Harrison and the Classics.* Oxford: OUP.

Stead, Jean (1980) 'Now is the time to stand up and fight', 5 December, reproduced in *Women of the Revolution* (2012) ed. Kira Cochrane, 79–81. London: Guardian Books.
Stein, H. (2005) 'What's Hecuba to me?', *Arion* 13, 179–94.
Steiner, Deborah (2002) *Images in Mind.* Princeton, NJ: PUP.
Stravinsky, Igor (1947) *The Poetics of Music.* Oxford: OUP.
Styan, J. L. (1983) *Modern Drama in Theory and Practice*, Volume 2, *Symbolism, Surrealism and the Absurd.* Cambridge: CUP.
Suhr-Sytsma, Nathan (2017) *Poetry, Print, and the Making of Postcolonial Literature* Cambridge: CUP.
Swift, Jonathan (1725–6) *Thesaurus Aenigmaticus.* London: John Wilford.
Talboys, David Alphonso (1820) *The Hecuba, Orestes, Phoenician Virgins, and Medea.* Oxford: Talboys.
Taplin, Oliver (1997) 'The Chorus of Mams', in Byrne (ed.) 171–84.
Taplin, Oliver (2002) 'An academic in the rehearsal room' in J. Barsby (ed.) *Greek and Roman Drama*, 7–22. Stuttgart: J. B. Metzler.
Taplin, Oliver (2005) 'The Harrison version: "so long ago that it became a song"?' in Macintosh et al. (eds.) 235–51.
Taplin, Oliver (2019) 'Tony Harrison's polygonal ode to Delphi', in Hall (ed.) 71–7.
Tarkovsky, Andrey (1986) *Sculpting in Time*, translated by Kitty Hunter Blair. London: Bodley Head.
Taylor, Christian James (2015) *Barbarian Masquerade: A Reading of the Poetry of Tony Harrison and Simon Armitage.* PhD Diss. Leeds.
The Greek Anthology (1916–18) text with an English translation by W. R. Paton (Loeb Edition). London/New York: W. Heinemann & G. P. Putnam's sons.
Thompson, N. S. (1997) 'Book Ends: public and private in Tony Harrison's poetry', in Byrne (ed.) 115–32.
Thompson, W. I. (1981) *The Time Falling Bodies Take to Light*, New York: St Martin's Press.
Thorndike, S. (1936) 'Gilbert Murray and some actors', in J. A. K. Thomson and A.J. Toynbee (eds.) *Essays in Honour of Gilbert Murray*, 69–77. London, G. Allen & Unwin.
Tommasini, A. (1996) 'Jacob Druckman, 67, Dies', *New York Times*, 27 May. https://www.nytimes.com/1996/05/27/arts/jacob-druckman-67-dies-a-composer-and-teacher.html.
Turnell, Martin (1947) *The Classical Moment.* London: Hamilton.
Tusa, John (2001) Transcript of interview with Harrison at the Barbican, 4 November, https://www.bbc.co.uk/programmes/p00nc89r.
Vallot, Antoine, Antoine d'Aquin, and Guy-Crescent Fagon (1862) *Journal de la santé du roi Louis XIV, 1647–1711*. Paris: Auguste Durand.

Vasunia, Phiroze (2005) 'Greek, Latin and the Indian Civil Service', *Cambridge Classical Journal* 51, 35–71.
Vasunia, Phiroze (2007) 'Aristophanes' Wealth and Dalpatram's Lakshmi' in Edith Hall and Amanda Wrigley (eds.) *Aristophanes in Performance*, 117–33. Oxford: Legenda.
Vasunia, Phiroze (2010) 'Introduction', in Hall and Vasunia (eds.) 1–12.
Vernant, J.-P. (1991) *Mortals and Immortals*, ed. Froma Zeitlin. Princeton, NJ: Princeton University Press.
Vines, Sherard (1930) *The Course of English Classicism*. London: Hogarth Press.
Volk, Katharina (2006) 'Cosmic disruption in Seneca's *Thyestes*', in K. Volk and G. D. Williams (eds.) *Seeing Seneca Whole*, 183–200. Leiden/Boston: Brill.
Warner, Marina (1982) 'Hall hath no fury', *Literary Review*, 44, 25–6.
Watkin, David (2006) *Radical Classicism: The Architecture of Quinlan Terry*. New York: Rizzoli.
Weil, S. (2005 [1940]), 'The Iliad, or the Poem of Force', in C. Benfey (ed.) *War and the Iliad: Simone Weil and Rachel Bespaloff*. New York: NYRB.
Whale, John (2006) 'John Keats and Tony Harrison: the burden of history', in Damian Walford Davies and Richard Marggraf Turley (eds.) *The Monstrous Debt: Modalities of Romantic Influence in Twentieth-Century Literature*, 63–80. Detroit: Wayne State UP.
Whitaker, Stephen (2013) *Prometheus to Revelation: Fire in the Work of Tony Harrison*. PhD Diss. Hull.
Wilmer, Clive (1992) 'Face to face', *English Review* 2, 31–5.
Wilson, D. (1987) *Gilbert Murray, OM*. Oxford: Clarendon.
Woodruff, P. [= P. Mason] (1953) *The Men who Ruled India: the Founders*. London: Cape.
Wroe, N. (2000) 'Man of mysteries', *The Guardian*, 1 April. https://www.theguardian.com/books/2000/apr/01/poetry.theatre.
Young, Alan (1984) 'Weeds and white roses', *Critical Quarterly* 26, 157–63.
Young, Edward (1759) *Conjectures on Original Composition*. London: A. Millar.
Zeitlin, Froma (1978) 'The dynamics of misogyny', *Arethusa* 11, 149–84.
Ziolkowski, Theodore (2015) *Classicism of the Twenties*. Chicago: Chicago UP.

Index

Abu Ghraib Prison 155
Achilleion (Corfu) 126–9
Achilles (mythical figure) 23, 29, 41, 44, 127–8, 155
acting, actors 26, 37, 39, 46, 54–5, 61, 65–7, 74, 91, 97, 120–1, 133, 158, 164, 187 n.31
Addison, Joseph 3, 5–6
Adorno, Theodor 151
Aeetes (mythical figure) 95
Aegisthus (mythical figure) 64, 66, 69, 76
Aeneas (mythical figure) 169
Aeschylus 99, 119, 158
   Oresteia vii, 9, 16, 59–77, 94, 97, 131, 152, 171, 195 n.59
   Prometheus viii, 121, 123, 132–44
   Suppliants 143
Afghanistan 42
Africa 12–14, 30, 37, 39, 161, 167–8
   West 36
African Americans 12, 128
Ahmedabad 57
Ahmadu Bello University (Kaduna) 38
Albery Theatre 154
Alcaeus 168
Alcinous 95
Alexander the Great 43
Alexander Nevsky (movie) 124
Alexandria 31
alliteration, alliterative 6, 33, 61–2, 65, 75, 82, 153, 155, 175
Alzheimer's Disease 176–7
   see also Dementia
Amazonia 12
Amazons 43
American Relief Administration 160
Amphis 9, 180 n.45
anaphora 50, 68
Anchises (mythical figure) 169
ancien regime 37
Andes 13

Angelopoulos, Theo (film director) 138
Anglican, Anglicanism 4
Anglo-Saxon literature 60–3, 175
anthropology 56, 64, 72
antisemitism 128
Aphrodite viii, 5, 15, 24–5, 45–6, 48, 51–2, 112, 165–6
Apollo 8, 26, 67, 76–7, 105, 107–9, 168, 175
Apollonius' *Argonautica* 93–5
Apuleius 24
Arabic 56
Archilochus 168
architecture 11, 56, 221, 28, 41, 148, 175
Archive of Performances of Greek & Roman Drama (APGRD) 55, 193 n.5, 186 n.118, 196 n.6
Ares 68
Arete (mythical figure) 85, 95
Argentina 135
Argonauts 84, 91, 93–6, 129–31, 164
Argos 64, 66, 68, 73, 76–7, 131
Ariadne (mythical figure) 23, 49
Aricie (dramatic character) 44
Aristophanes 101
   Clouds 101–2, 153
   Frogs 62, 99, 153, 178
   Lysistrata vii, 36, 65, 84, 124, 125, 156–7
   Plutus 57
Aristotle
   Poetics 2, 137, 151, 153
   Problems 66
   Rhetoric 153
Artemis 46, 48, 126, 147, 163–4
Arthurian literature 6–7
Aspyrtus (mythical figure) 95
Astraea (mythical figure) 22, 27
Astyanax (mythical figure) 154, 162
Athena 65, 77, 149
Athens, Athenian 36, 119, 129–31
   Acropolis 131, 194 n.36
   Opera House 154

refugees 131
atomists 110
atrocity 18, 53, 118, 155–6
Auden, W. H. 7, 138
Augustans, Augustanism (English) 2, 50, 55, 103
Augustus, Augustan (Roman) 9
Aurora (museum ship) 172
Auschwitz Concentration Camp 139–40, 151
Austria, Austrian 97, 114–19, 126
Austro-Hungarian Empire 22
Awtrey, Jonathan (academic) 3
Awyntyrs off Arthure (medieval romance) 6
Ayah (dramatic character) 39, 42, 44, 55

Bacchylides 29, 105
Bacchus, Bacchic
    see Dionysus
Bachofen, J. J. (anthropologist) 73
Bader-Meinhof gang 64
Baily, Edward Hodges (sculptor) 27
bakers, baking 29, 71, 72, 75, 82, 99, 141, 172
Balkan War 98, 119
Baluchistan 44
Bambi (Disney) 177
Bamford, Samuel 2
barber, barber's shop 11, 72
Barnard, John (academic) 12
Barnsley 62
Barrault, Louis (theatre director) 45, 54
Basra 150
Baths of Caracalla 134
BBC 5, 124, 125, 144, 149, 189 n.19, 196 n.7
Beerbohm, Max 162
Bell, Marie (actor) 54
Belov, G. D. (archaeologist) 165
Belsen Concentration Camp 6, 124
Bengal 42, 55
    Horse Artillery 42, 184 n.47
    Lancers 43
Beowulf 71
Berlin Wall 135
Bernini, Giovanni Lorenzo (sculptor) 24
bestiality 49, 52
Betterware Company 98

Bia (dramatic character) 133, 140
Bible, biblical 4
    Apocalypse 4–5
    Ecclesiastes 4
Billy Elliot (movie) 137
Birtwhistle, Harrison (composer) 62, 96, 187 n.10
Black Sea viii, 129–31, 142, 147–52, 164–6
blackness, black people 12–14, 37, 80
    actors 39
    classicism 12
    see also négritude
blackface makeup 39
Blackford, Richard (composer) 96, 133, 142, 145
Blackpool 13
Blair, Tony 171
'blowing from the gun' (punishment) 44–5
Boer War 161
Bogen, Nancy 177
Bolshevism 141, 172
Bonn 85
Bordin, Piero (producer) 115
Bosnia, Bosnian 98, 119, 121
Boston 3
Boswell, Laurence (theatre director) 154–5
Bower, Rachel (poet and academic) vi, 182 nn.3 and 8
Bradfield College 60
Bradford 5, 98, 178
    Omar Khayyám Restaurant 5
Bragg, Melvyn vi, 171, 180 n.37
Brassed Off (movie) 137
Braund, David (academic) vi, 165
Brazil 13
Brecht, Bertolt 9, 72, 74, 76, 189 n.80
Britain, British 11
    Army 35–57, 147–8
    class system 12–13, 16, 101, 135, 137, 141, 150, 173, 178
    Empire 11, 17, 21, 162, 164
    Museum 130
    Raj 35–57
    theatre 59, 151, 161
Britannia (Roman colony) 45
British Film Institute 50, 193 n.5
Bronx 128
Bronze Age 1, 6, 38, 63

Broun-Ramsay, James (Governor-General of India) 42
Brough, Robert (dramatist) 83, 180 n.57
Browning, Robert 46, 62
    Agamemnon 63
    'Artemis Prologuizes' 46
Bryden, Bill (theatre director) 61, 75
Buchanan, George (translator) 86, 89
Bulgaria 141, 144–6, 178
Burleigh (dramatic character) 40, 47, 51–3, 57, 154
Burn, George (sculptor) 27
Bushnell, Katharine (missionary) 53
bust, busts 20, 26, 99, 127
Butes (mythical figure) 94–5
'Butler' Education Act 16
Butler, Josephine 53, 185 n.104
Byrne, Sandie (academic) vi, 82, 187 m.37, 189 n.17, 192 n.28, 193 n.11, 198 n.4
Byron, George 2, 5, 20, 81, 176

Cabral, Luis (politician) 64
Cagney, James (actor) 177
Calchas (mythical figure) 62
Calcutta 43, 53, 56
Calderon, Pedro 83
Cambridge University Greek Play 59
Cameron, Alastair (cinematographer) 133
Canada 173
Canary Islands 14
cancer 13, 133, 175
capitalism 16, 130, 133–4, 138–9
Caractacus 173
Carlyle, Thomas 102
Carne-Ross, D.S. (poet) 74
Carnuntum vii, 10, 48, 97, 114–19, 126, 144, 174
carpenter, carpentry 29, 72, 169
cartography 27
Case, Sue-Ellen (academic) 66–7
Cassandra (mythical figure) 76, 156, 163, 171
Castalian Spring 174–6
catastrophe 6, 16, 31, 154, 159–60
Catholicism, Roman 4
Catullus 21–3, 25, 27–8, 101–2
Caucasus 142

Cavalli, Francesco (composer) 83
cavalry 42–3, 184 n.47
cement 119–23
centaurs 48
Cervantes, Miguel 19
Césaire, Aimé (poet and intellectual) 12, 14
    Cahier d'un retour au pays natal 12
Channel 4 Television 79, 132, 189 n.4, 193 n.15, 194 n.17
Charpentier, Marc-Antoine (composer) 83
Chartism, Chartists 2
Cherubini, Luigi 83
child, children 29–31, 91–2, 100, 110–11, 119, 121, 124, 131–2, 134–7, 144, 153, 156, 158, 162
Children's Employment Commission 1842 101
China, Chinese 3
Christianity 2, 4–5, 16, 21–2, 30–2, 51, 88, 104, 148
chorus, choruses vii, 2, 14, 27, 37, 46, 48, 62, 64, 68, 73, 75–6, 83–94, 105–6, 138, 153–7, 161, 184 n.63, 187 n.10
Cilissa (dramatic character) 76
Cimmerian, Cimmerians 151
    Bosporus 166
cinema
    see film
class, social
    conflict 60, 72, 80–3, 101–2, 108, 132–3
    consciousness 10, 17, 32, 79, 113
    middle 101, 143, 146.
    ruling 12, 20, 35, 42, 51, 75, 77
    working 17, 70, 72, 77, 80–1, 98–9, 101
Classic Stage Company 54
classics, classical vii–viii, 10–11, 14, 70
    curriculum 17, 51
    education 4, 12, 15–16, 54, 57, 71, 74, 81, 100, 149–50, 158, 169, 178
    Performance Reception 55–6
    postcolonial 56–7, 85
    Reception Studies 35, 40, 55, 85–7, 177–8
Classical Association 136, 178
classicism 4, 6–12, 19, 23, 38, 47, 54, 81, 136, 138, 177–8, 180 n.57, 185 n.110

Claudius (Roman Emperor) 45
Clavane, Anthony (sportswriter) 152
Clément, Catherine (philosopher) 86
Cleveland, John (poet) 14
cloaca, cloacal, Cloacina 100, 102, 111–14
Clytemnestra (mythical figure) 64, 65, 68–9, 74–7, 131, 160
coal 13–14, 76, 79–80, 134–5, 138
Coal Face (documentary) 130, 138
Colchis 93, 95
Cold War 140, 157
colony, colonial, colonialism 4, 12–14, 17, 22, 30, 36, 38, 40, 42, 56–7, 94, 167–8
Columbus, Christopher 14
comedy, comic 4, 9, 37, 55, 57, 84, 91, 98, 139, 114, 141, 143, 174
comics, comic strips 30–1
Commodus (Roman Emperor) 115–19
communism, communist 21, 72, 134, 136, 138, 140–2
concentration camps 128, 161
Confucius, Confucianism 4
Conservative Party 79, 135
consonants, consonantal 9, 61–2, 70, 75
Contagious Diseases Act 53
cooking 72
coprology
    see scatology
Corfu 92
Corinth, Corinthian 14, 40, 87–8, 90–2, 95, 163
Corneille, Pierre
    Médée 54
County Durham 137
Crete 40, 173
Creusa 85, 88, 90
Crimea, Crimean 147–52, 161, 164–6, 187 n.31, 196 n.2
Croatia 120
cross-dressing 37, 67, 148
crocodile 184 n.76
crusades 22, 143
Cuba 13, 20, 94, 167
Cukor, George 124
cunnilingus 84
Cupid 15, 21, 24, 32
Czechoslovakia 14, 21, 24, 26, 83, 140

Daily Mail 79
Daldry, Stephen (film director) 137
Dalpatram, Dahyabhai Travadi (poet) 57
Daly, Mary 69
Damas, Léon (poet and politician) 14
Dante 7, 20, 101, 191 n.14
Danube 115
Davis, Gregson (academic) 12
de Beauvoir, Simone 69
de Gaulle, Charles 37
Deane, Patrick (academic) 10
death 6, 9, 18, 19–21, 30–2, 44, 47, 62, 69–71, 86–93, 116, 169, 127, 131, 137, 139–46, 154–5, 171, 174–5
Deianeira (mythical figure) 93, 171
dementia 173, 177
Democritus 110
Demosthenes 76
Der ewige Jude (Nazi propaganda film) 140
Derby Playhouse 54
Deucalion (mythical figure) 176
Devereux, George (academic) 85
Dexter, John (theatre director) 17, 36–9, 83
dialects 8, 105
Dio Cassius 115
Dionysus, Dionysiac 5, 25–6, 51, 131, 150, 152, 172, 174, 178
dirge 6, 44, 46, 66, 68, 91, 131, 142, 169
Divus, Andreas 4
Dorsetshire Regiment of Foot 147
Dostoyevsky, Fyodor 177
Dougall, John (actor) 149
Dresden 132, 140
drinking, drunkenness 6, 14, 17, 91, 170, 176
Druckman, Jacob (composer) 84
drug addiction 128
Dryads 170–1
Dryden, John 3, 177
Dunbar, William (poet) 176
Duncan, Isadora (dancer) 159
Dudley, Bill (designer and actor) 61
Durbar Hall 40
Durham 28, 73, 114, 137
    Gulbenkian Museum 43
Düsseldorf 128

Earl of Chesterfield 111–12
Easington 137
East India Company 39, 41, 43, 57
Easterling, Pat (academic) 92
Eastman, Helen (academic and theatre director) vi, 186 n.118, 181 n.3
economics 1, 42, 73, 102, 134–5
Edinburgh Festival 61, 85
Edwardian 161–2
Egypt, Egyptian 105, 115
Egypt Exploration Society 105
Eisenhower, Dwight D. 16
Eisenstein, Sergei (film director) 124, 177
Ekphrasis 23, 29, 181 n.15
Elbe (river) 14
Elefsina 123
Eliot, T. S. 4, 164
  The Cocktail Party 54
  'The Journey of the Magi' 3
Elizabeth (Empress of Austria) 126–7
Elizabethan literature 50
Ellison, Ralph Waldo (novelist) 12
eloquence, ideal of 1, 71, 80, 159
Empedocles 175
Engels, Friedrich 73, 94
England, English 9, 12–14, 17, 27, 37–8, 45, 75, 79, 81, 83, 92, 99, 101–3, 116, 132–5, 138, 148, 153, 164, 172–3, 185 n.104
  Civil War 102
  Old 63, 73
Epicurean, Epicureanism 5, 98, 104, 109–14
epigram, epigrammatic 5, 31–3, 112, 123
Equity (actors' union) 55
Erinyes (mythical figures) 64–5, 69, 77
Eros
  see Cupid
Eton College 16
Euripides vii–viii, 36, 38, 57, 62, 97, 99, 147–66
  Alcestis 54, 91
  Bacchae 38, 51, 93
  Cyclops 152
  Electra 161
  Hecuba 154–6, 160, 162
  Herakles 91, 95, 157–9
  Hippolytus vi, 35–57, 46, 154, 161, 182 n.16, 185 n.80
  Iphigenia in Tauris 147–52, 161, 163–6
  Medea 84, 86–95, 160–2, 177
  Trojan Women 150, 154–7, 161–3
Europe, European 22, 27, 62, 123–4, 132, 138, 140, 166, 176
  Cultural Centre of Delphi 97, 119
  imperialism 13–14, 17, 22, 36, 41, 56, 161
Eurydice (mythical figure) 144
excretion 4, 97–119
Eyre, Richard 36, 79, 107, 171, 174, 189 n.4, 198 n.23

factories 27, 100, 133, 153
fairgrounds 13, 27
Falklands War 135
Faustina (wife of Marcus Aurelius) 118–19
Fawcett, Percy (explorer) 11–12
Feast, Michael (actor) 133
femininity 66, 85, 88, 95
feminism, feminist 53, 60, 66–7, 69–70, 73, 83, 89, 95, 144
Fenton, Roger (photographer) 147–8, 196 n.2
Festival Hall 174
Figgis, Mike (documentary maker) 136–7
filicide 92–3
film 11–12, 54–5, 60–1, 72, 79, 114, 123–46, 159, 173–5, 177–8, 189 nn.4 and 22, 195 nn.55 and 56, 196 n.6
film-poems vi, vii–viii, 5, 26, 32, 121, 123–46, 152
Finborough Theatre 191 n.1
fire 6, 13, 18, 32, 77, 114, 121, 123, 128, 132–4, 136, 139, 141
fire brigade 114
Flashar, Hellmut (academic) 55
First World War 125, 128, 162, 163
Florida 170
Fonda, Jane (actor) 144
football 72, 79–81, 104
Formby, George 177
Foundation of Hellenic Culture 129
FPÖ (Freiheitliche Partei Österreichs) 116
Fraenkel, Eduard (academic) 72
France, French 14, 36–7, 45–8, 59, 81–2, 86, 89, 102, 110, 127, 148, 150, 168, 181 n.9
  classicism 2, 7, 31, 35, 38, 54, 185 n.110

Frankfurt 128
Frascatorius, Hieronymus 168
Fraser, James Baillie (travel writer) 43
Freud, Sigmund, Freudian 85, 103
Fry, Christopher (dramatist) 59
funerals 4, 30, 32, 71–2
Furies 91–3, 105
    see also Erinyes

Gambia 39
gargoyles 25, 26, 28
Galatea (mythical figure) 23
Gay, John 114
gay people, gayness 93–5, 113, 144
    see also homosexuality
gender-blind casting 37, 67
Georgia 129, 141–2, 164
German, Germany 5–7, 62, 76, 115–16, 126–7, 139–40, 179 n.6
    imperialism 98
Gide, André 70, 72
Gladiator (movie) 115
gladiators, gladiatorial 48, 115–16, 118
Glasgow 161
gnomes 26
gods 6, 14, 23, 24, 31, 33, 48, 51–2, 57, 65, 66, 77, 94, 112, 132, 137, 178
Goethe, Johann 2, 5, 128
golden fleece 88, 131, 148
Goldhill, Simon (academic) 65
Gondwana 175
Gorgon (mythical figure) vii, 125–9
Gothic 21, 25
Götz, Johannes (sculptor) 127
Gough, Michael (actor) 55
Government of India Acts 41
Governor of Bengal (dramatic character) 39, 41–2, 44, 46–8, 50, 52, 54, 57
GPO 130, 138
graffiti 80
Granville Barker, Harley (theatre director) 161–4
grape, grapes 5, 170–1
Graves, Robert (writer) 85
graveyards 21, 80
Gray, James (film director) 11–12
Gray, Thomas (poet) 80–1, 171
Greco, Giovanni (translator) vi, 180 n.45

Greece, Greeks 6, 29, 31, 33, 37, 38, 56, 60, 62–5, 81–2, 88, 99, 104, 120, 129
    ancient language 4, 29, 33, 41, 45, 57, 62–70, 72, 75–6, 81–2, 88–9, 99, 105, 106, 115–16, 119–20, 123, 134, 139, 158–9. 161, 169, 178
    art 52, 148, 179 n.6
    drama 36–7, 49, 55, 57, 73, 119, 131, 168
    epic 23, 95
    epigram 19, 31–3, 99
    lyric poetry 4, 10, 29, 167
    mainland 38
    modern language 127, 130, 176
    music 96
    myth 47, 84, 127, 131, 137, 176
    philosophy 10, 22, 110
    satyr drama 26, 104–14
    tragedy 21, 25–6, 35, 46, 48, 54, 59–70, 66, 85–96, 119–20, 123, 132–43, 147, 162–6, 174–5
    vase-painters 10. 43, 139, 145
Greek Anthology 182 nn.26, 29 and 30, 191 n.5
Greenham Common 65, 156–7
Grenfell, Bernard (papyrologist) 104–5
Grey, Charles (Prime Minister) 27
Grierson, John (documentary maker) 130
Grillparzer, Franz (dramatist) 83
Grimethorpe Colliery Band 137
Grimley Colliery Band 137
Guardian 3, 119, 171, 197 n.33
Guiana 14
Gujarati 57
Gulf War 3, 119, 125–6, 150
Gunton, Bob (actor) 54
Guy's Hospital 100
gynaecophobia 67

Haider, Jörg (politician) 116–17
Haileybury 57
Haileybury Observer 57
Hall, Edith (academic) 55–6, 70, 147–8, 154–5, 164–6, 177–8, 186 n.6, 187 n.31, 193 n.5
Hall, Lee (dramatist & screenplay writer) vi, 74, 137
Hall, Peter (theatre director) 8, 38–9, 59, 75

Hapsburg Emperors 115
Harding, Emma (radio director) vi, 149
Hardwick, Lorna vi, 10, 196 n.23
Harrison, Anne 172
Harrison, Florrie 30, 60, 69, 71–2, 173–4
Harrison, Harry 60, 70–2, 82, 99–100, 111, 172
Harrison, Jane vi, 29–31, 165, 172
Harrison, Max 172
Harrison, Rosemarie (formerly Crossfield Dietzsch) 83, 126, 140, 172, 194 n.18
Harrison, Tony
  academic publications 9, 55
  alienation 10, 71, 169
  authorial persona 6–7, 9–10, 98–9, 167–77
  autobiographical poems 13–26, 167–77
  childhood 6, 11, 13, 110, 112, 124, 132, 152, 169, 178
  children 1, 17, 29–31, 83, 165, 172
  colloquialism 6, 8, 33, 49, 60, 74–7, 80–3, 91, 153
  erudition 6–7, 16, 93, 95–6, 98, 117
  fruit theme 25, 170–1, 173–4
  Geoffrey Faber Memorial Prize 17
  marriages 17, 30, 67, 83, 140, 172–3
  notebooks vi, 38–9, 41–3, 45, 49, 62, 64, 67, 69, 72, 74, 137, 139, 144, 154
  PEN/Pinter Prize 20
  political views 2, 9, 12–14, 17, 19, 21, 30, 32, 36, 56, 60–1, 64, 83, 88
  prose works 7, 15, 19, 26, 48, 63, 66, 94, 123, 134, 141, 157, 167, 178
  secularism 4–5, 11, 16
  suicidal thoughts 7
  theme of inarticulacy 8, 71, 75, 80, 97–8, 108, 123, 136, 151, 169, 177
  vital dates 6
  wit and humour 10, 21, 36, 37, 84, 86, 92, 104, 106, 112, 114, 117, 136, 141, 159
  works:
    'A Cold Coming' vii, 3, 119, 126, 128, 143, 149, 154
    'A Celebration of the Abdication of King Charles III' 20
    'A Fig on the Tyne' 25, 173
    'A Good Read' 70–1

'A Kumquat for John Keats' 25, 169–71
A Maybe Day in Kazakhstan 7, 26, 123, 129–32, 164
Aikin Mata vii, 36–8, 64, 124, 143
'Allotments' 21
'Ballad of the Geldsharl' 188 n.45
Black Daisies for the Bride 177
'Black Sea Aphrodite' viii, 165–6
'Blocks' 71
'Book Ends' 72
Bow Down 62, 177
'Changing at York' 67
'Classics Society' 11
Continuous 59–77
Crossings 138
'Cypress and Cedar' 169
'Dark Times' 188 n.61
'Doodlebugs' 4
'Essentials' 188 n.61
'Facing Up to the Muses' 156, 178
'Flicks and This Fleeting Life' 122
Fram 8, 16, 24, 147–66
From 'The School of Eloquence' 1, 12, 24, 31, 60, 70–2, 99, 168
'*from* the Zeg-Zag postcards' 167–8
'Fruitility' 25, 174
'Ghosts: Some Words before Breakfast. For Jane' 29–31
'Guava Libre' 143–4
Hecuba viii, 152–7, 160–1
'Initial Illumination' 119
Iphigenia in Crimea viii, 147–50, 161, 165
'Laureate's Block' viii, 171
'Loving Memory' 173
Loving Memory 125
'Manica' 21, 167
'Me Tarzan' 11
Medea: A Sex-War Opera vii, 56, 83–97, 129, 134, 144–5, 157, 161
Metamorpheus 123, 143–6, 178
'Newcastle is Peru' vii, 13–18, 27, 32, 150, 167, 169, 178
'On not being Milton' 7, 12
'On the Metre' 8
Oresteia vii, 8, 9, 59–77, 83, 84, 94, 96, 106, 146, 151, 152, 164, 174, 175, 177

Palladas vii, 8–9, 16, 31–3, 98–100, 112, 123
Phaedra Britannica vii, 32, 35–57, 59, 64, 83, 85, 134, 143, 154, 161, 177
Poetry or Bust 20, 99
'Polygons' viii, 167, 172–7
'Prague Spring' 21, 28
Prometheus viii, 26, 27, 32, 65, 85, 121, 123–5, 130, 132–44, 152, 165, 173–5
'Prometheus: Fire and Poetry' 123, 134, 141
'Queueing for Charon' 144
'Reading the rolls: an arse verse' 109–13
Square Rounds 65, 126
'Still' 11
'Study' 169
'Summer Garden' 23
'The Ballad of Babelabour' 75
The Big H. 124
The Blasphemers' Banquet 5, 189 n.22
The Common Chorus vii, 156–7, 161
'The Curtain Catullus' 21–28
'The Excursion' 110
The Gaze of the Gorgon vii, 25–5, 125–9, 144
'The Gifts of Aphrodite' 25
'The Grilling' 5–7, 176
The Kaisers of Carnuntum vii, 10, 48, 97–8, 114–19, 126, 144, 174
The Labourers of Herakles viii, 9, 32, 97–8, 119–21, 123
The Loiners vi, 8, 17, 19–33, 37, 71, 74, 104, 110, 121, 164, 167–8, 172
The Misanthrope 13, 17, 36, 37, 60, 182 n.14
'The Morning After' 169
'The Mother of the Muses' 173, 174, 177
The Mysteries 8, 59–61, 73, 74, 177
'The Ode Not Taken' 100
'The Pomegranates of Patmos' 4, 25
The Prince's Play 28, 35, 174
'The Railroad Heroides' 168
'The Red Lights of Plenty' 25, 188 n.61
The Shadow of Hiroshima 65, 123
The Trackers of Oxyrhynchus vii, 26, 32, 97–8, 104–9, 114, 119, 132–3, 135, 145, 150, 152, 174–5, 177
'The Viewless Wings' 172
'The White Queen' 30, 95, 167
'Them & (uz)' 75, 169
'Toasting Jocelyn' 174
'Turns' 99
'Travesties' 168
Satyrae 30
'Shango the Shaky Fairy' 94, 167
Under the Clock viii, 100, 192 n.45
U.S. Martial vii, 8–9, 16, 26, 101, 102, 106
'v.' vii, 7, 16, 24, 79–83, 104, 136, 172, 174, 189 n.19
'Wine and Poetry' 9
'Wordlists' 4
'Working' 76, 101
Yan Tan Tethera 187 n.10

Heath, Edward (politician) 135
Heaney, Seamus 9, 174–5
Hebrew 195 n.59
Hector (mythical figure) 3, 127–8
Hecuba (mythical figure viii, 154–7, 160–3
Heilbrun, Carolyn (academic) 87
Heine, Heinrich (poet) 2, 9, 26, 126–9
Hera 92
Herakles/Hercules (mythical figure) viii, 21, 33, 43, 50, 54, 91, 93–5, 97, 118–21, 123, 154, 157
Herakles General Cement Corporation 119–20
Herbert, Jocelyn (theatre designer) 26, 62, 97, 120, 133, 174, 183
Herculaneum 5, 112–13
Herman, Mark (film director) 137
Hermes (dramatic character) 107, 133–4, 136–7, 141–3, 145
Herodian 115
Herodorus of Heraklea 117
Herodotus 57, 120
Herter, Ernst (sculptor) 127–8
Hesiod 23, 139, 141
Heywood, Jasper (translator) 50
Hill, Jacqueline 69
Hindley, Myra 90
Hindu, Hinduism 51–2

Hippolyte/Hippolytus (dramatic
    character) vii, 35–57, 161–2
Hiroshima 64–5, 123
Hispanic Americans 128
Historia Augusta 115
Hitler, Adolf 111, 118, 140
Hobhouse, John (diarist) 176
Hobhouse, Leonard (sociologist) 162
Hoggart, Richard (academic) 168
Holloway Prison 163
Holocaust 44, 128, 132, 139–40, 151, 157,
    195 nn.55 and 59
Holub, Miroslav (poet) 9
homelessness 109, 114, 135, 154
Homer 2, 7, 20, 23, 29, 57, 63, 82, 105,
    126–7, 169
    Iliad vii, 3, 126–8
    Odyssey 4, 12, 13, 17, 29, 82
homosexuality 94–5, 144–5, 167–8, 172
Hoover, Herbert 160
Hope, Thomas (banker) 15
Hopkins, Gerard Manley 62
Horace 8, 20, 45, 57, 111–12
horror 7, 46, 92, 125, 141, 143, 147, 150–1,
    153, 156–60, 170
Hosidius Geta (poet) 96
Howarth, Gerald (MP) 79
Hughes, Ted 9, 35, 171, 174–5
Hugo, Victor 2, 9
    Le Roi s'amuse 28
    Les Misérables 103
    The Hunchback of Notre Dame 28
Hull 61, 77
humanism 103, 113, 140, 160
Humber Bridge 133
Hungary 114
Hunt, Arthur (papyrologist) 105
hunting imagery 47–53, 69, 114
Hus, Jan (Protestant reformer) 21
Hyderabad 40–1, 45, 51, 183 n.31
Hylas (mythical figure) 90, 93–5

Ibo people 36–7
Ibsen, Henrik 70, 72
Iceland, Icelandic 9
iconoclasm 31
Illustrated London News 147, 197 n.55
imperialism 14, 17, 21, 45, 56–7, 85, 98,
    115, 118, 161, 164

Independent 181 n.68, 192 n.27
India, Indian 3, 35–57
India Today Magazine 55
Indonesia 39
Indus (river) 47
intercultural theatre 36–7
inter-racial marriage 41
Io (mythical figure) 85, 133–4, 139–41, 166
Iphigenia (mythical figure) viii, 23,
    147–50, 161, 163–5, 187 n.31
Iran, Iranian 5
Iraq, Iraqi 3, 128, 143, 150–1, 154
Ireland, Irish 36, 53, 64, 147, 174
Iron Curtain 23
Islam 5, 43, 98, 119, 121
Italy, Italian 2, 57
ITV (Independent Television) 138

Jacobean literature 50
Jarecke, Ken (photographer) 150
Jarry, Alfred (dramatist) 102
Jason (mythical figure) 84, 87–92, 94–5
Jebb, Eglantyne (philanthropist) 159
Jews, Jewish 126, 139–40, 142, 195 n.59
Jones, William (Indo-Europeanist) 56
Jonson, Ben 3, 8, 101, 191 n.12
Jalalabad 40, 42
Japan, Japanese 36, 69, 169
Jobberns, Joseph (Sergeant Major) 149
Johansen, Hjalmar (explorer) 158
Joseph II (Emperor) 116
journalism, journalist 40
Jung, Carl 85
Julius Pollux 115–17
Juvenal 30, 94, 101, 167–8

Kafka, Franz 21
Kalais (mythical figure) 144
Kali (Hindu god) 52
Karl V (Emperor) 116
Kaufmann, Walter (philosopher) 151
Kazantzakis, Nikos 176
Keats, John 2, 9, 25, 100, 167, 169–72,
    198 n.12
Kelleher, Joe (academic) 106
Kerch 151, 166
Kern, Otto (academic) 144
Kershaw, Patience (mineworker) 76, 101
Khomeini, Ayatollah 5

Kidel, Mark (film director) 130
Kiev 151, 165
King Edward VII 36
King Louis XIV 37, 104
King's College London vi
Kingsway Theatre 13
Kipling, Rudyard 20
Kirkby 135–6
Kirkpatrick, James Achilles (colonel) 41
Kleisthenes 130
Kluge, Alexander (academic) 4
Knossos 6
Knottingley Palace Cinema 138
Koran 5
Koun, Karolos (theatre director) 131
Krajina 120
Kramer, Reinhold (academic) 101
Kratos (dramatic character) 133, 140
Krishna (Hindu god) 52
kumquat fruit 25, 169–71

labyrinth 49
LaFargue, Paul (revolutionary) 73
lament
   see dirge
Latham, Caroline (teacher and scholar) vi, 75–6, 186 n.118, 187 n.28, 188 nn.48 and 73
Latin, Latin literature 2, 4–5, 7, 14, 21, 24, 29, 45, 48, 50, 54, 47, 71–2, 81, 86, 89, 92–3, 100–1, 109, 111, 147, 168, 178
   prose composition 11
Latin America 13
Laurel and Hardy 153
Lawrence, D. H. 173
League of Nations 159, 162
Leeds 13–15, 100, 124, 172
   accent 152, 169
   Brotherton Library
   City Art Gallery 15
   City Square 15, 124
   Empire Theatre 35
   Grammar School 15–16, 80, 152–3, 178
   market 153
   music hall 153
   News Theatre 124
   Tetley's Brewery 153
   University 16, 35–6, 80, 124

Leeds United Football Club 80–1
Legouvé, Ernst (playwright) 83
Lehmann, John (poet) 141–2
Lemnos, Lemnian 84, 93–4
Lemprière, John 170–81
Leningrad (St. Petersburg) 24–5, 31, 124, 164, 172
lesbian 145
Lesbos 144–5
Lessing, Gotthold 22, 181 n.13
Levi, Peter (academic) 74
Levi, Primo 140
Lévi-Strauss, Claude 86
lexicography 6, 63
Libération 150
Libya 136
Lilimani (dramatic character) 39, 44–7, 51
limericks 104
Lind, Jenny (soprano) 173
linguistics 56
lions, lion-tamers 76, 114, 116–17, 120
Littell, Jonathan (novelist) 139
Livy 112
London Corresponding Society 1
London Review of Books 5, 165, 167
LSJ (*A Greek-English Lexicon* by H.G. Liddell, R. Scott and H.S. Jones) 139
Lucretius 5, 98, 109, 111, 113, 124
lyric, lyrics, lyric poetry 4, 10, 29, 45, 124, 155, 163, 175
Lyric Theatre 161

McCarthy, Lillah (actor) 163
McCowen, Alec (actor) 38
McDonald, Marianne (academic) 56
MacGregor, Ewan (actor) 137
MacGregor, Ian (magnate) 79–80
Macintosh, Fiona (academic) vi, 56, 85, 66, 182 n.9, 186 nn.115 and 118–19, 190 nn.23, 25, 30, 41, 44, 197 nn.44–5, 51 and 55
Macromanni (Germanic tribe) 115
Mann, Thomas 2
Marcus Aurelius vii, 10, 115–19
Mars, Mlle 20
Marshall, Cécile (translator) vi, 180 n.45, 181 n.9

Marshall, Hallie (academic) vi, 179 n.10, 187 n.12, 191 nn.2 and 4, 196 n.22, 198 n.6
Marshall, Toph (academic) vi, 188 n.62
Marsyas (mythical figure) 25–6, 108
Martens, Henry (artist) 184 n.47
Martial vii, 7–9, 16, 26, 101–2, 106, 191 n.10
Martinique 12
Marx, Karl 26, 40, 70, 72–3, 110
Marxism, Marxist 60, 70, 72, 133–4
masculinity 51, 67, 68, 75, 93, 137
mask, masks 25, 62, 127, 133, 150–1, 156, 158–60, 187 n.12
Match, Franz (painter) 127
Mathers, Edward Powys (translator) 177
matriarchy 69–73, 85, 94
Mauriac, François (writer) 38
May Day 25, 129
May, Thomas (poet) 5
Medusa 63, 81, 138–9, 157, 172–4, 177
Mendès, Catulle (poet) 83, 89
Mercouri, Melina (actor) 129, 131
medieval 6, 61, 73, 82
    guilds 28, 73
    masons 28–9
Mee, Charles (dramatist) 143
melodrama 38
Melpomene 127, 174, 176
Memsahib (dramatic character) 42, 44, 46, 48–50, 52–3
Meredith, George 7
messenger speeches 76, 88, 90, 147, 151, 154–9, 164–5
metaphysics, metaphysical 5, 104
Metcalfe, Thomas Theophilus (civil servant) 39
metre 2, 7, 8, 33, 43, 66, 74, 105, 124–5, 175
    see also verse forms
Metropolitan Opera 83
Miletos 120–1
Millett, Kate 70
Milton, John 4, 7, 9, 12, 20, 171
    'Ad Patrem' 71
    Paradise Lost 124
miners, mining 13, 32, 79, 101, 132, 135–9
Minoan-Mycenaean 7
Minotaur 49

misogyny 66–7, 69–70, 83, 85–6, 91–4, 144
Mitchell, Adrian (poet) 36–8
Mnouchkine, Ariane (theatre director) 36–7
Modernist, Modernism 4, 23, 54, 164
Moiseiwitsch, Tanya (theatre designer) 37
Molière (Jean-Baptiste Poquelin, playwright) 3, 5, 17, 20, 36–7
Molyneux, Andrée (TV documentary maker) 124
Monteverdi, Claudio 177
Morgan, Lewis H. (anthropologist) 73
Morley, Sheridan (journalist) 45
Morrison, Blake vi, 180 n.34, 189 n.2, 191 n.7
Morrison, Toni (author) 12, 180 n.57
mosaics 118, 165
Moscow 158
mothers, motherhood 24, 30, 43, 52–3, 59–61, 66, 68, 76, 82–5, 87–8, 90, 114, 118–19, 121, 134, 150, 154–5, 172–4, 194 n.18
Moul, Victoria (academic) 8
movies
    see film
Muhammad 5
Munro, Hector (Commander of British Army in India) 44
Munro, William (Colonel) 147–8
Murray, Gilbert (academic) 151, 157–64
muse, muses 71, 125, 127, 129, 145, 156, 172–4, 176–8
museums 22–3, 28, 43, 118, 126, 130, 147, 165, 172, 184 n.47
Muslim, Muslims
    see Islam
Mussolini, Benito 118
Myron (sculptor) 22

Nagasaki 64
Naiads 170–1
Nansen, Fridtjof (explorer) 158–60
Nashe, Thomas (playwright and poet) 191 n.11
Natal 39
National Army Museum 147
National Coal Board 79, 135
National Union of Mineworkers 79, 135

National Theatre 9, 17, 28, 36, 37, 38, 39, 55, 59, 60, 61, 67, 74, 97, 109, 152, 159–60, 187 n.42
    Cottesloe 61
    Olivier 60, 109
    Studios 119, 187 n.31
nationalism 2, 116, 145
Nazi, Nazism 82, 127, 140, 151
négritude 13–14
Nelson, Horatio 21–7
neoclassical, neoclassicism 11, 23, 35, 43, 54, 56–7, 84, 161, 183 nn.31 and 43
Neptune 27, 51
Nero (Roman Emperor) 38, 91, 182 n.16
Nessus (mythical figure) 170–1
New England 3
New Statesman 187 n.34
New Testament 57
New World 14, 168
New York 26, 37, 54, 70
New York Daily Tribune 40
New York Times 70
Newcastle upon Tyne vii, 13–27, 32, 150, 167, 169, 174, 176
    Grey Monument 27
    Old Fish Market 27
    Royal Victoria Infirmary 29
newsreel 6, 124, 128
Nicholson, John (poet) 20, 99
Nietzsche, Friedrich 25, 102–4, 150, 196 n.12
Nigeria 13, 38, 124
Nigerian-Biafran War '16
Nilsson, Sten (academic) 56
Nota, Alberto (dramatist) 2
Nowa Huta 141
nuclear power 133
Nymphaion 166

O'Brien, Sean (poet) 79
obscenity 16, 79–80, 82, 84, 160, 169
Observer 150, 186 n.111
Oceanids (mythical figures) 27, 133–4
Odysseus (mythical figure) 4, 12, 13, 17, 29, 82–3, 138, 140
Oenone/Nurse (dramatic character) 42
Offenbach, Jacques
    Orpheus in the Underworld 178

Ogun (Yoruba god) 51
Old Norse 9
Old Vic Theatre 37–8, 162
Olive, Edythe (actor) 163
olives, olive trees 29
Omphale (mythical figure) 93, 117
Onitsha 16–17
opera vii, 55–6, 67, 83–96, 114, 129, 134, 144, 154, 157, 161, 177, 187 n.10
oratory 3, 50, 133
Orestes (mythical figure) 66, 69, 73, 76–7, 105, 165
Orff, Carl (composer) 177
Orpheus viii, 118, 143–6, 178
Orphic, Orphism 144–6
orthography 24
Orthwein, Jake (film critic) 12
Osborne, John (playwright) 59, 102
Otway, Thomas (dramatist) 50
Ovid 175, 178
    Heroides 50, 95, 168
    Metamorphoses 23, 95, 45, 96, 176
Oxbridge 56
Oxford University 51, 55, 70, 161–3, 178, 193 n.5, 196 n.6

pagan, paganism 5, 16, 31–2
Page, Raissa (photographer) 157
Paine, Tom 3
painting, paintings 11, 19, 23, 43, 127–8, 173, 183 n.43, 184 n.47
Palazzo del Te (Mantua) 183 n.43
paleogeology 173
Palladas vii, 16, 19, 31–3, 98–100, 112, 123
Palladian architecture 11, 40–1
Pandora (mythical figure) 23
Pangaea 175
Pannonia Superior (province) 115, 118
pantomime 74
Paris 12, 20
    Comédie-Française 20, 28, 37
    École Normale Supérieure 12
    Théâtre Essaïon 54
Parker-Bowles, Camilla 36
Parkyn, Lottie (academic) vi, 186 n.118, 192 n.35
Parliament 41, 79, 102
Parnassus 167, 175–6
Parthenon 130–1, 194 n.36

sculptures 130
Pasiphae (mythical character) 43, 49, 52
Pasolini, Pier Paolo (film director) 124
pathetic fallacy 46
Patmos 4, 25
patriarchy 11, 66–7, 73, 85–9, 92, 177
Pausanias 92, 95
Perloff, Carey (theatre director) 54
Pelopidas 154
Peloponnese 38
Penelope (mythical figure) 87
Persia, Persian 120–1
personifications 24–5, 52, 80, 94
Peru vii, 13–17, 27, 32, 150, 167, 169
Peshawar 40, 42
Petrarch 23
Phanocles (poet) 144, 195 n.70
Philodemus of Gadara 112–13
philosophy 5, 10, 57, 86, 98, 104, 110, 112–13, 116, 137
photograph, photography 19–20, 23, 49, 125, 137, 147, 150–2, 159–60, 163, 181 n.2, 196 n.2
Phrynichos (tragedian) viii, 9, 119–21
Pillars of Hercules 115
Pindar 29, 93–4
Piso 112
Plato 10, 105
  Republic 99
Plautus 112
pleasure 5, 6, 25, 52, 99, 116, 133, 164, 170
Pliny the Elder 112
Plutarch 153–4
pollution 137, 141
Polymestor (dramatic character) 156
Polyxena (dramatic character) 155
Pompeii 5
Poole, Adrian (academic) 177
Pope, Alexander (poet) 3, 101–3, 191 n.11
Poseidon
  see Neptune
postmodern, postmodernism 12, 139
Pound, Ezra 4, 144, 164, 195 n.68
  Cantos 4
  Electra 54
poverty 10, 138, 173
Povolzhhye famine 159
Powell, Enoch (politician) 41, 183 n.38
Prague 13, 15, 21–3, 25–8, 140, 164

priest, priests 4, 5, 52
Prince Charles 11, 20, 36
Princess Diana 36
prisons 28, 54, 154, 162–3
Prochorus (early Christian) 4
Prometheus (mythical figure) 124–43, 175
Proserpine (mythical figure) 171
Protestant, Protestantism 4, 21
Psyche (mythical figure) 24, 171
Punjab 39
Punkah fans 35, 43
Puri, Rajika (dancer) 55
Pygmalion (mythical figure) 23
pyramids 20
Pythian priestess (dramatic character) 74, 76, 110

Quadi (Germanic tribe) 115, 117
Queen Elizabeth II 171
Quick, Diana (actor) 39

Rabelais, François (author) 103, 110–11
Racine, Jean 182 n.15
  Bérénice 50
  Britannicus 45
  Phèdre vii, 35–57
racism, racist 12, 39, 80–1, 85, 118
radical, radicalism 2–3, 10–12, 40, 53, 54, 75, 85, 126, 132, 164, 167–71, 180 n.57
Rajput clan 39, 43–4
rape 53, 154–5
Rawson, P. S. (academic) 43
Received Pronunciation 75
Red Army 130
Redgrave, Vanessa (actor) 154–5
Reformation 22
Regan, Christine (academic) vi, 81, 182 n.5, 188 n.61, 189 nn.12 and 14
Rembrandt (Rembrandt Harmenszoon van Rijn) 23
Renaissance 4, 14, 55, 60, 183 n.16
republican, republicanism 1, 3, 4–5, 9, 28, 71, 171, 174
revolution, revolutionary 1, 3, 9, 32, 60, 72, 73, 85, 132, 134, 167
rhetoric 1, 49, 50, 65, 68, 76, 101, 102, 154–6

rhyme, rhyming 6, 8, 10, 65–6, 74, 83, 90, 98, 106, 110–11, 114, 116, 131, 141–2, 155, 163, 171
Richardson, Tony (film director) 196 n.6
Richmond, Yorkshire 54
Rigg, Diana (actor) 37
Rihm, Wolfgang (musicologist) 3
Rimbaud, Arthur (poet) 2, 9, 81–2, 189 n.13
Ritson, Blake (actor) 149
Ritsos, Yannis (poet) 9
Rockefeller Center 139
Romano, Giulio (artist) 183 n.43
Romantics, Romanticism 2, 7, 134, 171
Rome, Roman 3–5, 10, 32, 45, 51, 56–7, 91, 98, 102–3, 114–18, 169, 173, 177, 182 n.4, 185 n.89
    Cloaca Maxima 112
    Empire 14, 31, 42, 45, 151
    entertainments 35, 46, 48–9, 55, 91, 97
    forum 112
Rowland, Antony (poet and academic) 82, 144, 195 n.68
Royal Court Theatre 59
Royal Holloway University of London 1, 148
Royal Shakespeare Company 54, 154
Royalism 14, 102
Royalty 77, 171
Rump Parliament 102
Rusbridger, Alan (journalist) 119
Rushdie, Salman 5, 101
Russell, Thomas (Irish radical) 53
Russia, Russian 23–4, 36, 131, 147–8, 159, 164, 166, 172, 176
    see also Soviet Union
Rutter, Carol (academic) 181 n.2
Rutter, Barrie (actor) vi, 61, 97, 105, 117, 186 n.7

Sabbath, Julian (film editor) 130
Saltaire 26, 97
Salt's Mill 97
Samarth, Alaknanda (actor) 39
Sanskrit 57
Sappho 105, 145, 167, 195 n.68
    'Pleiades poem' 4
Sarajevo 121
satire, satirical 3–4, 14, 16, 36–7, 101, 113, 191 n.11

satyr, satyrs 5, 8, 26, 97, 105–9, 175
satyr drama 91, 97, 108–9, 113, 132, 152, 177
Savarkar, V. D. (historian) 40
Save The Children Fund 159
Savoy Theatre 161–3
Scargill, Arthur (Trade Unionist) 80, 136
scatology 98–14, 191 n.11
Schiller, Friedrich (poet) 128
scholia, scholiast 92–3, 95
Schumann, Robert (composer) 125
Scotland, Scottish 42–3, 45, 57, 124, 135, 176
Scott, Ridley (film director) 115
Sea of Azov 166
Sevastopol 147–51, 164–5
Second World War 6, 23, 125, 128, 139, 151, 159
Secretan, Dominique (academic) 7
Seferis, George (poet) 176
Sejanus 102
semen 17, 67
Seneca, Senecan 38, 46, 90–1, 116, 182 n.16, 185 n.89
    Agamemnon 54
    Hercules Furens 54, 91, 93
    Hercules Oetaeus 54
    Medea vii, 86, 95, 91–3
    Phaedra vii, 35–57, 185 n.80
    Phoenissae 54
    Thyestes 90
    Troades 54
Senegal 13–14
Senghor, Léopold Sédar (politician) 14
Service, Robert (poet) 124
Settis, Salvatore (academic) 3
sex, sexual 7, 13, 16–17, 19, 18, 21–2, 30, 36, 52–3, 66, 75, 84, 94, 114, 133, 143, 163, 168
    bestial 43, 52
    explicit 4, 10, 79, 173
    imagery 15, 32, 48, 94
    repression 4–5, 30, 35, 51
    war 67, 70, 83–96
sexism, sexist 10, 69, 85
Shakespeare, William 20, 54
    Macbeth 50
    Much Ado about Nothing 54
    Sonnets 131

Shelley, Percy Bysshe 2, 9, 134, 152, 160
  Prometheus Unbound 134
Silenus (dramatic character) 105–9
Silkin, Jon (poet) 35, 180 n.31
Simferopol 151
Simmons, James (poet) 36, 182 n.8
Simon, Rainer (film director) 139
Simpson, William (artist) 148, 196 n.6
Sind 39
Siva 48, 52, 154
Skalla-Grímsson, Egil (poet) 9
Skinner, James (Colonel) 43–4
Skinner, Hercules (Colonel) 43
Slavery 12, 13, 53, 56, 73, 94, 103, 153, 155, 178
Slovakia 114
Smetana, Bedřich (composer) 83, 177
Smith, Fern (actor) 85, 139
smoking 133
soap opera 59
socialism 32, 132, 141–2
Solanas, Valerie (feminist) 85
soldiers 15, 16, 22, 24, 41, 53, 72, 127, 139, 147–8, 150–1, 153
sonnets 7–8, 23, 25, 61, 72, 101, 131, 180 n.34
Sophocles 57, 104–8
  Antigone 46
  Electra 54
  Philoctetes 142
  Trackers vii, 97, 152
  Women of Trachis 93, 171
South Bank 114, 159
Soviet Union 13, 22–4, 26, 129–30, 136, 140–2, 164, 172
Soyinka, Wole 35
  A Communion Rite 38, 51
Spain, Spanish 14
  Civil War 127
Sparrow, Walter (actor) 133
Spencer, Luke (academic) 67
Speranza, Robert (academic) 129, 194 n.43
SPQR 11
Srebrenica 120
St. James' Theatre, New York 37
St. John 4
St. Paul, *Epistles* 10
St. Vitus' Cathedral 13, 27
Stalin, Joseph 118, 129, 151

statues, statuary 11, 15, 17, 19–33, 48, 52, 102, 115, 121, 123, 126, 127–8, 130, 133, 138, 141, 144, 147, 175, 181 n.15
Stead, Henry (academic) vi, 127, 178, 179 n.10, 180 n.10, 185 n.103, 186 nn.120–1, 189 n.80, 194 n.25, 195 n.56, 198 n.29
Stead, Jean (poet) 69
stichomythia 65–6, 90
stoic, stoicism 10, 51, 114–19, 185 n.89
Stratas, Emmanuel 173
Stratas, Teresa (opera singer) 67, 83, 173, 189 n.22
Stravinsky, Igor 8
Strindberg, August (playwright) 20
Studley, John (translator) 50
Suda 119
Suffragettes 162, 164
Sunday Times 187 n.13, 194 n.43
Suzuki, Tadashi (theatre director) 36
swan, imagery of 171
Swanee (river) 169
swastika 126, 140
swear-words 72, 75, 96, 99
Swift, Jonathan 102–3, 113–14
Sydney University 41
Symes, Peter (film director) vi, 125–6, 5

Tacitus 45
Tagore, Satyendranath (civil servant) 57
Talboys, David (translator) 89
Talthybius (dramatic character) 155–7
Taman Peninsula 166
Taplin, Oliver (academic) vi, 55, 63–4, 144–6, 179 n.26, 186 nn.117–18, 187 nn.10 and 16–17, 198 n.25
Tara (dramatic character) 47
Tarkovsky, Andrei Arsenyevich (film director) 32, 177
Tatars 151
Tauric Chersonesos 147–9, 164–5
Tel Aviv 195 n.59
television 59–61, 79, 83, 123–5, 129, 132, 138, 145, 159, 174
Tenerife 168
Terpsichore 129
Terry, Quinlan (architect) 11
Tertullian 96

Tethys (mythical figure) 14
Thackrah, Charles Turner (surgeon) 100–1, 109
Thatcher, Margaret (politician) 135
The Battle of Orgreave (documentary film) 136–7
The Battle of Maldon (poem) 61
The Case for Decision Ö (movie) 139
The Red Flag (anthem) 131
The Shawshank Redemption (movie) 54
The Times 39, 79
theology 52, 56–7
Theophilus, Thomas (dramatic character) 39, 42–3
Thera (Santorini) 6
Théramène (dramatic character) 40, 47
Theseus/Thésée (dramatic character) 42, 47, 49, 50, 57, 158
Third Reich 116
Thoas (dramatic character) 149
Thomas, Sian (actor) vi, 160, 165, 173, 174
Thomson, George (academic) 72
Thorndike, Sybil (actor) 158, 160, 162–3
Thrace, Thracian 64, 94, 144–5, 156
Thucydides 57
Thule 14
Tibullus 6
tigers 47–50
Tilley, Vesta (music hall artist) 177
time, representation of in art 22, 33, 51, 138
Tinley, Robert (Lieutenant-Colonel 148
Tischbein, Johann (painter) 5
Titan Cement 123
Titian (Tiziano Vecellio, painter) 11
Tobacco Factory (theatre)
Torre Nilsson, Leopoldo (film director) 177
Trafalgar Square 21, 27
trapeze, image of 7
trochees, trochaic 66
Troezen 38
Trotsky, Leon 72, 73, 130
Tsar, Tsarist 23, 24
Tuareg people 168
tuberculosis 101
Turkey, Turkish 22, 145, 154
Turnell, Martin (academic) 38
Tyne (river) 13, 17, 25, 27, 29, 173

Ulster 36
Ulysses
    see Odysseus
Ulysses' Gaze (movie) 138
Unsworth, Barry (novelist) 60
USA 83, 128, 169

Valerius Flaccus, *Argonautica* 95–6
vases, vase-painting 10, 43, 139, 145, 147
Vasunia, Phiroze (academic) 56–7, 183 n.44, 185 n.90, 186 nn.127–30
venationes 148
venereal disease 21, 53, 126, 168
Venus
    see Aphrodite
Verdi, Giuseppe (composer) 177
verse forms 6–8, 19–20, 33, 36–8, 46, 50, 54–5, 59–63, 66, 74, 76, 79, 104, 110–12, 124, 125, 129, 136, 138, 145, 155, 161, 163
Vesuvius, Mount 5–7, 176
Victorian 15, 27, 36, 38, 48, 51, 83
Vienna, Viennese 97, 116
Vietnam War 144
vine, vines 5
Vines, Sherrard (academic) 2
Virgil 9, 41, 55, 57, 96, 100, 170, 175, 182 n.4
Virgil Society 9
Volcano Theatre Company 85
Volga (river) 159
Voltaire (François-Marie Arouet) 5
    Oedipe 54
Vulcan 15, 23

Wagner, Richard 94
Wales, Welsh 45, 135
Walters, Jimmy (theatre director) vi, 191 n.1
Warner, Marina (academic) 67
Warren, Joseph (American revolutionary) 3
Washington, DC 25, 155
Watchman (dramatic figure) 68
weapons 17, 68
    chemical 127
    nuclear 64, 156–7
weaving 25, 87, 121

Weil, Simone 127
West, Benjamin (painter) 11
West Yorkshire Playhouse 97
Westminster Abbey 16, 24, 158
Wharf Theatre (Sydney) 97
Wheatley, Phyllis (poet) 12
White Heat (movie) 177
Whitehouse, Mary ('decency' campaigner) 79
whiteness, white people 12–13, 24, 30, 39, 41, 51, 56, 72, 80, 94, 135, 167–8
wildlife 145
Wilhelm II (Kaiser) 126–9
Winckelmann, J.J. 179 n.6
wine 5–6, 9, 146, 171, 173
Wolf, Christa (novelist) 87
Women's Experimental Theatre Co. (New York) 70
Women's Parliament 163
Wordsworth, William 81

Wright, Joseph (philologist) 178
Würzburg 6

Xenophon 11, 57

Yeats, W. B. 70, 20
Yelland, David (actor) 39
Yerushalmi, Rina (theatre director) 195 n.59
Yorkshire 61–2, 70, 100, 105, 137
    Playhouse 54, 97
Yorkshire Post 16, 181 n.67
'Yorkshire Ripper' 69
Yoruba people 36–7, 51
Young, Alan (poet) 8
Young, Edward (writer) 11
Ypres, Battle of 126

Zargana, Maung Thura (poet) 9
Zeitlin, Froma (academic) 70, 140
Ziolkowski, Theodore (academic) 2

www.ingramcontent.com/pod-product-compliance
Lightning Source LLC
Chambersburg PA
CBHW050514020526
44111CB00052B/2015